The Dingoes' Lament

Published by Melbourne Books
Level 9, 100 Collins Street,
Melbourne, VIC 3000
Australia
www.melbournebooks.com.au
info@melbournebooks.com.au

NATIONAL LIBRARY OF AUSTRALIA
CATALOGUING-IN-PUBLICATION ENTRY

AUTHOR: Bois, John, 1950-

TITLE: The Dingoes Lament / John Bois.

ISBN: 9781922129062 (pbk.)

SUBJECTS: (country rock band)
Country rock music.
Rock groups.

DEWEY NUMBER: 781.642

The Dingoes' Lament

John Bois

M
MELBOURNE BOOKS

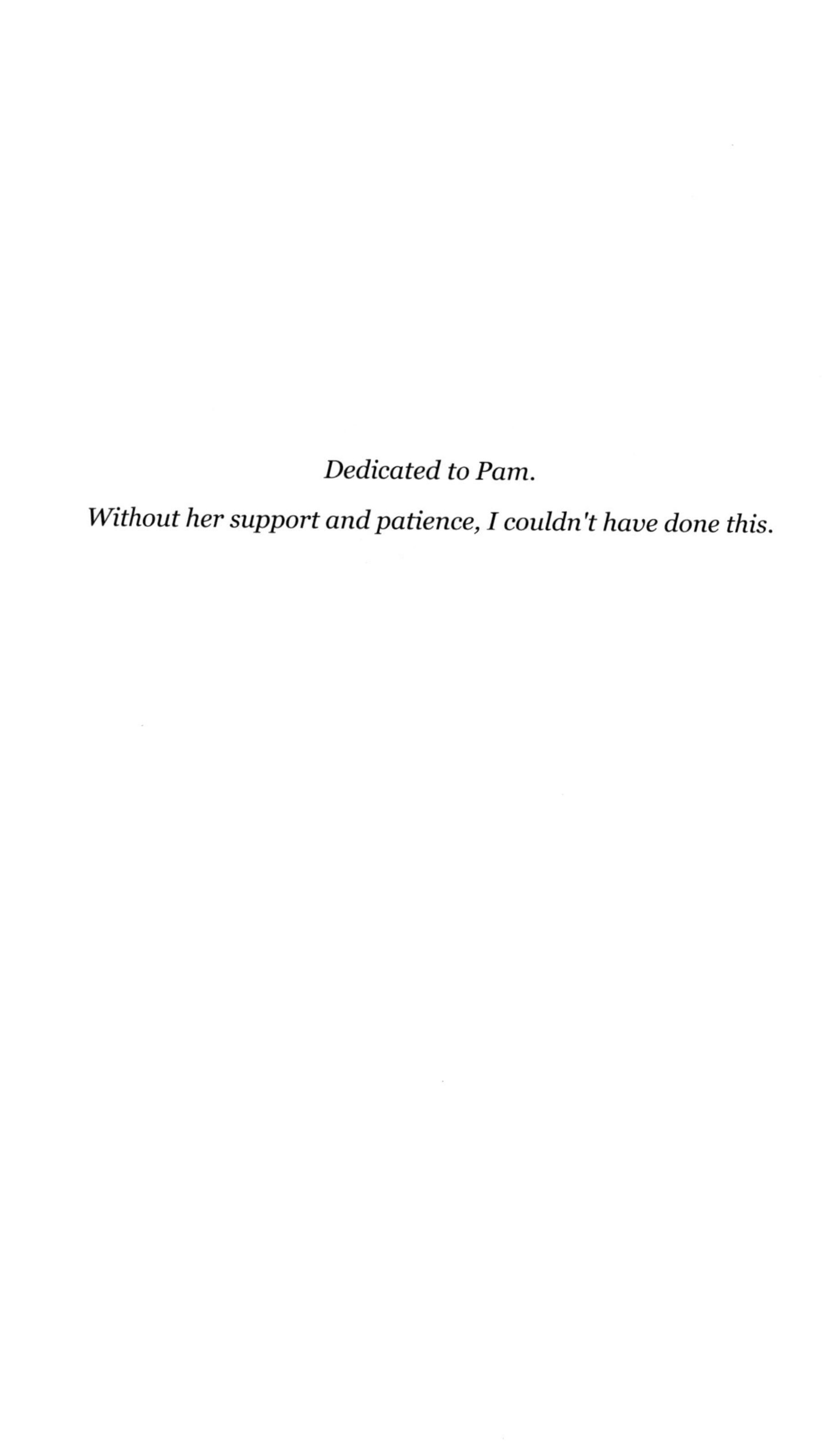

Dedicated to Pam.

Without her support and patience, I couldn't have done this.

Acknowledgments

Thanks to:

Greg Quill for rescuing the book from my desk drawer.

Chris Stockley for providing photos and memorabilia.

Kerryn Tolhurst for jogging my memory and giving advice on an earlier manuscript.

Broderick Smith for photos and encouragement.

Kevin MacLean for photos.

To all living Dingoes for allowing this yarn to bear their names.

John Lee, if you're listening, for your groove.

Donna Verdier for early editorial advice.

Janice Azrak, Philip Morris and Andrew Chapman for photos.

Duncan Kimball for putting two chapters on his 'Milesago' website.

John Tait for reading those chapters and wanting to read more.

Brian Wise for asking me to read them on his 3RRR radio show.

Jenny Darling and John Tait for their work in finding a home for the book.

Anne Tait for pre-editing.

Philip Quirk for the iconic cover shot.

Adolfo Aranjuez for his editorial perception.

David Tenenbaum for taking a chance on the band and the book.

Everybody for turning up at the 2010 Dingoes tour.

Foreword

I knew John Bois when he couldn't talk his way out of a paper bag, let alone write a work of such infectious whimsy and great cultural import as *The Dingoes' Lament*.

Boisy was the glue that held my band, Country Radio, together for about four years back in the early 1970s. He was the best bass player I've ever worked with. Great timing, intuitive sense of feel, melodic and punchy all at once.

He was a quiet guy, not much of a talker, but never unhappy. He never seemed to have much ambition, no big dreams beyond the next gig down the road. But he always delivered ... sometimes a little ragged around the edges, sometimes without shoes, sometimes in need of deodorant, sometimes with an entourage of dubious followers in tow ...

It was one particular gaggle of Boisy's friends I was thinking about when out of the blue I heard his voice on the phone around 1997. He just wanted to catch up, he said. He'd been drinking some classy Australian shiraz, got a bit homesick, and wanted to share the afterglow with an old mate. We were both exiles, lost abroad, me in Toronto writing for a big newspaper, Boisy in Maryland teaching high school science.

My mind immediately reeled back to sometime in 1972, when Country Radio was at the height of its meager powers, following the unplanned success of our single, *Gypsy Queen*, to which Boisy and drummer Tony Bolton had contributed a powerful and unique rhythm arrangement.

He probably doesn't remember the night, a few months later, when we had the opportunity to stay — at long last, and after years of infested, infected digs — in a real, high-class hotel, somewhere in Sydney's Potts Point area. Around one in the morning, the door flew open and in lurched Boisy, smelling like jet fuel.

'I've brought some friends,' he blurted. 'They don't have anywhere to stay tonight, so I said they could sleep in our lounge room!'

He beckoned, and out of the corridor gloom stepped half a dozen grizzled battlers, all scars, scabs, bloody knuckles and bleary eyes. Feral dudes with shaky hands and itchy grins.

'I met them in the park,' Boisy explained, his tongue suspiciously thick. 'They are very nice men who've fallen on hard times. They have so little, and we have so much!'

Needless to say, Boisy's new mates were repelled, and in an indignant show of solidarity, our bass player departed with them, to spend what remained of the night in their company under the stars. It was a typical Boisy stunt: well-intentioned and potentially catastrophic.

Forty-odd years later, I still see flashes of that irrepressible free spirit whenever we meet. And it infuses this fantastic account of the Dingoes' almost mythical rise and fall — and I mean that in the literal sense, because *The Dingoes' Lament* is partly a coded fantasy, partly chaotic catharsis, in the best Australian yarn-spinning tradition, inhabited by real characters and circumscribed by actual events.

No-one in either The Dingoes or Country Radio saw this coming, this canny, funny, loving and self-deprecating account of an odyssey undertaken in the late 1970s by a band almost prophetically doomed from the start.

I had no idea he'd written a book. I confess I would not have thought this happy-go-lucky rambler was up to it. Yet, not long after that 1997 phone call, chapters started arriving, one a week, in my email inbox, without comment or explanation. I was captivated, mesmerised. I couldn't wait for the next installment.

It wasn't just the story. It was the quality of John's storytelling that grabbed me, and his uncanny ability to focus in on the idiosyncratic qualities and foibles of characters I knew so well, on the very sound of their voices, on the unique language and eccentric culture that musicians develop when they spend so much time together in isolation.

This was not a sterile diary, not a collection of war stories, not a self-aggrandising *we coulda been heroes* reverie. This was literature, its standards as noble as those The Dingoes had practised in their art. I can't think of a rock'n'roll yarn that's as convincing, as absorbing, as *The Dingoes' Lament.*

In the decade since I first read it, bits and pieces of the book have been passed around like totem fragments among fans of The Dingoes. The band's induction into the ARIA Hall of Fame in 2009 — a well-deserved testament to their indelible contributions to the shape and substance of Australian music — prompted huge interest in a story that had never been, and was, indeed, long forgotten.

By very deliberately and very unsentimentally embracing the Australian vernacular, laying bare the austere, reckless and unhappy experience of life in the Lucky Country, conjuring up the harshness of the Australian landscape, and wrapping it all in an appealing and somehow familiar musical package that bridged rock, country music and R&B, The Dingoes were ahead of their time. But they were destined to be misunderstood — in their own country and in America — as a damned hot pub band.

They were that, but they were so much more. And underlying the ribald stories and richly drawn characters in *The Dingoes' Lament* is the sad sound of a wreck down the line. Boisy heard it long before it happened, and started paying close attention to what was going on around him ... gathering in details and memories before they were scattered and forever lost.

This book is those memories reassembled with candour, humour, sorrow and a lot of love.

It's also another typical Boisy stunt: well-intentioned and potentially catastrophic.

Greg Quill
Toronto

1

Perth

Barefoot, hungover and vacant, I sat on Sandy Beach and looked out across the Indian Ocean toward Africa. Seagulls patrolled the slate-grey troughs of the trade-wind swell just before it spent itself on the coast of Western Australia. A squall was whipping up whitecaps and driving a powerful onshore breeze right in my face. It was laced with sand.

I put my head between my knees and strained the sand with my fingers and toes. I had just had a breakfast of milk, tea and tomato juice. I was ministering to my hangover. You see, last night we agreed that this was to be our last tour, and that when we got back to Melbourne, The Dingoes, my band, would be no more. And so we spent the night drinking in a post-mortem sort of way.

Back in Melbourne I didn't drink so much. I had things to do there. But what was I going to do after Perth? The Dingoes had a good shot, but we had gone as far as we were going. I thought for an instant what it would take hours to tell: I was glad we were finished — I was ready for something new.

Kerryn, our main songwriter, called me from our beachfront hotel. He was shouldering the glass door to hold it open against the heavy westerly. He was beckoning me to come over.

Buffeted by the almost-cold wind, I picked up my shoes and scuffed across the street and into the protective stillness of the hotel lobby.

Kerryn held a piece of note paper; Stockley, Brod, and J.L. looked on expectantly.

I walked over to them.

'What's up?'

'How do you like this for a message?' Kerryn said, as he handed me the note with the Sandy Beach Hotel letterhead.

I read it aloud, 'Ring Paul McCartney at the Rolling Stones' office.'

'What do you say to that?' asked Kerryn.

'Poor sort of joke,' I said.

'Yeah,' said Brod. 'That's what we thought. But the receptionist swore it was America calling.'

I could hear the muted percussion of the wind against the plate glass of the motel front.

'But we can't ring 'til six tonight,' said Kerryn. 'It seems it's still yesterday in America.'

We looked stupidly at each other until Stockley shrugged and said, 'Well, there's nothing else for it. Who wants a beer and who's a poofter?'

We walked briskly to the bar of the Sandy Beach Hotel.

The bar, which had just opened, consisted of three areas: a dingy little lounge with a cranky old bartender elbow deep in dishwater; a beer garden; and off to one side of the bar, a pool table on a parquet floor. The bartender was too intent on his work to notice us.

Stockley tried to get his attention, 'Excuse me. Could we have five pots, please?'

Without acknowledging him, the bartender wiped his sudsy hands on his apron and poured our beers.

As we sipped, we quickly exhausted all the possibilities of the phone call. It was a hoax. It wasn't a hoax. It could be either Paul McCartney or the Rolling Stones. Or, it could be Paul McCartney and The Rolling Stones teamed up especially for a joint project: The Dingoes.

'They're all impissabolities,' slurred Stockley, staring into his glass and impersonating his favourite Melbourne drunk, Maury.

'Anyone for pool?' I asked.

'Rack 'em up, John,' said Stockley as he slotted money into the table.

The balls dropped with a resounding thud. I searched for the triangular pool rack.

'Where's the thing?'

'Here it is,' offered Brod as he came over to watch.

As soon as I finished racking up the balls, Stockley propelled the white ball into the pack with a shattering force. Only two balls broke free.

'Christ, what's a bloke gotta do?'

'It's all finesse in this game, mate,' I said. 'That's why you're pist'ry!'

I dropped a low ball and left myself without a shot.

Stockley stood with a beer in his left hand and the pool cue in the crook of his left elbow. His shirt was open, as usual, to reveal his scars — he was stroking them. Only a year ago, he was the victim of a weekend shooting spree by two prison escapees. They fired two bullets into a crowd just for fun. One of them got Stockley in the back and the operation to remove it left three huge, vivid, purplish scars. He stroked them constantly: he was very proud of them.

'Would you mind not stroking your scars so loudly?' I said, walking around the table, trying in vain to find a shot. I fired into a pack and left him with good position.

Stockley smiled, 'Thanks for the po, John.'

I sat down as he made a great show of not being able to decide which easy shot to drop first. Brod gave me a look of pity as Stockley sunk his first ball and winked at me. Kerryn and J.L. sat talking at the bar.

I thought about the message. It was probably a horrendous mistake, a fabulous garbling of syllables by the receptionist.

Six months before I would not have been so sceptical. Then, at the Station Hotel, in Melbourne, we were a five-piece dynamo. Derelicts and dole dependents normally peopled the Station, as well as besotted bon vivants who claimed it was a haven of mateship, a place where men could be men out of earshot of nagging women. But to the untrained eye it looked more like a place of banishment.

Nevertheless, on Saturday it was transformed into a subcultural temple. The gods of that subculture were ... The Dingoes. The Station was licensed to seat eighty persons, but when we played there the only crowd restriction was the amount of discomfort people were willing to bear. However, the only *intolerable* discomfort was inability to get to the bar.

At two in the afternoon, three hundred people and five gods converged on the bar. At six, three hundred drunks and five drunk gods waded across the beer-soaked carpet and out into a world strangely untouched by the four hours of sweat, inebriation and rocking music.

We were not stars. We satirised stardom. The Station audience loved us because we refused to take anything, including ourselves, seriously. We disdained the slick professionalism of nightclub bands; and as we argued and clowned around between songs, we happily exempted ourselves from superstar status as well.

But this overt anti-professionalism, while it was one cause of our celebrity at the Station, drastically limited our appeal. When we played anywhere else, people stared at us as if they were watching a foreign-language film without subtitles. And our manner and dress were so un-star-like that often, when we arrived at a new place, people would ask us what time the band was coming — they thought we were the road crew!

On stage we had no light show, no props, no choreographed moves, no staging of any kind. We didn't vomit blood, or leer like trolls while rolling our tongues lasciviously at the audience. Our strengths were our personalities and our music. And at the Station, the room was intimate enough for both to count. On a good day, we believed, our characters and our music formed an irresistible winning combination.

The central element of this winning combination, our lead singer Broderick Smith, sat next to me as Stockley dropped his second gift-ball. Brod's hand shook as he lifted his glass to his lips. He had a very complex and puzzling personality. As fantastic as he was onstage, offstage, and particularly behind the wheel of his vintage Land Rover, he was stodgy and anxious. Maybe, I thought, he was trying to keep his zany side at bay, as if it were a strange beast — a mercurial, abnormal thing, which could only be released safely at showtime when outrageousness is customary. He must keep it in check lest his veneer of sanity cracked. If I had his gift, I thought, I would revel in it twenty-four hours a day.

Stockley dropped his third cinch shot.

Brod had a complexion that was prone to ashenness. He had grey-blue eyes and a large, expressive jaw that jutted out heroically. He had a dimple in his chin. Brod resembled the Germanic ideal, but he had an endearing scruffy quality — like an Aryan the cat dragged in.

The contents of his flat affirmed his zany side. His formal need to cling to sanity was apparently abandoned amid the eccentric clutter of his collection of bric-a-brac. A Remington statuette of a cowboy on a rearing horse stood in as a heroic paperweight. It was on a large glass museum display case, which, supported by antique filing cabinets, was used as a desk. Inside the glass case, hundreds of lead military miniatures were lined up in chronological order from Roman Centurions to Patton's Eighth Army. The desk was an island in a sea of dolls, exotic hub caps, rolled-up maps, old cameras, wood and metal puzzles, and antique scientific instruments. He was a voracious reader: comics, individually wrapped in clear plastic, were stacked in hallowed corners; a huge bookshelf sagged under the weight of science fiction paperbacks, which were crammed into it at the rate of one every two Earth days. And, with his collection of books on the history, customs and conquest of the North and South American native peoples, he sought the fantastic in the real world too.

Brod's wife was a seamstress. Pieces of material, quilts and cloth-filled cane hampers added plushness, a buffer to Brod's clutter that was appreciated by the third denizen, Ronald, a lithe Persian cat. Ronald, if he wasn't asleep in some dark, cushioned nook, could be seen bouncing from object to object in search of one or another of the infinite possibilities of its Broderickian universe.

But, as used to the wacky world of Broderick as Ronald was, I think he would have gone stark raving mad if he just once saw his master in action at the Station. At the end of *Sydney Ladies*, a song Brod wrote about American GIs on R&R from Vietnam, he would blow a ten-minute harp solo into his refurbished taxi-driver's microphone. As he walked out onto the audience's tables, people cleared their glasses to make way for his tattered tennis shoes. Girls mockingly clutched at his crumpled jeans. His hair stuck to the sweat on his cheeks and forehead as his frenzy increased. At the climax of his solo, the audience cheered as if someone had scored a go-ahead goal in the final second. Brod would affect smug appreciation for the applause and saluted the crowd like Hitler at the Nuremburg rally. Then he would introduce the next song:

'Die fumph zong nicht einer kraftwerk von Chris Stockley, Achtung! Mein Kamerades die tempo: ein, zwei, drei ...'

Stockley would play a lightning-fast introduction while Brod slid across the stage on his knees, prostrating himself before the guitar hero.

After this song, as I was tuning my bass, Brod would whisper into the microphone in the voice of a golf announcer, 'John is moving onto his D string ... no. Wait just a minute ... I'm sorry. He's changed his mind. He's on the A string. He's pulling it up ... up ... up ... until it's just right. Ooh, that was *nicely* done.'

On it went from a seemingly bottomless well of comic patter. And Brod never repeated himself — that was anathema to him.

What theory of personality could accommodate the contradictions in this man, this man who sat next to me with his elbows on his knees, wringing his hands in anxiety over life in general, and the phone call in particular?

He wasn't sweating over the pool game, though. He stood up, 'I'm going for a walk along the beach. I'll see you back here about six.'

'Okay, mate.'

'See ya, Brod,' said the others.

And he disappeared, worrying out the door.

Stockley looked at his fifth giveaway shot. It required him to put the cue behind his back with just one foot touching the floor. He grunted. 'A little ... tricky, this one, mate.' He pocketed the ball with a motion that said: Take that! But he left himself in poor position for the next shot. He made a gallant shot off the cushion but just missed.

Then, to reach the white ball, I had to use the extension stick to rest my cue on.

'Need the poofter stick, John?' He stood leaning against the wall with his cue, his beer and his scars.

'Would you mind buttoning up your shirt,' I said. 'It's like trying to play next to the bloody Aurora Borealis.'

'No way, mate.'

My ball went down but I had a long shot for the next one and I missed by a mile.

'Too bad, mate.'

I left him in good position for his last two balls. He had not beaten me in quite a while so he took his time deciding which ball should go into which hole. He made his first shot and was nicely in line for the next, but, in trying to hit it too hard so the white ball would carry back up the table to the eight ball, his last ball bounced from side to side of the pocket and dribbled out impotently. 'I was fucking robbed.'

'Bit too much english, mate.'

By this time J.L. and Kerryn were watching. 'Another round of beers?' asked Kerryn.

'Thanks, mate,' we all said.

Stockley went to the bathroom and I punched in three balls while he was away. When he came back he looked at the table and said, 'Was anybody watching this bastard?'

Next, instead of trying to make a difficult shot, I put the white ball behind my ball snookering Stockley. He was genuinely miffed.

Kerryn laughed. 'I'm next,' he said as he slapped some coins on the table.

Stockley couldn't recover and I sank my last ball and then sent down the eight ball with a feather-touch side shot. It was a fluke.

'See, mate? Finesse. You gotta have class in this game.'

'You're a ratbag, John,' he said. And he guzzled down his beer. 'I'm going upstairs. I'll see you in the lobby at six.'

'They're dropping like flies, Kerryn.'

He collected the balls and looked for the rack. 'Where's the thing?' he said.

I passed him the rack. 'A thing by any other name is still a thing.'

Kerryn's smile, like my sense of humour that day, was notable for its economy — only the corners of his mouth needed to turn up to indicate amusement. He positioned himself to break and pumped the cue vigorously. He thrashed the white ball and sent it ricocheting off the pack and bouncing off the table.

'Okay, you blokes,' whined the bartender as the ball bounced across the linoleum and smashed into the bar. 'What do you think this is, cricket?'

'Mind your own business,' retorted Kerryn angrily. Then, instantly composed, 'Sorry, mate. Can I try that again?'

'Have at it,' I said.

I had never seen Kerryn hit anyone, but I have often thought that he would be a good friend to have if things got rough. Perhaps his badly chipped front tooth gave that impression, or maybe it was his cocky stance and attitude. His posture and clothing bore a striking resemblance to the male dancer in Renoir's *Dance at Bougival*. But Kerryn's hair would not have fit under that gentleman's hat. Kerryn, like the dancer, wore a beard, but his hair was long and frizzy and naturally assumed the shape of a toadstool. Apart from his hair, there was no extravagant sign of his driven creativity. For that you had to hear his songs.

No single reason for our success stood out. But Kerryn's songs provided the intellectual justification for that success. We were praised in the rock press for charting new territory for Australian bands — we actually sang about Australia. To understand why this was so important you have to appreciate the unique history of Australia's popular culture. Australian/European culture was only about a hundred years old before it was inundated by radio and, later, TV. The fully developed American and English popular cultures tended to wash aside any nascent local varieties. As a generation, we felt a keen sense of embarrassment at our lack of homegrown art forms. This embarrassment even had a name: *the cultural cringe*. Our songwriters avoided all mention of Australia in our popular songs.

But Kerryn found a voice. Though his music was heavily derivative of American blues, country and rock, his lyrics used Australian place names, situations, characters and language. This, in a serious tone, was new. Certainly, plenty of songs had been written about the outback, but they were novelty songs like the great *The Pub with No Beer*, and the not so great *Red Back (spider) on the Toilet Seat*. Now Kerryn had written a serious song about a man who went oil drilling in the western desert. It made the charts towards the end of 1973. In a later song, about people stuck in limbo, *Waitin' for the Tide to Turn*, Kerryn put a woman's plight in an Australian setting:

> I know a girl livin' way out west,
> Havin' trouble just keepin' her head.
> Home on the range in the kitchen — bitchin'
> Cursin' the day she was wed.
>
> 'Cos her man don't seem to understand
> That you can't get nothin' from a sunburnt land
> Day after day, you know it's gettin' her down.
> She knows she won't even make it the long way around

Kerryn's songs had wit, and for our fans — who gave us fierce loyalty in return — they validated a tentative nationalistic pride. The Dingoes' songs could be seen as harbingers of a growing cultural confidence, among the first sedimentary islands to settle after the denuding cultural flood that emanated from wood, Bakelite and plastic boxes sitting in the corner of every Australian living room.

Kerryn had absolutely no airs or pretensions of greatness. He was strictly one of us. Nor did we feel he was superior in any way. Although he had the most to gain from any success we might have had, we would allow no leader to rise above the rest. I felt that Stockley, Kerryn and, to a lesser extent, Brod each thought they should exert more control over the band's decisions. Whenever one of them complained about our lack of leadership it was tinged with regret that they had not taken charge themselves. Since I had come to the band last, and I was not the lead songwriter, the lead guitarist, the lead singer ... the lead anything, I was not a contestant. But my judgment was well respected and I could have handed power to either of them had I wished. But I felt none of them had natural leadership qualities around which we could gather in admiration and respect.

Perhaps this conviction was affected by my own repressed hunger for power and envy of those who held it. I had had a miserable experience as a sixth-grader.

In a meteoric rise to power I was voted captain of the Chatham School football team. But immediately after my ascension, the team of eleven-year-olds refused to submit to my overambitious regimen of push-ups, jumping jacks and fifty-yard sprints. In any case, we were half the size of all our opponents and we went on to a completely scoreless season — in a game where a low score is thirty points.

The next year, I returned to brag to my teacher about my success in high school mathematics. He invited me into his classroom and said, 'John Bois is going to show us how a mathematical wizard solves a problem.'

With that, he wrote one of his most convoluted word problems on the board. I choked. He asked one of the sixth-graders to solve the problem and she did it easily.

I must have looked crestfallen as I walked down the corridor. Another teacher stopped me and asked what had happened. After I told him, he explained that Mr Evans didn't like me because he blamed me for our losing season last year. He said that he felt this was wrong because, while Mr Evans didn't come to a single game, he *had*. And he thought I was a good captain.

This is a previously unexamined memory. And it's only now that I realise how absurd it was to blame one person, me, for the performance of our hopelessly mismatched team. Yet it was Mr Evans's judgment that I accepted. And until now it has stood there like a hazard sign whose simple message reached my subconscious: *Remember the disaster that befell you the last time you went down this road — turn back!*

Leadership was a recurring problem with The Dingoes. Stockley, Kerryn and Brod each had a valid claim to it, but they couldn't step forward for certain knowledge that they would be knocked down again. And, since none could claim it, all denied it. This was often embarrassing. When an interviewer asked us who our leader was, we all froze for a revealing second.

Then we blurted out that we were democratic. The interviewer looked at us as if to say, 'I don't care who the big chief is — I just want to know who to ask the question. Geez, guys! Get your act together.'

And so, when six o'clock came around, when we met in the lobby of the Sandy Beach Hotel, I was wincing from apprehension of the delicate tussle about to take place — who should make the call to America?

'Well, then. Let's do it,' said Kerryn, as we stood around the lobby.

'Who should ring?' asked Stockley.

'I don't mind. Do you want to do it?' said Kerryn.

'No, mate,' said Stockley. 'You do it. You know Paul better than I do.'

Kerryn snatched the phone message from his own hand as if to say, *Come on. Let's not play one of these ridiculous games.*

'Come on,' he said.

'He's a ratbag,' said Stockley.

The issue was in the open but it was never addressed. I sometimes wondered what would have happened if one of us had said, 'Look. We know power in this band is shared. No one of us is going to run off with all of the goods. Let's just say that one of us, say me, is the leader. No leader gets everything his way. It's usually no more than a formality — just like we agree to drive on the left side of the road. There's nothing inferior about the right side. We just drive on the same side to avoid accidents. Having a leader would do the same thing — it would make the path to a common goal easier.'

Then we could have gone outside and done push-ups, jumping jacks and fifty-yard sprints.

Even if we had had such a leader there could be no inspirational element — we were far too equal for that. And where would such a leader take us — our common goal wasn't formulated beyond wanting to make lots of money doing what we wanted to do. Besides, at the Station, the obvious power vacuum within the group was endearing, perhaps even the cornerstone of our highly prized anti-professionalism.

The leadership question was a conflict that remained with us. Though we felt we needed leadership, we rationalised our democratic dynamic with an attitude that said authority was for children and right-wing governments — we were gentlemen and boon companions; we needed no conch shell.

We tramped upstairs to the room Kerryn and I shared. I reached the door first and knocked on it. They stood still for a Pavlovian second.

'Boisy!' said Brod, as he shoved my shoulder.

I unlocked the door and we went in. Stockley came in last, having stopped at his room to get some beer. He opened one. Pretending to be drunk and talking to Paul McCartney on the phone, he said, 'G'day, Paul. Chris here, mate. Yeah. Chris fuckin' Stockley. How the fuck are ya. I'm good, thanks, mate. How's John, George and Ringo ... Fuckin', eh!'

I walked over to turn off the air conditioner in the frigid room. I listened to the wind buffeting the salt-begrimed window as Kerryn talked to America, 'Hello? ... Hello ... Yes. My name is Kerryn Tolhurst. I'm ringing on behalf of The Dingoes.' He spoke too loudly — he had never spoken to anyone that far away before. 'We got a message to ring someone called ... Paul ... McCartney.'

We snickered.

'Yes ... I see ... Yes ... No Paul McCart ... *Billy* McCartney ... No, that's alright. Our mistake. Is he there? Thank you.'

We knew Billy McCartney. He was a road manager who had gone overseas to crack the big time. It was nice to hear from him, but not at the expense of my destiny.

'How dare he not be Paul McCartney,' I said.

'He's a fuckin' ratbag,' said Stockley.

Kerryn held up a silencing finger. 'Billy! How are you, mate? ... Good, thanks. Listen —we got this message to ring the Rolling Stones' office ... Yeah ... I see ...'

My heart sank as Kerryn sat on the edge of his bed with a poker face, saying 'Yeah' and 'I see' for the next ten minutes.

I looked at Stockley. He had on dark sunglasses that were supposed to turn transparent indoors. But they stayed dark and he looked like a heroin addict as he sullenly sipped his beer. He stood up, walked over to the window and gave me an exasperated look. I took great pride in the personalities of The Dingoes, and as I looked at Stockley I felt sadness that the world would not, after all, it seemed, come to know him. I thought of him arriving at the Station with Jen, his girlfriend, and his guitar case. He had a slight build and was five-foot-three-and-a-half. Jenny was five-foot-nine and voluptuous. He was engulfed in her sexuality and was, in this respect, a very happy man.

Stockley had a closely manicured beard but his hair rambled down to the middle of his back. His shirt was open and he had on the leather jacket he was shot in. A hole the size of a spider bite was in its back. All this added to his legendary stature.

When we played he had a little cluster of fret watchers — The Stockley Faithful — gathered immediately in front of him. On his small frame his guitar looked immense, but he handled it with ostentatious ease. He was legendary for his lightning fingers, for being in some of Australia's biggest groups, and for being shot in the back.

Stockley came to Australia from England when he was ten and I think he got his ambivalent attitude toward class from his hometown of Winchester. He had wedged the attitude of a working-class hero and a dandy into one contradictory personality. This showed up in big ways: he had a dogmatic socialistic philosophy, yet he adored such perquisites of the capitalist running-dogs as he could lay his hands on. And it showed up in little ways: after playing a devastatingly down-home blues lick, he shook his wrist with a motion that brought attention to his gold watch. Stockley had a fetishistic love of beer and its ancillary culture, yet he was a wine aficionado and a diligent epicurean. All of this was paradoxical. But I had to admit that his desire to be of the people, yet enjoy the privileges of the upper classes, was consistent with the idea of success in his chosen career: rock'n'roll.

I don't know how he came upon it, but he seemed to believe in a kind of paganistic animism. He was bedevilled by what he called 'electrickery'. An amplifier worked fine until he tried to use it. Then it would pop, crackle and hum brutally. Anything electrical conspired against him, and every time it happened he would look at me and say, 'See, mate. It's got it in for me. Thy electrickery.' Then he would blow on his ring finger to ward off the evil spirits.

But, if the spirit of electrickery bedevilled him, the spirit of beer was his ally. On a Sunday, when his fridge was stocked up against the blue laws, he talked to his little friends. He shook the fridge gently until the bottles jingled against each other.

'My little jumblies,' he said. 'Yes, it won't be long now, my babies.'

Then he shook the fridge to make them answer him.

'All right. But just one of you now.'

He took out a bottle and stroked it, smiling at the others like a proud father.

Stockley's house at that time was called Rat Manor. It was the home of one in a long line of Stockley's assumed comic personas, Maury. Stockley's inspiration for Maury was an old drunk who lived in an abandoned house opposite the Station with some other derelicts. We knew, via Stockley, only a few things about Maury: he believed that the only nutrition one needed was beer; he routinely urinated in the corner of his living room; and he either loved or hated people. Maury cast his judgment on others in this way: 'He's number one in my book, Mr Murray. Number one in my book!' To express disapproval it was: 'He's a ratbag,' or, the even more expressive: 'He's a fuckin' ratbag, Mr Murray.' As far as Stockley could tell, Mr Murray was a figment of Maury's alcoholic dementia.

Stockley took these characteristics and invented his own Maury, a kind of derelict anti-sage. Whether at Rat Manor, the Station or on the road, Maury became a constant companion. We begged Stockley to be Maury, or we planted lines for him to respond to.

So, as we listened to Kerryn grunting to America, I whispered to Stockley, 'Geez, mate. You didn't have a meal before that beer, did you? You should take better care of yourself, mate.'

Stockley replied in the high, whiny voice of Maury, 'No worries, mate. There's a steak in every glass.'

'I see ... Mmmm ... Yes,' said Kerryn to America.

J.L., our drummer, impatiently picked up a rock magazine. The day before, he was reading the same magazine, when Stockley, in his Maury character, said, 'Here, what are ya? Ya don't wanna read a bloody book, mate. You're gonna turn into a bloody poofter. Yer don't need books. All you need is beer, footy and mates ... and beer for ya mates, o' course. Did yer want people to think you're an ineffectual or somethin'. Don't be a smarty pants, mate.'

J.L. didn't read. Not that J.L. was anti-books — rather, he was possessed by music. From waking up, until after he was asleep, J.L. played tapes of Al Green and reggae music. He grew up in a West Indian suburb in London. He said he learned to play drums by banging sticks on the sidewalk in time to the strange and wonderful rhythms of the Caribbean.

His natural shyness offstage left you unprepared for his onstage presence. Onstage he shone. He was possessed by the groove and he exuded an open pride that was catching. He played with his nose tilted slightly above the horizontal, and his head rocked back and forward making his hair swish below his ear. The motion of his head and hair reminded me of an Irish setter trotting out its victory lap at a dog show. J.L.'s confidence was so infectious that, whenever I felt my attention drifting off the groove or felt a mild paranoia that it simply wasn't there (oh, will-o'-the-wisp), I just had to watch him and it solidified once again. Together we made the moment live. When we were playing on a good night I wasn't thinking about yesterday or tomorrow — I was in the groove, in the moment. Winston Churchill said he felt that way as he rode into battle with the bullets whizzing by his ears. Playing with The Dingoes was not quite as heroic, but, at the Station, with a glass of beer on my amplifier, a girl or two in the audience catching my eye, and a rock-solid bass-and-drums combination thumping out the beat, I was deep inside the moment.

At twenty-three, those bacchanalian good times were reason enough for self-satisfaction. But even then, self-doubt, and doubts about the worth of The Dingoes, had begun to eat away at my contentedness. We had released an album, *The Dingoes*, and it had charted and peaked at number seventeen. We had given it everything we had, and now it was off the charts. So where did we stand in the overall scheme of things? At the Station we still felt like we were at the top — but what hierarchical structure were we at the top of? Could our success at the Station be trusted? No, I thought. We were merely the beneficiaries of the arrival of large numbers of people of our generation at an age when their innate need of culture made them latch onto anything that resembled it. As a mere cultural enzyme I couldn't claim too much credit for The Dingoes — yet, seen in this light, we had as much right as Mozart to success, if not longevity.

But the pressure of self-doubt was nothing compared to the growing problems surrounding The Dingoes. Though our pre-eminence remained at the Station, we began to get bogged down in unfriendly bars, 600-mile road trips and empty concert halls. And each time we came back to the Station, a little of our shine had worn off. By degrees we came to see ourselves as victims of a small and saturated market. We had played the same songs to too many of the same audiences. We had to admit we were going nowhere. We had decided to split up after our Western Australian trip. And then came the call.

Kerryn hung up the phone. 'Well. That's that, then.'

'What's what?' I said.

'Nothing. Who wants to go down and get a beer?'

He was toying with a very big and delicious piece of information. Understanding the need for an organised presentation of big news, we followed him downstairs. We went out into the empty beer garden.

This garden was surrounded by white trelliswork. Grapevines had threaded their tendrils into every available space. The beer garden was roofed over with green corrugated plastic, and when the patchy cloudiness occasionally gave way to the sun, everyone turned a deep shade of green.

I volunteered to get the beers. 'It's my shout. But you're not to say a word about the call until I get back.'

'Okay, mate.'

When I came back, Kerryn was saying: 'And then I hung up.'

I scowled and put the beers down on the white wrought-iron table.

'You're number one in my book, Mr Murray,' said Stockley, grateful as ever for a beer.

Kerryn began to spin out the phone conversation, 'It seems that young Billy McCartney got a job working for Elvis Presley's road crew — that's what got him overseas, anyway. After that, he got a job with this band called Lynyrd Skynyrd. They're apparently big in the South.'

He took a long draught of his beer and cleaned the foam off his top lip leisurely with his bottom lip. 'He took our album with him and he used to play it over the PA before Lynyrd how's-your-father played. Well, their manager, a guy called Peter Rudge, heard it and thought it wasn't bad. It seems he also manages ...' he took another sip, cleaned his top lip and went on, '... The Rolling Stones.'

'No!'

'Yes. And apparently Peter Rudge played it for Mick. Mick thought it was alright, too.'

'No kidding,' said Stockley. We were all flabbergasted. No-one else had touched their beer.

'And so ... so?' I said.

'Well, Rudge wants to cut a deal with A&M Records in Los Angeles. Billy wants us to set up a lawyer. He says contracts are on their way over.'

'Doesn't this Rudge guy even want to see us?' I asked.

'No. Our man in New York has sold us to him. Remember, about six months ago, when Billy used to hang at the Station?'

I could remember Billy leaning, beerless, against the back wall of the bar, with a grin a mile wide.

'My mate, Billy,' said Brod.

Just as intimates yawn together, we all sipped our beers at the same time. The clouds moved away for a minute and completely exposed the trellis to the sun, the beer garden became infused with green.

I looked at green Kerryn and said, 'Come on. You were on the phone much longer than that. What else?'

'That's not enough?' he said.

'When do we leave?' asked J.L.

'As soon as the lawyers take care of the contracts, I suppose.'

'Christ, this is unbelievable,' said Stockley, and he blew on his ring finger five times. 'I'm off to ring Jen.'

'Good idea.'

One by one the green Dingoes left to telephone the good news back to Melbourne. Presently I was alone in the beer garden. The squall had disappeared as quickly as it had come, and now the unobstructed sun's rays flooded me with still, green warmth. As I drained my glass, I was filled with an almost tangible sense of wellbeing. As soon as I put it on the table it was replaced, by Kerryn, with a full one.

'I think this is called for, don't you?' he said.

'Capital.'

'I suppose we shouldn't break up just yet, mate?'

'I suppose not, mate.'

2

Melbourne

In the green beer garden, after everyone had phoned our good news back to Melbourne, we agreed to keep the call secret. We realised people would find out, but we didn't want to make a big announcement until the contracts were signed.

As soon as we returned from Perth, a friend of the band said he knew a lawyer who knew something about the music business. His name was Seymour. No. He didn't know *international* music law but our friend was sure he could handle it. He had only been practising for two years, and we should have been sceptical, but we thought that all we needed was someone who could make sure the contracts were fair and legal.

Seymour's office was above a barber shop in Carlton. His desk was in front of a window that looked over the street; the window rattled every time a tram went by. The light coming through was so bright you could barely make out Seymour's features, except in silhouette.

On his glass-topped desk sat a huge ashtray filled with pipe paraphernalia. He smoked a pipe constantly. Even lying dormant in the ashtray, his Doctor Petersen pipe gave off an acrid odour.

I surreptitiously tried to read his diploma as Seymour said, 'It's really very simple. They will offer us a percentage. We'll send them back some higher figure. And we'll compromise somewhere in the middle. It's no different overseas.'

As he spoke he stuffed his pipe. He was slightly rotund and wore a beard and a brown corduroy suit of studied casualness. He took some matches and lit his pipe. Between incendiary puffs he said, 'They can afford to give you ... a good deal ... they want you bad enough to ... bring you, lock stock and ... barrel to America ... they must have ... money is not an issue.'

A great pall of smoke, courteously blown over our heads, hung a foot thick below the ceiling. His pipe was now fully lit. He put it in the ashtray, where it smouldered. A thin, pretty, grey plume replenished the smoke up by the ceiling; it began to diffuse throughout his office.

He looked at us to make sure we understood the fundamental wisdom of his statement. 'When do you expect the contracts to arrive?'

He turned to look each of us in the eye. For a second, no-one answered. Then Kerryn said, 'Well, Billy said they were sending them over straight away. They're fairly standard, he said. And he thought Peter Rudge was going to cut us a decent deal.'

Seymour let out a pompous laugh, 'Haw! Don't let them tell you that. There are no such animals as standard contracts.'

He fired up his pipe. 'From now ... on ... you can't trust ... whatever they say ... At least until we sign the contracts.'

He placed his pipe down again, and, with an air of finality, said, 'Look, perhaps it's better if you don't talk to them. Tell them to make all their communications through me. I think then we'll get the best bargaining position. Okay? Okay!'

Outside the barber shop we held an ad hoc conference.

Stockley said, 'I dunno, do you think he's okay?'

'Who knows,' I said. 'But we've got to have somebody. And who else do we know? There just aren't any international music lawyers here. Australia isn't international.'

'But do you reckon he was right about not talking to Billy?'

'No,' Kerryn jumped in. 'But we have to be careful. We can trust Billy, but their lawyers are going to be doing all the talking. It's best if they do it through Seymour. They could be nasty pieces of work.'

'Agreed by the party of the first party,' said Stockley.

'And agreed by the party of the second party,' I said.

The contracts came three weeks later and Kerryn took them to Seymour, who was going to take a couple of weeks to look them over. I imagined Kerryn sitting in Seymour's office, marvelling at the clouds of smoke as Seymour muttered an all-knowing 'Hmmm'. But then I thought Seymour probably wouldn't even sit at his desk. He would rather usher Kerryn out quickly and do the all-knowing in private.

During this time rumours about our deal began to flourish. Paul McCartney was writing songs with Kerryn; The Rolling Stones were to tour the world with The Dingoes. We decided to do an interview to straighten things out. After the interview, every second promoter billed his place as the site of *The Dingoes: Final Farewell Performance.* It became a running joke. We tried to stop it, but, although we thought we were about to be lifted up into a fabulous new life, we were broke — we had to work.

You can believe yourself to be great when you are not — but once you believe you are mediocre, it is hard to re-convince yourself of your greatness. Even though The Dingoes had been hailed as 'great' in the rock press, at the Station and at the New York office of The Rolling Stones, we had a bad case of creative block. As much as we told each other maybe we were great, we could see in our averted looks and hesitant rehearsals that the magic of the creative dynamic was, for the moment at least, no longer with us. Nobody expressed it this way, but I'm sure we all thought the same thing: *When we do an album overseas they'll probably get us to do our old material and arrangements. Let's make it on our past laurels. If we are successful internationally we will have to admit we are great. We can take it from there.* This attitude, impossible though it was to avoid, was going to make for a lengthy and soul-destroying stay in limbo — that is, unless we could make a quick exit.

A thick pall of smoke dissolved slowly into the air as Seymour tapped out the slag plug from the bottom of his Meerschaum's bowl. He took a velvet-green pipe-cleaner from a stand next to his ashtray and expelled a thick globule of black tar from the stem. Putting down the pipe, he picked up the folder with the contracts and gave them a cursory look.

He lobbed the folder onto the desk. 'You can sign these if you want ...'

They landed with a *thwack* that blew ash onto my thighs. Then he pushed himself deeply into his plush office chair and fondly stroked his upper lip: '... but you're fools if you do. Seven-and-a-half percent is bull. We're going to ask for fifteen. I bet that's closer. And let's up the advance money while we're at it. It's The Rolling Stones and A&M records, for God's sake. They can afford ten times that,' he said, pointing his nose at the contracts.

As we passed the contracts around, Seymour picked up his pipe and began to scrape it out. Black shards of carbon, bearing the residue of a week of Seymour's smoking, cascaded into the ashtray and onto the desk. He used his matchbox as a blade to gather the errant carbon into a pile near the edge of his desk. He pulled up his wastepaper basket and scraped the carbon into it. The contracts forgotten, we watched, spellbound by Seymour's excavations.

'Let me make a counter-proposal. All they can do is say no.'

Outside the barber shop, J.L. was adamant: 'I think we ought to sign and get out, now.'

I said, 'But we can't. We have to let Seymour try and get the best deal he can.'

'Does he know what he's doing?' said J.L.

'Good question. We haven't got much choice, mate — still,' said Stockley.

'I wish we knew how good seven-and-a-half percent is,' said Brod. 'It doesn't seem like much.'

'Seymour's position is that it's just an opening offer,' I said. 'Let's wait and see what reply he gets from them. Then we'll know where we stand.'

J.L. rolled his eyes.

Seymour had insisted that all negotiations be done by mail. Verbal agreements, he said, were useless. And furthermore, you knew where you stood if everything was down on paper. Seymour took two weeks to frame his reply. The laggard international post took another two weeks to get it to the lawyers in America. They took another two weeks to get to our contracts and advise Peter Rudge how to respond. Six weeks after our meeting their response came and we were summoned to Seymour's office.

As we walked up the stairs, the aromatic stench of his Private Bin #72 tobacco flooded our senses and evoked Seymour in a way his actual presence never could. As he opened the door, eddies of smoke whorled about our bodies. It was worse than usual today. The thick, overcast ceiling had been disturbed by the suction of the open door and was now seething with Gothic potential. Seymour had no pipe, but telltale wisps of smoke vivified his beard. He asked us to sit and, walking behind his desk, pulled an airmail letter from a drawer. He was still standing and, while he leaned on his desk with one hand, he slapped the letter against his trouser leg with an action that fanned up a few flakes of ash.

'They're just not playing the game — they've thrown this right back in our faces. We were looking for some good faith and they gave us nothing!' He shook with passion. 'Nothing!'

He threw the letter down onto the desk and fell back into his chair. One by one we read the letter. Stockley passed it to me like it was a hot potato.

Seymour had said, 'Seven-and-a-half? They can do better than that. Let's ask for fifteen; maybe we'll get ten.'

'We feel,' the letter said, 'our initial offer was more than fair. We made this offer in order that you would sign quickly. Please reconsider and get back to us as soon as possible.'

'Maybe the offer is fair, Seymour,' I said. 'Do you know what is standard?'

Seymour had lit another pipe and smoke was streaming from his nostrils. Everyone looked at the smoke-enshrouded lawyer for a reply to this reasonable question. He tapped the mouthpiece of his pipe against his cheek:

'Don't be tricked by their letter,' he said. 'I deal with contracts all the time. All this means is that we were a little high on our fifteen. You know they can't say, 'Well, we thought that fifteen was a little high. Why don't you ask us for ten and we might go for eight or even nine. This is a standard tactic. We'll just hit them a little lower next time, that's all.' Seymour thumped his pipe down in his ashtray like a gavel as if to say, *Case closed.*

But Kerryn contemptuously said: 'But you just said they weren't playing the game.'

'Oh, they're playing a game alright! They call it hardball. These are top-flight people. Savvy ... and ruthless.'

'I'm worried,' said Brod. 'I'm worried we're gonna blow 'em off.'

'You have to trust me,' said Seymour. 'This is the way it's played. You can't let them roll over you now — if you do they'll have you for breakfast later on.'

But Brod came back, 'Do you mind if we step outside for a couple of minutes? I think we ought to talk between ourselves.'

Seymour couldn't stop us from doing that and we walked a block away from his office, to a pub. We sat in a semicircle around the bar. When we got our beer we began.

'Ring Billy — all we have to do is find out what's fair. It's obvious Seymour doesn't know.'

'He should have gone lower to begin with.'

'Yeah. They might have given us nine.'

'It's too late now.'

'This being in limbo is killing us — we've got to get out soon or it will be too late, no matter what percentage Seymour can get.'

'Yeah. Let's take the seven-and-a-half and run.'

'Seven-and-a-half of something is better than fifteen percent of nothing.'

'God! You're wise, Stockley,' I said.

Kerryn brought the meeting to conclusion, 'Let's up and down these beers and give the good news to Seymour.'

'Man, he's gonna love this.'

Brod knocked on Seymour's door. The room was clear of smoke. I think he knew what we were about to say. Brod spoke, 'We've decided to sign now. We've got to get over there soon or we won't have anything left for America.'

'Very well.' Seymour was disgruntled. 'That's fair enough, I suppose.'

He picked up his pipe and started to fill it.

'But there is something else.'

He put the filled pipe on top of a box of matches and handed out five xeroxed copies of page five of the contracts. As we read them he lit up, and spoke between draughts of air:

'The second ... sentence in para ... graph three.'

The flames from the pipe, dimly visible through the smoke, shot six inches above the bowl when Seymour released his sucking pressure. *When he was sucking,* I thought, *those flames must be blasting right on his tongue.* As he spoke I tried to get a glimpse of it, but the light streaming in from behind, and the smoke, made it difficult to see anything. I imagined that he had a kind of asbestos sheath that he slid over his tongue, and this gave me a mild case of the giggles as I was apparently reading the contract.

'This wouldn't be so funny, John,' said Seymour, 'if you understood what it was that was being said. That line means you have to pay back any advances they give you — whether or not you make it. Do you know what that means? You're going to be paying them back for the rest of your lives — unless, of course, you're phenomenally successful.'

We carefully read the clause. To me, and everyone but Seymour, it seemed to mean the opposite. It said that advanced money was non-returnable royalty — it should be paid back only if we made money on the contract. But Seymour insisted that it said we had to pay back no matter what. 'Here, you read it.'

> Subject to ARTISTS fully performing all of ARTIST's respective obligations pursuant to this Agreement, and all of the ARTIST's warranties and undertakings hereunder, COMPANY agrees to make to ARTIST the following non-returnable advances against royalties:

He picked up his pipe. It had been smouldering in the ashtray. The small amount of time it had lay there allowed the tar to settle in the bowl and soak up into the remaining tobacco. The smoke produced was ten times more acrid. As he fired it up we winced in anticipation of another burn.

'The percentage is okay ... but you can't ... go with ... this ... they will screw you royally ... mark ... my words.'

'But it doesn't say that, Seymour,' I said. The others nodded in agreement. 'It says non-returnable — *non-returnable*, right?'

'Yes. But look at the words before it. 'Subject to artist fully performing ... That's badly defined. They can say you didn't fully perform and make you pay back everything. You can't trust them.'

'But it ...'

'Now, look. Would I tell you how to play guitar? You hired me to interpret contracts for you. That is what I do.'

He tapped his pipe on the ashtray and slowly cleaned it out.

'I'll tell you what we'll do. I know a Queen's Counsel. I'll take it to him and get an opinion. Fair enough?'

We supposed so. We should have said no at every step, but each time it seemed to be just another two weeks on a very crucial point. We walked out into the world of plaintiffs and defendants.

'I dunno,' said Stockley. 'I agree with you, John. But we've waited this long already. And it is a pretty important point. And, you know, contracts do have their own language. Maybe only lawyers understand them.'

'I fuckin' hate this,' said Kerryn, as he kicked a can out into the busy mid-afternoon traffic.

'Yeah,' said Brod. 'But Stockley's right.'

'I think that genius is full of it. But we can't take the risk of his being right,' said Stockley.

'It's a jerk-off,' said J.L.

'This is like *The African Queen*,' I said. 'We're bogged down in the swamp at low tide. We think there is no escape and we lay down to die not knowing that the lake is a stone's throw away. So, instead of waking up dead, we will be lifted up by the high tide and swept into the lake.'

'But not until Seymour sees the African Queen's Counsel,' said Kerryn.

We would see what happened in two weeks. In the meantime, there were jobs to do.

As we trundled up the Hume Highway between Albury and Gundagai, on our way to Sydney, I lay on a mattress in the back of Brod's

World War II vintage Land Rover. Stretched out like fallen heroes of El Alamein, Kerryn, J.L. and I were trying to urge Brod to go faster than thirty-five. In buying the Rover, Brod had selected style over speed, comfort and utility — style, and fighting chance should we run into the Rommel's Afrika Korps. Brod, who was quite dashing in other ways, drove with palpable anxiety. He fidgeted to make sure he was still in gear, that the choke was in, the handbrake wasn't on, and that the rear-vision mirror was properly adjusted.

Kerryn whispered into my ear, 'He drives like somebody's aunty.'

'Try telling that to Field Marshall von Rommel,' I said.

Brod drove with his foot slightly depressing the clutch, a move that, though rough on the clutch, was an excellent defensive tactic. Nobody could make him go faster than thirty-five and, so far, despite several near-misses from behind, Broderick had got us through.

Stockley, who was up front, had given up conversation and was nodding off. But sleep, for him, was impossible, since to rest his head anywhere on the violently shaking metal was to risk severe injury.

'Stockley,' I offered. 'I'll swap places with you. I can't sleep anyway in this rattletrap. Sorry, Brod. This very *strategic* rattletrap.'

'Here,' said Stockley, using the voice of Maury. 'You're number one in my book, Mr Murray. Number one.'

After we changed places, at about 3am, I started to reflect on our legal situation. Seymour had tried to up our percentage by too much. This was a forgivable error in judgment; he was, after all, only trying to get us the best possible deal. He had called into question a crucial sentence about non-returnable royalties, and he had hired a Queen's Counsel to write an opinion on it. If all this was taking too much time, he was erring on the side of caution. That the QC had gone on vacation, and couldn't give his opinion until after we returned from this series of final-farewell performances in Sydney, wasn't Seymour's fault. I didn't like Seymour, but I shouldn't, I thought, let that interfere with my opinion of his conduct.

On the other hand, though I was cowed by the bigness of our contractual dealings and my ignorance of law, I felt that Seymour was wrenching away our destiny by trying to make the negotiating process more arcane than it need be. I had a growing suspicion that he was like a dubious and unskilled motor mechanic who thinks he can do any work he wants to because you can't tell he doesn't know what he's doing. Any complications only made his cover deeper. Maybe Seymour felt that by invoking the QC any arguments about legal syntax would be stymied. But I wasn't so sure that law was as esoteric as engines — despite the efforts of lawyers to make it so. However, though these were concerns to keep in mind, all things that were presently being done, I thought, had to be done.

'Where are we, driver? Any sign of the bloody Krauts?'

'No, sir,' said Brod. 'We should reach Cairo at about 0800 hours.'

'Very good, Corporal. Carry on.'

'Thank you, sir.'

'By the by, Brod. Do you know you're in second gear?'

'Thanks, mate.'

He changed into third, but soon after, the Rover died on a hill. The same gear ratio that enabled it to pull six-inch howitzers out of the mud, robbed it of power on the highway. Brod pushed the pedal down to the floor with a clang, clang, clanging sound. The futility of that action reminded me of The Dingoes' efforts to throttle up and climb our current hill — Seymour and the contracts.

We arrived in Sydney at ten in the morning looking as deprived of sleep as the Rats of Tobruk. No sleep would be had before our first job, an afternoon open-air concert. As if we didn't have pressure enough, we had extra pressure in Sydney. Our record had not been played there, yet we were known to have a big overseas deal in the offing. We were either ignored somebodies or celebrated nobodies, and no-one, least of all ourselves, knew which. And this hung like a giant question mark between us and every audience north of the Murray River.

At the concert, the radio station had thoughtfully provided a tent and free beer in huge garbage pails filled with crushed ice. Our common sense was anaesthetised by our lack of sleep, and it was a very hot and humid day — we drank deeply. When it came time to play, we were barely capable. To ourselves we were hilarious. Behind the curtain of amplified sound we shouted jokes about Aunty Broderick and the Nazi threat. I was tired and became hysterical easily. I buckled up with laughter. The audience must have thought we didn't care if we were appreciated or not. We received polite applause as we hit the tent for another round of heavy beer drinking. Stockley stood in the corner of the tent in a pensive mood.

'What's the matter, mate?' I asked.

'Nothing, mate.'

'You don't look like you're having such a good time.'

Stockley answered in the whiny voice of Maury, 'We didn't come here to have a good time, Mr Murray. We came here to get fuckin' drunk.'

With a full head of steam, and fearful of a devastating early-evening hangover, I kept on drinking. As I drank I had, somewhere in the back of my mind, the foolish idea that I was only maintaining my state of inebriation — that I was keeping constantly, mildly, drunk. But later that night, I attempted to pinch the bottom of every girl at the Trocadero Club. The companion of one of them punched me in the face. I wept for Man's inhumanity to Man, and by four o'clock in the morning I sobered up enough to realise I was on some suburban porch singing Elvis Presley songs. My audience of three included an auto accident victim who wore a cast on his leg and needed crutches. Like a Pied Piper of brotherly love, I led them through the streets to my hotel room. Kerryn, roused from his drunken sleep, promptly shooed my boon companions away. I passed out almost immediately.

The next day we had to drive north of Sydney to the Hunter Valley Wine Festival — of necessity another all-day drinking affair. We began playing an hour before sunset; the sun shone directly into our faces as we played. I was so drunk, dirty and exhausted that I had to lie down as I played. In the morning the others told me I had made an idiot of myself. But I had made no mistakes. I was tempted to praise my musicianship for maintaining its standard even under befuddled adversity — but then, I thought, I had played those songs so many times that my brain worked like an old pool table that had channels leading to its pockets: even the blind shots went down.

The next two days were a blur. But I remember Newcastle. On the way to the job, I said to everyone in the Rover, 'Does anyone feel as bad as me? We really shouldn't drink so much.'

'Naw,' said Stockley, as Maury, 'A bloke's gotta have a bloody beer, mate.'

'But why does a bloke have to drink so much bloody beer, mate?'

'Because when a bloke's had a bloody beer he feels better than when he hasn't had one.'

Kerryn sneezed. 'Christ! I think I'm carrying my cold to Newcastle.'

That night at the club, our warm-up act was a male stripper. Members of the Vice Squad were in the audience, so he had to stop his act at his G-string. When he came offstage he was livid. Retaining his G-string had stripped him, as it were, of his artistic integrity. Having protected everyone from his unsightly genitals, the Vice Squad left, and Stockley hatched a wicked idea.

The stripper ranted backstage with sibilance as we were introduced: 'Soon to be off to America, and signed to a big overseas recording deal — let's hear it for their final Australian performance ... The Dingoes.'

The audience, fully aware of the stripper's plight, cheered convulsively as we shuffled on stage with our pants down around our ankles, revealing all.

After the set, I had a tryst with a redheaded motorcyclist (she must have been impressed by my genitals). She took me speeding out on the Newcastle breakwater. As the huge Pacific rollers crashed a couple of feet below us, we made love, which was wonderful until she asked me to pinch and scratch her. My desire fizzled; we dressed. As I was about to get on her bike, she sped off. I found my way back to the hotel by sunrise.

At ten we had to leave for Sydney and an early afternoon sound check. We were the warm-up band for the English group Bad Company. After the show, we all went to a late-night club for a jam session. When the club closed we challenged the Englishmen to a test match — a beer-drinking test match. I think Australia won.

The next day was a rest day, except for an interview with a writer for the Australian section of *Rolling Stone* magazine. We decided to meet her at a posh restaurant. Our conversation was sparse and unfocused as we sat waiting for service. Instead of making brilliant comments like, 'Pop music is the soundtrack for a generation,' I said, 'So anyway, how long have you worked for *Rolling Stone*?'

We ordered food and wine. The waitress brought a delicious Chateau Tahbilk and our soup. Stockley, who sat at the opposite end of the table from me, was dressed in a dandy blue-velvet suit. He had put his jacket on the back of his chair and rolled up the cuffs of his floral body shirt in one meticulous roll, so as to admit no impediment to his epicurean enjoyment. He delicately tasted his wine and nodded appreciatively to no-one. Then he tasted his soup. He froze, 'This soup is canned,' he said.

'It tastes fine to me,' I said.

'It's canned, mate.'

'Stockley, they wouldn't serve canned soup in a place like this.'

'It's canned.'

'Ask the waitress. I'll bet you it's real soup,' I said. 'I'd stake my professional reputation on it.'

'Professional reputation as a rat?' said Stockley.

'No. As a professional knower of the difference between canned and real soup.'

I was half joking, and half berating Stockley for making such a big deal over the soup. But, like a play fight that turns ugly, I became unable to tell whether we were still joking. The flatness of my wits, dulled by six days of high jinx, made me say, as I looked at the journalist, 'Working-Class Hero Likes Soup Just So.'

I had meant it in a joking way, but I realised, after the first word, that my faux headline sounded malicious. Stockley kept looking, with furrowed brow, toward the waitress station. By the time the waitress came over, all conversation had ceased and our table was charged with an embarrassing tension.

Stockley said, 'Excuse me. Do you know if this soup is canned or not?'

'Yes, it is,' she said matter-of-factly, as she busied herself at our table.

All faces turned to me.

'Waitress,' I said. 'This soup is *excellent*. What brand *is* it?'

After the soup and some more wine, we recovered our humour — enough, anyway, to make it seem that drinking was a fun thing to do.

The last day in Sydney we were to play a live radio show. After the first note we realised we had made a mistake in trying to play. Halfway through the first verse we looked at each other like drowning men. Broderick's voice was completely raw; I opened my mouth to sing a harmony but nothing came out; no rhythmic connection existed among any of the instruments — we fell apart. One by one we stopped playing and looked pathetically at the audience. The producer cut to one of our recorded tunes and came out of the control room with his arms outstretched.

'What's going on?'

Kerryn and Brod tried to explain our problem to him. To the confused and embarrassed audience we must have appeared to be undergoing a group nervous breakdown. Stockley's glasses seemed darker than ever that day as he and I sat on the edge of the stage with heads in our hands; J.L. sat on his drum stool staring straight into space. I longed to be an audience member who could casually walk out of my life and into their trouble-free existence of limitless possibility. But I was stuck.

'You want to go outside for a walk, John,' said Stockley in a tremulous voice.

As our equipment was being packed up, Stockley and I were both experiencing a terrifying anxiety attack. The more we tried to comfort each other, the more validity we gave our attacks. Our anxiety was fuelled by exhaustion, the compounding effect of seven days of drinking, and fresh guilt. And though the attacks were rooted in our pressure-filled reality, they seemed to override reality and take on a life of their own. The rest of the day was a day of going through the motions of life, but feeling only fear.

My attack lasted three more days — all through the Rover ride back to Melbourne (if Rommel had known our state he could have cut us to ribbons) and in my rented room where I sequestered myself and vowed I would never feel that way again. But even as the days became tolerable, during the nights, since I was no longer sleeping in a drunken stupor, I developed worrying symptoms. I woke up several nights in a row in a cold sweat. I was convinced that my heart had stopped beating. I sat bolt upright in bed and clutched my wrist to feel a pulse. But I was grappling with tensed fingers and could feel none. I leapt out of bed and breathed feverishly to jump-start my heart. Of course my heart had not stopped beating, but, try as I might to convince myself of the logic of this, my emotions shoved the apparent fact of impending doom in my face every night.

Another consequence of my battle to cling to reality was that I clung more tenaciously to things I believed to be rational in everyday life. And one of these was the sentence that said that advances had to be paid back out of non-returnable royalties. I was building a parallel with my anxiety attacks. If I perceived the sentence correctly, if my powers of logic could prevail over a lawyer, a QC and four men (for, by now, everyone was prepared to go along with the QC's opinion), then perhaps they could also prevail over the irrational nocturnal tigers of anxiety and beat them back to their primitive den.

We parked opposite Seymour's office in J.L.'s white Morris minivan. The day was hot and Seymour had his window open; smoke was billowing out. A pigeon alighted off its air current and onto Seymour's window ledge. It flew off immediately.

'I've read that sentence so many times,' said Stockley. 'It could say *Eat at Joe's* for all I know. I say we go along with the Queen's how's-your-father.'

'I think we have to,' said Kerryn.

'Even if it means we go nowhere,' said Brod, 'I think we have to take the QC's opinion seriously. We can't risk being ruined for life.'

'Let's see what the Q-fuckin'-C says,' I said.

We climbed up and out of the mini. Seymour had heard our footsteps on his stairs and was waiting at his open door. He had a smile that desperately tried to show concern but was smug beyond the hiding.

'Come in and sit down,' he said. 'How was Adelaide?'

'Good,' I said. 'How was the Queen's Counsel?'

'Ah, yes,' he said. 'I'm afraid he thinks we have a problem. He says that at best the sentence is ambiguous, and that it probably means you have to pay back whether you make it or not.'

We were silent. J.L. buried his head in his hands.

Kerryn was exasperated. 'Well, where does that put us now.'

'We're fucked,' concluded Stockley. 'That's where it puts us.'

'It's up to you. If you sign these contracts you'll have to be prepared to pay back for the rest of your life. Of course, you can gamble that you'll make it. But if you want my advice — I wouldn't sign for anything.'

'I think you're wrong,' I said.

'Well, as I said, it's up to you. It's your risk, not mine.'

'I think you and the QC are wrong. The sentence means we don't pay back if we don't make money.' My voice was shaking with exhilaration; I made no effort to hide it.

Seymour looked at me with a bemused expression and said, 'Wait a minute. Where did you say you got your degree from, John?'

'Hey! Don't talk to him like that,' said Kerryn menacingly. 'He's not an idiot.'

'I can understand English as well as you. And that's what these contracts were written in.'

'And what about the Queen's Counsel? I suppose you can read law as well as him, too.'

'*He*, Seymour. I don't know anything but that that sentence is a protection for us. It's common sense.'

The others were a silent but appreciative audience.

'Come with me,' snapped Seymour as he snatched up his pipe and lit it. He headed for the conference room. I walked out last, and the single file of bobbing heads, with Seymour's sending out clouds of smoke, looked, for all the world, like a train of heads. But this time I didn't get the giggles.

We sat at the conference table while Seymour wrote, on a blackboard, the disputed sentence. After twenty minutes of his syntactical browbeating, the blackboard was covered with underlined syllables and arrows pointing from preposition to conjunction. I calmly said, 'I'm sorry. But it says just the opposite, in plain English. I haven't got a clue what you're talking about, but you must have made a mistake somewhere.'

Seymour shouted, 'John, if you can't see it now you're a bloody moron!' He quickly withdrew. 'I'm sorry. Look, I don't blame you. That's why you hired me. But you're not letting me do my job. Would I tell you how to play drums? Ha, ha. I hope not. No. But let me interpret the law, won't you?'

But the more he carried on, the stronger my conviction became. I felt as I would if Seymour was a doctor and we were all studying an X-ray. Everyone was saying the dark spot is a tumour. I can plainly see it is a fly.

'There's only one thing to do,' I said. 'You reword it to your satisfaction, and I'll ring their lawyers tonight. If they agree to your change, we sign. If they don't, I'll bring the cyanide tablets to our next meeting.'

'What do we have to lose,' said Stockley.

'Cool,' said Brod.

At one in the morning I rang Peter Rudge's lawyer. She agreed to the change without a quibble.

I saw Seymour only once after that. The amended contracts were mailed to him and I had the privilege of picking them up.

'I've looked at that sentence again. You might be right,' he said.

So six months after the first call, we signed, sealed and sent off the contracts. Two months after that we boarded a jumbo jet bound for America.

3

Toronto

Our new American manager, Peter Rudge, had a master plan. We were to live initially in Toronto. There we would be able to rehearse and play far enough away from the blanching New York spotlight, yet close enough for him to monitor and foster our progress. Record producers would fly in and we would record at whatever studio the best producer wanted. After that we would move to New York and tour. Starting in small clubs, we would cause a small buzz of excitement. Then we would step up to big halls and stadiums with Lynyrd Skynyrd and, perhaps later, with The Rolling Stones. By then we would be household names.

But when our plane touched down in Vancouver, there was no-one there to meet us. After all the other passengers had been processed, we sat alone in the middle of an acre of fluorescent-lit linoleum, like resting Sherpas, among our equipment.

'Did you think Rudge would be here to meet us, Stockley?'

'That ratbag?'

Kerryn and Brod walked over to the Immigration desk and tried to persuade the officials to let us into their country. Everyone, from Rudge down to us, had assumed that you could travel without a visa between Commonwealth countries. The officials could have turned us around and sent us home at our own expense. Instead they gave us a two-week interim visa. We flew on to Toronto.

Thirty-two hours after we took off from Melbourne, we arrived at the quasi-US city of Toronto. We left in the Australian winter. It was summer over here. July 1976.

The Rolling Stones' office — actually, Sir Productions, or 'Sir' for short — had dispatched someone to help us set up house in Toronto. Janice was a tall woman with a Marilyn Monroe mole and waist-length, jet-black hair. Amid the bland Torontonian accents, her Brooklynese reminded us of the Promised Land just south of the border. She was charmingly overenthusiastic to see us. We were her promotion and she was in 'a mass state of psychness' to do good things for us. At times she had a quizzical expression. I imagined that this expressed her mighty puzzlement that these five unspectacular men were about to become stars. For Peter Rudge's ability to make this miraculous transformation was an article of faith among all his employees.

Janice drove us to our hotel.

I walked into my room, dropped my suitcase, and sat on the edge of the bed. I leaned over and turned on the television. A porno movie was on; a couple was going at it.

Stockley knocked on the door. In the voice of Maury he said, 'Here, mate. What's that yer got on the telly?'

'I think they're married, mate. So it's alright. What are those?' I asked, pointing to the green bottles under his arm.

'Some of the local variety. I suppose we really ought to try them.'

'Alright. But only in the interest of international goodwill.'

We sipped the beer.

'A bloody poofter's beer,' said Stockley.

'You don't want it?'

'I didn't say that, now, did I?'

Kerryn walked in bringing six more opportunities for international goodwill.

'Just like any other tour,' he said.

We finished the beers and went to bed. The TV stayed on as I dreamed a dream of frustrated curiosity. It was a dream I had had several times in Australia. I flew, riding an airplane like a bronco, over North America. Instead of familiar terrain, I saw only a vast anonymous map sprawled beneath me in political pastels. I woke up and thought, *Christ! My subconscious doesn't even know I'm here yet.* We had sat, stagnating in time, for so long, and now we were sucked into the desired maelstrom. I needed time to catch up. Ten hours later I awoke to the porno channel and the feral sounds of human ecstasy.

After two days of recovery, I started to feel better. But we were all getting zapped by tremendous static-electricity shocks. I theorised that these came as a result of us moving from the southern to the northern hemisphere; our electrical polarities were out of phase or something. Stockley said it was electrickery up to its usual devilry. He stood, blowing on his ring finger as he moved his key towards the lock of his room. But a visible spark arced across the gap and zapped him ferociously.

'Thou sinister jumping fire!' he snapped.

By the second day, Janice had found our dream home. It was in an outer suburb called Unionville. This was a once sleepy village that was now in the process of being swamped by lower-middle-class developments. The house had a gambrel roof and a two-car garage. It was in a cul-de-sac with five other identical units.

On the first day, Stockley, after a trip to the store, entered next door's house by mistake. On the second day, this very forgiving neighbour brought us a bottle of blue wine as a welcoming gesture to his neighbourhood. As Kerryn switched on the fireplace, the man plunked himself down in our flimsy rented furniture and said, 'So, you're a band, eh? Are you going to be playing aboot here?'

I slipped out to pour the wine down the sink. Stockley caught me and whispered, 'Save that, mate. We can use it for the dishes — it's Chateaux Ajax.'

The kitchen window looked out onto the backyard and abandoned farmland beyond. Our ensconcement into the neighbourhood coincided with the development of this land. A team of surveyors marked the positions of future roads and houses among the thistles and dandelions. But none of this concerned us. Apart from the congenial Canadian next door, we had nothing to do with the neighbourhood — we had nothing to do with anything, except ourselves.

We settled into domestic bliss. With a nutritional diet of eggs, eggs and eggs, we rehearsed the same old songs in the basement in preparation for our onslaught on America. And when we stopped rehearsing, which was the instant any of us could come up with the flimsiest of reasons, we often went for a delightfully rewarding cultural stroll through some of the local shopping malls. We had dinner at an Italian restaurant where the waitress brought the red wine perfectly chilled; or at that distinctively Canadian establishment, McDonald's. Stockley saw the *Three Billion Sold* sign and thereafter referred to McDonald as 'The Great Chef.' Some days we tried one of the many great family restaurants. Stockley marvelled at the chrome potatoes as we indulged ourselves in a friendly game of waitress baiting. We said *thank you* at every opportunity and wagered on how many times she would say *you're welcome* in response.

And beer had to be obtained. Stockley and I went to our local Liquor Control Board of Ontario. This looked more like an off-track betting facility than a beer store, and I have never seen Stockley more depressed as when he was filling out his request form for beer. He stood in line grumbling about the intrusion of the state, 'Nineteen eighty-fuckin'-four,' he muttered.

Stockley was hit hardest by all this crassness. He saw his lifestyle being brutalised by the disappointing lack of culture of the Canadians, and by the already well-established lack of culture of The Dingoes. He was revolted by the state of disarray and uncleanness of the house. Signs began appearing. 'Don't use beer glasses for milk', said one. He became morose, defeatist and whiny. And though the rest of us loathed his whining as unproductive, we thought it was the appropriate response. I even entertained the idea that I would have moaned as much as he did — if only I had the class to feel as outraged.

And then we got several reminders of our reason for being there. Emissaries from Sir and A&M came to examine their investment.

Biff Epstein was the Artist and Repertoire man from A&M Records. Historically, A&R men have acted like editors: they helped their artists select and develop their recording repertoire. But in Biff's time, this function was usurped by record producers and the artists themselves.

The job of the A&R man had been relegated to acquiring and rejecting artists for their label. We had been handed to Biff as a *fait accompli*. I don't know if this made him naturally antagonistic towards us, but it seemed as if he had been given just one directive by his recording company bosses: 'Get in their face!'

When he rang our doorbell we had been drinking a quiet late-afternoon beer and watching the Olympic Games on TV. The Scottish commentator for the 100-kilometre bicycle race had just said, 'Gianelli is in first place now, but he had better be careful. He's making it easy for the man behind him because he's breaking a lot of wind.'

When Biff entered the living room I was rolling around on the floor and Kerryn was laughing like a hyena. Biff was visibly gauging his first impression. He was not amused.

He was dressed in impeccably pressed denim. He wore red-rimmed glasses and had long blond hair that was untidy just so. This snazzy intellectual hipster opened the leather briefcase on his lap and peered at us over its lid. He looked at us with a dubious expression. We knew he was coming, and we had tried to look nice for him, but we had been hanging around the house all day like bored housewives. We were rumpled and frumpy. He said, 'Now. You *are* signed with Peter Rudge, aren't you?'

'Yes,' said Kerryn.

'He is your manager, isn't he?'

'No,' I said. 'I understood he was going to be our dentist.'

'Then you've signed contracts — and can I see them, please.'

I ran upstairs and brought down a copy.

'Good,' he said, and he made a little notation in the privacy of his briefcase. It was plain that the reason A&M was interested in us was that we were signed to Rudge. I took an instant dislike to Biff for revealing this, even if it were true. He kept on with his kindergarten questions.

'Are you a cover band?'

'No. We do our own stuff. Haven't you heard our album?' asked Kerryn incredulously.

'Are you sure? Because we already have hundreds of them over here. Cover bands.' He put up his hand to silence our nonexistent protest. 'I'm not putting them down — they are very good at what they do. But we wouldn't be signing a cover band.'

'Well,' I said, 'we only do three tribute medleys. One Beatles, one Stones and one Led Zeppelin. But all the other songs are ours — not counting *The Mexican Hat Dance* and *Zorba*, of course. Well, and *Ave Mar—*'

'All right, John,' said Stockley.

'Not ... a ... cover ... band,' said Biff as he wrote in the recesses of his briefcase. 'Can you play me some of your songs now?'

We walked down to the basement and started playing. Biff sat on the floor making notes and offering a noncommittal 'Okay' after each song.

After we played our only cover song, *Something Else* by Eddie Cochrane, Biff said, 'Now can I hear *Zorba*?'

I liked him a little better after that.

But then he said, 'But you wouldn't put a cover song on your record, would you?'

'Gosh, no!' I said.

Playing to an audience of one can be very uncomfortable and Biff didn't make it any easier. After we played a song by Brod and Stockley (*Boy on the Run*, which had my favourite bass part), he said, 'But you can't just play an ascending line through those chords — you, on the bass.'

You on the bass was yours truly.

'What would you suggest, *you on the floor*?'

Kerryn laughed and then intervened, 'No. We're not going to break down each and every song. We're going to get a producer, right? Let's leave something for him to do.'

Even if Biff was trying to be constructive, he gave us the distinct impression that he thought we were no good. At the time I thought he might be right. Now I believe he showed destructive incompetence. No matter what he thought, he should have given us the opposite impression — and I can only conclude he was either very stupid or he was trying to torpedo us.

The next visitor was from Sir. He was their accountant and he was refreshingly drab. His name was Bill Szisblatt; he was so detail-conscious that Stockley dubbed him Bill This-and-That.

Bill's favourite pastime was telling us how huge we were going to be. Ours was listening to him.

'There's no way you guys aren't going to be very wealthy.'

We sat at his feet like devotees of a guru, enraptured by his prophecies. But he didn't hang around. As soon as he got all the information for our life insurance and health policies, he had to be going.

We had arrived in the summer. By the time we met Peter Rudge, autumn was in progress. He was staying at an opulent hotel in downtown Toronto, and we drove into town in a state of high curiosity, eagerness and some apprehension. He opened the door of his suite.

'Hello boys. At last, eh? Heh, heh, heh.'

He was a small Englishman with eyes that craved action. His clothes were rumpled and skewed by his constant agitation. We knew that he owned a soccer team and he had the look of a player who, while graceful on the field, was the soul of awkwardness in a shirt and tie. He seemed ready at any moment to spring into action and score the immortal goal.

We stood waiting for him as he rifled through his bags for his credit cards. When he found them, he said, 'We might need these. Heh, heh, heh.'

In the elevator we all stared stupidly at the floor numbers above the door. And at the restaurant, after we exhausted pleasantries, we fell silent. We had been delivered to him like mail-order brides and we hardly knew what to say. He had to like us — and it appeared that he did — but even at that first meeting, when we became more familiar, Stockley suggested a new name for the band: Rudge's Folly.

Rudge laughed and said, 'Don't say that. It might be true.'

Rudge's Folly was not a foreign concept for him.

Unrestricted by our allowances, we ordered food and wine. When the wine came Stockley sipped his glass of Chateau Neuf du Pape. He groaned quietly with delight, like a prisoner of war who had been smuggled a cigarette.

We listened as Rudge told us, at our prompting, the story of his life. He had wanted to be a spy for the British agency, MI5. He had passed every exam but one. For the final test he was to be locked in a house for a week and visited by stressful situations. He was rejected from the agency because he was rude to one of the servants!

'How awfully British of them,' I said.

He sublimated his desire for covert action and high drama on the world stage by managing The Who and, later, The Rolling Stones. But I think he felt his greatest coup was to be the rise to world prominence of ... The Dingoes.

I remember a nervous but warm and mentorial presence from Peter Rudge that day. I can't remember any more conversation, however, except a run-in I had with Stockley. The day before, he and I had discussed education ('intellectual pricks' that we were). I argued that bright kids should be put together so they wouldn't be dragged down by slow, uninterested and disruptive children. He argued — shouted, actually — that this was an elitist attitude and, as such, it shouldn't be considered.

At Rudge's dinner table Kerryn was saying, 'In Australia we've gone as far as we could go. You know there's so much more music over here — well, not here, but in the US — the competition has just got to force you to be better. I really think it's going to improve us.'

'Yes,' I said. 'It's like our elitism discussion, Stockley.'

'*Peter* doesn't want to hear about that, John.'

'Stockley! You come from a lower-middle-class background. It's making you do confusing things. You Englishmen and your bloody classes! Here you are paying lip-service to social equality while you're in the middle of an orgasm over this fine wine and posh place. And another thing: don't pretend there's any pecking order in this band. Just because you're suffering in Unionville, don't think you're the only one who's outraged. Don't think you're on any aesthetic high ground or anything. How dare you brush me aside so rudely. You think I won't say anything because we're trying to impress Peter Rudge here. Au contraire, my dear fellow, Peter is plainly mortified, as you can see, by your total lack of class — you peon.'

This, anyway, is what I imagined saying as I tried to rid myself of poisonous feelings that night in bed. At the table, I was effectively neutralised for the rest of the dinner. Stockley and I had a tradition of sniping at each other, but we had never been forced to live so close for so long. We were suffering all the tensions of marriage and had none of its mechanisms of release. At Unionville, we were more like five animals in a cage than a social unit in its natural environment. A zookeeper would lose his job if he put five alpha males in a single cage. But, I thought, as I looked at our benefactor, Rudge was oblivious to this.

At the dinner, we petitioned Rudge that we had to work or bust. Three weeks later, as autumn turned to winter, we were playing in Toronto and Montreal and all points in between. All of a sudden we had a road crew, a roster with complete logistic information — all materialised as if we had asked it of a genie. Out in the backyard at Unionville, earthmovers worked feverishly to get as much done as they could before the soil stiffened with cold. Eager to show our wares, we took to the road.

All went well for a while. But, after a time, we realised we weren't connecting with the audiences. We didn't take this personally; we blamed the audiences. After a particularly flat performance in Brockville, Ontario, we were invited to a party. In Australia we were used to having a little cachet at parties, enough at least to freely express our opinion on bad music. At this party the host was at one point playing the song *A Horse with No Name*. I looked at Kerryn and pinched my nose.

He said, 'Supposed to be about heroin.'

'That don't make no never mind,' and I made the finger-in-mouth vomit sign.

The host must have seen me and taken exception to my criticism.

'Who do you think you are!'

He was right. I had forgotten my place. That record was a million-seller and I was just playing his dumb club in Brockville.

On that tour of the Saint Lawrence Seaway, most of the clubs were dumb. We would often play to empty houses. The few people that were there invariably preferred watching ice hockey on an ever-present TV set.

Montreal seemed a cultural oasis in a mind-numbing desert. Our visit coincided with the first flexing of René Lévesque's separatist movement. In every café and bar, concerned citizens and avid drinkers were talking animatedly about politics. Since we weren't from Ontario, they were eager to impress us with their cause. They embraced us. On our first night there, Stockley and I went on a pub crawl. At every bar, with our Australianism as our only credential, we were feted and bought free beer.

In the smoky Galois haze, as a patriotic French-Canadian song erupted, Stockley rubbed his scars, held up his free beer in a toast and shouted, 'This is alright, I reckon!'

At last, here was a place that was different, foreign. We had travelled nine thousand miles to Toronto and found only a pallid version of Melbourne. Now, outside my hotel window, people behaved differently. Normal social intercourse was carried out under a different set of rules. People spoke with more and different gestures. They touched each other (heaven forbid)! They stood closer to each other. And in the hotel itself, a simple trip to the bathroom led to discoveries.

'This is a funny water fountain, mate,' said Stockley, pretending to drink from a bidet.

At the Hotel Nelson, we stayed and played for a week. On the third night a clean, white blanket of snow covered the city. It was the first real snow we had seen. We ran out between sets and played in it like children. We yelled at the patrons standing in line to see us that we were Australian and that this was our first snow.

'Ah. Oui!' they cried, and clapped for our delight.

After this night, I went home with a pretty Montreal girl. She matter-of-factly took off her clothes and bathed herself in front of me, cleaning her body gracefully and unabashedly. After, she complained that, in a rash youthful decision, she had destroyed her 'petit tétons' with a silicon breast implant.

'Zey were beautiful,' she said.

I replied, 'Mais les grands tétons sont très beaux, aussi.'

But we had to return to beloved Unionville. After a week, Kerryn snapped. Rather than Stockley's slow, festering disillusionment, Kerryn put a quick, surgical hole through the living room wall with his fist. A few nights later, he and I decided to sublimate our violent urges the way many Canadians do — we went to an ice hockey match.

It was between the Toronto Maple Leafs and the Detroit Red Wings. As we went to get our tickets we were astounded to see grown men chirping like sparrows. They were pretzel sellers and this was their way of advertising. Kerryn asked for some pretzels and half-a-pound of birdseed to go. Inside, our repressed violent urges were satiated vicariously — but not, at first, on the ice. Two fans caught, with their faces, vicious slap-shots that flew over the Plexiglas barrier. Each was carried out on a stretcher. Then the action switched to the ice. A Maple Leafer delivered a beautiful high-stick shot to the side of a Red Winger's head. He was a good bleeder, and before they carried him out, before his blood was frozen, a phantom organist hidden somewhere in the rafters thrilled the crowd with an interpretation of *Tie a Yellow Ribbon Round the Old Oak Tree*. Everyone clapped in time as the sacrificial Red Wing was borne from the ice.

Then the game started in earnest as the Red Wings sought revenge for their fallen comrade. The crowd roared encouragement as couples paired off to fight. Kerryn and I cheered as we once had at Australian Football matches.

'You bloody mongrel!'

'He's a girl, Ump!'

'Come on, ya bloody choirboy!'

'Have a go, yer mug!'

But the crowd was so loud; our unique cultural contributions went unappreciated.

When everyone was satiated, the game was stopped. We walked out of the game feeling a renewed composure, an enhanced ability to deal with life's vicissitudes.

Then came the Stanley Cup. We were playing at a club sixty miles west of Toronto. It was a big place, but only two tables were full. Everyone else was at home watching the Cup. In protest, Brod dressed in a smoking jacket and dragged an overstuffed armchair on stage. For the whole first set he sang every song in an overdramatic, theatrical tone, like Noel Coward.

In our break, one of the patrons came up and introduced himself, 'Frank Walcott, A&M Canada. Sorry about the crowd. I'm sitting over at that table with Jerry Moss. Hey, you guys must really be going somewhere for him to come all the way from LA just to see you.'

Jerry Moss, the M from A&M, had indeed flown from LA and then driven sixty miles in snow to see us. Brod lay low as Stockley and Kerryn went over to the table. After a couple of minutes I went over and introduced myself to this inscrutable personage. I stood, not hearing a word over the recorded music, and then I faded away. A tribute had been paid to us. Jerry Moss was paying us special attention. So, the next set we played full-on rock'n'roll. With two people watching, this felt more ludicrous than the Noel Coward set.

The Noel Coward set was just the kind of legend-building faux pas that Rudge loved. When he heard about it from Jerry Moss, he called to congratulate us. He also reported that Moss had liked Stockley's song the best. This made life with Stockley more tolerable. But the biggest news was that Rudge said it was time to record. He had persuaded a hot producer — Elliot Mazer, whose last record was Neil Young's *Harvest* — to see us at the Nelson. Elliot came, he saw, and he wanted to record us at his studio in San Francisco.

Just beyond our backyard in Unionville, as we packed for San Francisco, I could see men working. The surveyors had long finished their task — and so had the earthmovers. Now, the builders were laying the foundations for a whole new population of mall-shoppers. They would certainly thrive — but they would have to do it without us. We packed our meagre possessions and were driven to the airport. We boarded a jumbo jet bound for the USA.

4

San Francisco

'Move it or lose it, buddy!' yelled a cop outside the San Francisco Airport. Like awed dogs on a freeway, we crossed the no-man's-land pedestrian crossing. A red, white and blue tour bus pulled out from the curb and rolled towards us.

'Move it!' shouted the cop.

We sprinted to safety and huddled together against a concrete column. Amid the noise and the smells of the busy airport, we exchanged glances that said, 'Yeah! Just like I pictured it.'

Our new producer, Elliot Mazer, met us inside the airport and had to make some calls. Now, like a parent who had let his children wander too far, he came rushing out to save us. He led us to his Citroën and we five bundled in (by this time all of our equipment was taken care of by our road crew). The Citroën wheezed and elevated its suspension a couple of inches. Elliot was tall, dark and bookish. He had glasses that perched on the bridge of his nose. They made his eyes look small and focused, penetrating and scientific. Whenever he took them off you were astounded how big his eyes actually were. He had produced several successful records and had a name as a brilliant engineer. The dimensions of the US music industry overwhelmed us, and by now we were feeling very lacklustre. We were counting on our producer to uncork our creative juices.

As we drove out of the San Francisco Airport, a song from the number-one-selling record of the year came on the radio.

'Your record is going to sell more than this,' said Elliot.

In Australia we had, for a while, the zealous adulation of a small cognoscenti. We almost took them seriously when they said we were great. But in the US, the only believers, true or not, were the men who were vested in us: Peter Rudge, the M from A&M and, now, Elliot Mazer. And since they all stood to gain from our success, they could and did say anything that might help us achieve it. So Elliot's compliments were not yet to be believed, nor his predictions.

And so, as we drove toward our new individual apartments next to the ancient Mission Dolores, Elliot tried to make us feel welcome and confident. But, as the stench of a joint filled the car, I dwelt on this question: *What does he really think of us?*

I was certain that he did not see in us the potential of mythic character. He was far too familiar with the likes of Bob, Neil, Linda, Robby, Janice, Levon and Garth. He was like a scientist who, knowing how everything works, was in awe of nothing, least of all The Dingoes. He had met the myths and found them to be human. And yet his familiarity with the stars gave us the heady sensation that we were actually on their level. When he talked of BNLRJL&G, he spoke with no special emphasis. A visit to BNLRJL or G's place was spoken of with the matter-of-factness of a visit to the cornerstore. Elliot made no kind of caste distinction between them and us. At least he is smart, I thought, as I remembered how Biff Epstein had belittled us by betraying his lack of respect.

Elliot dropped us at the apartments. They were within walking distance of the studio and he was going to pick us up in about an hour to show it. In the meantime we checked out our new homes. Mine had beige carpets, jute walls, a refrigerator the size of a cardboard box, and a sliding door that opened onto a pool. Stockley's pub had the same decor, including identical paintings. He thought this might have something to do with The Great Chef, McDonald. He went over to the designer painting and looked in vain for a plaque that said, *Over One Billion Sold.*

'Housewarming beer, mate?' he asked.

I had inspected my apartment. Stockley inspected the corner liquor store and found some Budweisers.

'The genuine American article,' he said.

'The septics are civilised after all.'

'Let's not be too hasty. This requires a *thorough* inspection, John.'

Soon Elliot arrived. We crammed ourselves into his Citroën and drove to the studio. Sandra and Smiggy were there. Sandra, a slight English woman, was the tape operator and Elliot's wife. Smiggy was Elliot's engineer. He was Scottish and wore a bushy Ben Turpin–style moustache and wispy hair down to the middle of his back. This nearly compensated for his incipient baldness. Smiggy had been in many bands and we recognised him instantly as a kindred spirit.

The studio, named His Master's Wheels because Elliot had made his name recording on location, was immaculate. It was in a two-storey building. The upper floor was still the Alembic guitar factory. But back in the main recording room, the second floor had been removed to make a high ceiling with a skylight. This room in the middle of the city was soundproofed and perfectly quiet. And yet ethereal daylight flooded in to reveal a rock musician's heaven. All our equipment was set up, along with the extras we had ordered: a Rickenbacker slide guitar, an electric twelve-string guitar, a Cajun accordion and, for me, the very latest in bass-amplification technology: a Crown. In front of the amps, around the drums, near the ceiling and lining the walls was a score of microphones to collect ambient sound. And each of these was the ultimate in sensitivity and sound quality, some with fine silk meshes to protect their ribbons from the ruthless 'p' sound of vocalists, and others whose sensitive elements were held by a spiderweb-like net to insulate them from the low rumbles of passing trolley cars going down Market Street. Off in one corner was a glassed-in booth with a grand piano.

All of this was a backdrop behind a scrim of lazy dust drifting through a shaft of sunlight. In the centre of the room, flooded in sunlight, was a cloth-covered pool table. On the table was a not-quite-classical still life: grapes, oranges, apples, bananas, red and white wine, champagne, Heinekens, cold cuts, camembert and brie, French and Italian breads, a bouquet of roses and another of daffodils.

Stockley was beside himself. He made a delicate sandwich and poured a fine Napa red, then put them on top of his amp. After a dreamy sip, he rolled up his cuffs, put on his Stratocaster, and played rock'n'roll guitar on full blast. At first the effect was as if someone had started a jackhammer. All conversation was halted. The classical delicacy of the visual scene was eradicated by his toxic guitar. Elliot's glasses slid down his nose and his eyes appeared big and round as he cast them around the studio to see what damage was being done. Suddenly Stockley stopped; all the other instruments vibrated in sympathy with the Strat. J.L. took his cue from Stockley and struck up a great beat. I was embarrassed to play anywhere other than onstage, in rehearsal, or at a recording session. But I did the right thing. I picked up my bass and we jammed. In another day, another era, the engineer could have raced into the control room and started the tape machine. But the modern studio had reached such technical perfection that Elliot, his engineer and his tape operator would need a further three days of setting up. So The Dingoes rocked on, surpassing the brilliance of BNLRJL&G, creating new worlds of musical excellence, and not a note of it was recorded.

We played for about thirty minutes while Elliot, Sandra and Smiggy looked on approvingly. I hated myself for not being able to surrender to the moment. I was unable to become lost in the music just whenever I would have liked to, and I was more keenly aware of the social setting, the big business stakes (our backers were committed to dropping about a million on us) and in reading the aesthetic judgments of our audience of three than I was in the music itself. And while these thoughts rattled around (invisibly, I hoped) inside my head, I had to pretend to be absorbed and on the edge of musical inspiration. How was it then that I could feel completely uninhibited in front of twenty thousand people, and yet, practically paralysed by three?

We had about a month to finish the record. The next day we sat with Elliot and talked over song selection and arrangements. We had only two criteria for picking songs: first, the song of Stockley's that the M from A&M liked must get on; and, second, we must put on the best songs whether or not we had recorded them before. In this and in practically everything else, we relied on Elliot's expertise and vested him with more authority than we gave ourselves. Whether out of trust and admiration for Elliot, or because we had played those same songs for so long that we couldn't make dispassionate decisions, we gave over control of our artistic destiny: The Dingoes rolled over.

We had Saturday and Sunday off. This was part of Elliot's plan to keep the hours as normal as possible. He was performing an experiment that has been tried many times and usually fails: that of living with a family and rock'n'roll simultaneously. He had stopped recording away from home, normalised the hours during which recording took place, and made his wife the tape operator. So, instead of being able to make the studio your own private pigpen, you felt that you must always be on your best behaviour, as if you had been invited for dinner. But Sandra was not familiar with the studio and had been recently taught by Elliot how to fast-forward, reverse, shuttle, splice, play back and record on the refrigerator-sized tape machine. The Dingoes were to be her first job.

On Monday we arrived, sleepily, at 10am. J.L. was already out in the studio banging on his snare drum. He had an expression like the dog in the His Master's Voice logo. Smiggy lurked about in the shadows connecting this cable to that patch bay. From a technical standpoint, drums are the most difficult instrument to record. A kit has at least four drums, each with twenty lug nuts for tuning two skins; a high hat; pedals; ride and crash cymbals. It was a recording engineer's kinetic nightmare when clattering sticks and rogue overtones would not go gently into the good night of technical thrall. But producers and engineers, with duct tape, pads, strategically placed microphones, and baffleboards, spent hours and days fiddling to get the sound just right. Sound engineers use the drum sound as the true indicator of their skill. On Wednesday, we were getting punchy after three days of *boom-boom*, *tish-tish*, *thud-thud* and *toc-toc*. Yet Elliot, J.L. and Smiggy remained rapt.

At last, at around nine at night, Elliot said, 'John. Can you play?'

I plugged my bass right into the control board and in five minutes I was finished.

'You feel like getting guitar sounds tonight? Actually, it's a little late. Let's start fresh in the morning. And tomorrow we can work on basic tracks.'

For all the advances in sound recording, making the basic tracks was still susceptible to the human element. Yet without a solid bass-and-drum combination, all further instrumental add-ons, or over-dubs, would sound bad. So the pressure was on the bass player and drummer to play for four or so minutes without making a mistake, without speeding up or slowing down, and with intensity and taste. Sometimes a producer will decide that rhythmic accuracy is crucial and make the musicians play to an electronic metronome in their headphones, a click-track. When I have played with a click-track, I am like an upside-down chicken that becomes hypnotised by a straight line drawn away from its beak. All I could focus on was the click. No such thing as music entered my mind. Instead, I felt something like vertigo as I tried to match the bass notes exactly to the click. If I hit one, I missed the next. Was I in front of the beat or behind it? On a bad day, in a slow song, I resorted to pretending the beats were clay pigeons going by.

Pull ... pull ... pull.

Yet some musicians (the good ones?) embraced the click and performed as naturally with as without it. I distrusted their ability to do this. I was a romantic. I believed that good music sounded good because of the interplay between musicians. Surely, playing along with a machine should sound sterile. Once upon a time I was eating dinner with an actress and she bragged that she could make herself cry whenever she felt like it. I dared her to do it there and then. She did. While I admired her skill and was a little envious of it, too, her gift belittled the nature of real emotion. It was as if emotional response were a modular faculty that she had learned to switch on and off independent of an emotional context. Yes, in her acting training she had to look into her own pain, but now she could skip that step. So, when she cried on command on stage it wasn't the play that affected her. In the same way, I distrusted the ability of musicians who could switch on their musicality, who could play with a click. This was irrational of me. Later, I swore I could tell the difference between a drum machine and a real drummer. I could not.

To Elliot's great credit, he recognised that we weren't this kind of band. So he sent all of us out in the studio to play the songs just as if we were on stage but with the likelihood of saving only the bass and drums and over-dubbing the rest. The lights were dimmed. We drank a little beer. Elliot and Sandra came out of the control booth and into the studio where they danced with abandon. I closed my eyes and tried to put myself in a state of artistic transport.

But when the red light went on, I choked. I immediately became nervous and tic-ridden. I compulsively pressed the bass string against the fretboard as hard as I could. I moved my finger back away from the fret to see how far it would go before I got fret-rattle. I don't know how I got by with these mental deficiencies.

Sometimes, instead of allowing itself to surrender to rapture, my mind dwelt upon the irrelevant realities of the recording process. A signal travelled from my ear to my brain, down my arm to my fingers. The string was plucked and its vibrations were converted into an electrical signal by the pick-ups on my Fender Precision. The signal, now moving at light speed, shot down my guitar cord and into a direct box. Here it was split in two. The first path went to my amp where it agitated the speaker, causing air waves to pulsate and, in turn, vibrated the ribbon in a microphone. This ribbon converted the sound back to an electrical signal that travelled down the wire to a patch bay, and from there along another wire, into the control room, the terminus of all wires. The second path took the signal directly to the patch bay and on into the control room. These two signals each had a volume control and Elliot could blend them if he wanted to. The blended signal was sent to the tape recorder, where it was converted to an arrangement of tiny metal particles on magnetic tape. The final arrangement of these fragments could be played back and either copied onto a smaller cassette tape or converted to vinyl bumps on a record. If we did our job, people would hear magic in them.

A signal travelled from Stockley's brain, down his arm ... down his guitar cord ... No! There was something wrong with his cord. His guitar sounded distorted and electrical crackles sputtered out from it. Stockley pulled out his guitar cord. As he did so, it popped and hummed. Elliot, Smigggy, and Sandra looked up in horror.

Elliot spoke to us softly in our headphones, 'Chris. Let us know when you're going to do that.'

'Sorry, mate,' said Stockley as he put the cord back in, causing an even louder pop.

Elliot dived for the fader but pushed the wrong button. A monstrous feedback tone spilled into our headphones. In the interest of survival, I slapped them off and nursed my stunned ears as they rang for the next five minutes.

'Thy evil electrickery,' said Stockley. 'Thou dost vex me.'

Smiggy brought him out a new cord then the signal went to his amp ... but it was still breaking up. Stockley, bringing his own expertise to bear, punched the top of his amp. The springs of its internal reverb unit clattered like thunder. We cowered in fright as he played some power chords.

Between chords he shouted, 'Get thee behind me, foul entity! Behave thyself!'

But still it was breaking up.

'Try the Marshall, Chris,' whispered Elliot in our headphones.

'No, mate. This Fender ... if ... I just had it checked out.'

In the failing daylight, Stockley's glasses appeared to darken as he battled the mysterious forces of electricity. I put down my guitar and, with J.L. and Kerryn, walked into the control room. Elliot was regaling Brod with stories of our favourite session players.

'Yeah. But in Nashville they all take uppers. Muscle Shoals is all downers. That's why they play the way they do ... they're behind the beat. In Nashville they're on top of it.'

'What about us?' asked J.L.

'You guys are in the best tradition of English bar bands. You have this good-timey, haphazard, behind and before the beat. But, no! It's great.'

Then he looked lovingly at Sandra and said, 'Sandra, rewind to the start of that last take. It was jolly good, wasn't it, darling?'

Sandra, with one hand in the back pocket of her jeans, gracefully manoeuvred the tape. We listened to the playback and were immediately seduced by *us* coming out of the high-tech studio speakers. But then Elliot switched us down to his tiny radio speaker.

'This is how most people will hear it,' he said.

What a letdown that was, and Elliot quickly put the playback up on the deluxe speakers.

When the song finished we could hear Stockley's guitar bleeding through into the soundproofed control room.

Just then Peter Rudge walked in.

'Hello, boys. How is it going? Do you like the studio? Hello, Elliot, Sandra, lads. This is Emmett Grogan.'

As animated as ever, today he was showing us off to the pugnacious Irish New Yorker, Emmett Grogan. Emmett was famous for his exploits with the Diggers, a benevolent organisation that thrived in the pollen days of Haight-Ashbury and which helped create the fabulous hippie non sequitur that if you loved enough, your food and rent would be taken care of. He was a nice man without airs, but he was notorious. I had no idea why. Rudge apparently thought it would be a bit of a coup to get him to do the liner notes on our record. I had no idea why.

Emmett did do our liner notes. Here is what he wrote:

> The Great Wall of China was built as a defense against Barbarians. It is very high, very thick, and 1,684 miles long. But the longest, highest, deepest barrier in the world is in Australia. It is a wire-meshed fence 6,000 miles long also built to defend the land from barbarian droves. There are no gaps in this fence. Only a few get through from down under. Five who did it alone, banded together, and chose to call themselves what 6,000 miles of fence could not contain.
>
> 'Listen to their bite, for you won't hear their bark.'

He might have got his idea for this in the studio that day as he heard Stockley's barking or biting guitar, now more vitriolic than ever. We made small talk with Rudge and Emmett as distorted, crackling and humming feedback reached us from beyond the aural barricades.

Somehow we were talking about the Queen of England. Brod told a story about what was supposed to have happened at the opening of the Sydney Opera House.

'So this photographer was in line to be presented to the Queen. "Your Majesty. This is Joe Bloggs. He is a well-known photographer." "Oh," Her Majesty said. "What a coincidence. My brother-in-law, Lord Snowdon, is a photographer, you know." "That *is* a coincidence, Your Majesty," the photographer said. "My brother-in-law is a queen."'

A cymbal crashed out in the studio. It was snagged in Stockley's guitar cord. He gave up on the Fender amp; Smiggy put the Marshall in its place. It was even louder, and Rudge smiled as its sheer volume pierced the polite control-room conversation.

'Stockley sounds like he ate his Wheaties this morning. Heh, heh, heh,' said Rudge

Elliot leaned into the talkback microphone, 'Chris, can you turn it down? I'm getting too much of you bleeding into the other microphones.'

'Sorry, mate. No fuckin' way. It's got to be loud to get the right sound. It's a bleedin' Marshall, mate.'

'Heh, heh. He's right about that,' said Rudge.

'Smiggy, pull out some more baffle boards and put them around his amp.'

Soon Stockley was set up. We went back out into the studio. Elliot, Rudge and Emmett came out too. When we started playing, Elliot danced to get us in the mood. He danced like a college student — the tertiary trot — with more enthusiasm than grace. Curse me if this didn't make me even more self-conscious.

With Sandra and Smiggy running things inside, we went for some takes. But nothing was happening. After a while Rudge and Emmett left. 'Keep up the good work, lads. It's sounding good.'

The way he said 'good' expressed his belief that it was nearly sounding good.

Elliot, back in the control room, whispered into the talkback mic, 'I'm going to close it down for today. We'll get this one first thing tomorrow. It's almost there.'

It was 9pm.

Kerryn and I walked up Market Street. Outside the studio, the real world of music was just waking up. We stopped at a small club where a zydeco band, headed by Queen Ida, was playing. She played an old button accordion. Her percussion player had thimbles on his fingers and played dance rhythms on a washboard and a triangle. All of the musicians were unpolished. They sounded as if they had been pulled off the front porches of Louisiana and Texas. And yet strange half measures, melodic twists, trills, licks and many other mutually understood idiosyncrasies made this deceptively simple-sounding music more complex than anything on a sophisticated pop record.

'Wow! Can you keep track of that melody?' I said into Kerryn's ear.

'No.'

And when the music stopped we both sat sipping a Guiness.

'It makes me wish I was born on the Bayou ... or the Ozarks, or the Appalachians ...'

'Or in Chicago in 1921,' Kerryn mimicked Muddy Waters.

I eyed a very pretty girl sitting alone at a table. She returned my gaze and smiled. I smiled back. But then her boyfriend appeared and sat between us.

'Once in Melbourne,' I said, 'I was hanging around with these Irish musicians. They were going to a jam session ... they didn't call it that ... and I, as a fab and successful local musician, said, you know, "Can I come too, and play?" Those bastards told me I could come but that I might not want to risk the humiliation of trying to play with them.'

'Did you?'

'Yes, I did. I had had just one Terry Deer too many. I thought, *Shit. It's just folk music. Any moron can play that.* They were brutal. They put me right in my place. It's incredible. They know so many tunes and each one is ...'

'Laissez les bon temps rouler!' Queen Ida, with her gold-filled smile, summoned the dancers onto the dancefloor.

'These tunes are handed down from father to son,' I said as the music began.

'I didn't hear my first note of blues until I was thirteen.'

We were shouting now.

As much as The Dingoes worshipped and imitated the rawness of true folk music, we were not for real. We were not born on the Bayou or in Chicago. We were not even American. In Australia, we were far enough away from the source that we took the foreign music and turned it into something of our own. But here, watching and listening to the Cajun funkiness, after a day of musical baffling, isolation and sterilisation in the sophisticated technical studio, only one word came to mind as I compared our music with Queen Ida's: bland.

The next morning, Kerryn and I found a breakfast place in the Mission District. We had been told that it was a homosexual ghetto, and since no such thing existed in Australia (Rule #1: No Poofters), we were curious. But, for now, we just wanted breakfast. I took the local paper off the top of a cigarette machine, and we sat down. Holding the paper up, I read through it. I noticed two or three men staring intensely in my direction. *Why do they have to be so pushy*, I thought. I put the paper down and there on the back page I saw what the men had been looking at. A perfectly proportioned man was laying prone while a huge lion was on top of him and penetrating him from behind. It was an advertisement for a local club. 'Struth!' I said.

'He's got the lion's share, alright,' said Kerryn.

Back at the studio I showed the paper to Stockley. He assumed the Maury character. 'Here, what's this?'

'It's homosexuals, mate.'

'Homysexuals?'

'It's when two men love each other.'

'Yer mean like mates?'

'Sort of, Maury. Except they have sex together.'

'I told you, Mr Murray. He's a ratbag. A fuckin' ratbag!'

Stockley stormed off in mock disgust. Maury's denial of homosexuality was like that of Queen Victoria's, who, when she was asked to sign a law banning lesbianism, refused on the grounds that it didn't exist.

Soon we got playing and we nailed the first basic. We started on the second, but it was another painful delivery. Sometimes, when I was in this situation, a kind of automatic response would kick in. I took on some leadership! I could rethink the song and come up with another rhythmic approach or a melodic hook. So I felt strangely able. Before I knew it I was drawing from a small well of good ideas. Where the song had sounded uninspired, it now sounded new, and that caused us to play it even better. And J.L. was so very open to new ideas; when we were working out a new arrangement or bit he was unbelievably focused and positive. I suppose this allowed your internal editor — that entity that threatens to reject every single thought you ever had — to take a break and allow a trickle or two of creative juice to flow. These are the best moments for a musician, the sense that you are on exactly the same wavelength. J.L.'s attitude was one of invitation to communicate, to exist in the same moment. On only the second take of the new arrangement we nailed that one too.

All of yesterday's self-conscious silliness and stupid thinking was gone. I was on. With this aberrant creativity, I glimpsed the me that was possible, and a certain part of my consciousness sat back and said to itself, *That's my boy!*

When we listened to the playback, Smiggy seemed tickled.

Sandra said, 'That was wonderful, John.'

But Kerryn's was the face that I most often looked to for validation. This was one of his songs, and he was beaming.

During the playback he confided, 'Nice one, John.'

He was referring to the little bass tickle at the start of *Smooth Sailin'*.

We took a break, and as Elliot cleaned extraneous human sounds off the tracks, I found myself pining for a more stable supply of creativity. But it would come when it would come, and that was that. I cringed inside when I thought of how I had tried to force it. Once I believed my creativity was stymied by my prevailing self-consciousness. If I could only find a place where no-one, absolutely no-one, could hear me ...

Back in Australia, Windy Saddle on Wilsons Prom was, in winter at least, a lonely, desolate place. I took my guitar there to communicate, alone, with the winds and the muses. On a ridge between two of the highest mountains on the promontory, the air raced eastward, forced up by the rising ground and suddenly released to rush down to the sea. From the Saddle you could see the ocean to the east and the west of the promontory. There was no evidence of humankind — except for a screaming idiot with a guitar and a bottle of port. Surely I had all the ingredients of a creative act: a guitar, some grog to loosen whatever inhibitions remained, the inspirational setting of a mountain before and behind me, and an ocean to my left and right, as pure and fresh a wind as ever flowed in the Southern Hemisphere, and, most important of all, solitude.

The table was set for the muse, but the muse didn't come. The more I tried to be possessed by the creative spirit, the more stupid and dull were the words and music that came forth. Finally, humbled by the majesty of my surroundings and the contrasting poverty of my own contributions to them, I put down the guitar and the bottle. Seeking escape in the entertainment nature could provide, I headed east, down toward the sea. Between the sea and the saddle was a swamp. It was deeper and broader than I thought and it took a good hour to penetrate the thick vines, undergrowth, and overhanging boughs. At last, the sodden ground gave up its water to a slow-moving creek and the dense forest gave way to tussocks and reeds. Soon I was walking on the sand of a small inlet and in the full light of the afternoon sun. I rolled up my jeans and discovered ten leeches having me for dinner. *At least I am good for something*, I thought, as I burned them off. The effect of the wine was wearing off, and in its place an ugly little mid-afternoon hangover loomed. I curled up under a tea tree and fell asleep ...

Now here I was in the studio actually being creative. If I could just hold on to that spirit a little while longer ...

That's how the basics went — in fits and starts — a nice idea here, a creative block there.

When they were finished we started over-dubbing the guitars. Most of the solos had been allocated to either Stockley or Kerryn, but some were still up for grabs. Every age has its cultural heros. In the sixties and seventies it was rock'n'roll musicians and, in particular, lead guitarists. Our lead guitarist was Stockley. But Kerryn may have believed it suited himself just as well or better than Stockley. It was possible that Stockley was like a successful politician whose power resided more in the perception of the electorate than in his skill. In other words, just because Stockley thought of himself and had the reputation of a lead guitarist, this didn't mean he was a better player than Kerryn. Stockley had a fast and loose approach that wasn't always precise, but its idiosyncrasy embodied the rogue spirit of rock'n'roll. When he took a solo, it leapt out of the song and grabbed your attention. Kerryn's solos, on the other hand, were embedded in the arrangement and aimed to complement the song. Two very different approaches. And, just as in our leadership dynamic, there may have been a pecking order. It was just that no-one was exactly sure what it was.

'I've got a great idea for this one,' Kerryn said, as they stood out in the studio facing each other with their guitars slung around their shoulders.

Kerryn ripped a solo. Stockley's glasses darkened, and when Kerryn had finished, Stockley, in a tone that betrayed as much boredom as possible without being obvious, said, 'Hmm. I dunno, mate. I think this song suits the Strat sound better.'

Delicacy and dimly perceived power made this lethargic comment as much a command as if he had said, *This spot is mine. Touch it and I'll smash your teeth in with a sledgehammer!*

Kerryn came into the control room looking peeved. But of course he couldn't express his frustration. He had to be content with rotating back and forth in the engineer's chair as Stockley played the solo.

Something was going wrong with Stockley. On one of our weekend breaks we had visited Mill Valley on the other side of the bay. We had heard about this party through A&M records in Los Angeles. It was an afternoon affair. The house was set among the giant redwoods. But it was on the side of a steep hill and several trees had been cut away to reveal a view of Mount Tamalpias. As we arrived a gentle breeze nudged a dogwood in late blossom. A shower of petals fluttered down on us and our feet sank into a cushiony layer of pine needles.

'God's country, mate,' said Stockley.

The people there were uniformly bright, beautiful, and successful. Several of them were the sons and daughters of showbiz families. Stockley, small and licentious, stood out among their homogenous beauty. A well-read man and a connoisseur of the good things in life, Stockley was a great raconteur and he came alive at parties. After a while, half the party was gathered around him as he told the story of our rise to fame-that-was-to-be. I sat glumly on a tree stump and worked on a tasteless beer. Like a husband whose wife, tiresome and bored around him, becomes the soul of vitality and charm around others, I watched Stockley with envy and some jealousy. For, with the pressure of all we were going through, Stockley was indeed withdrawing. At this party I recognised the Stockley of old. One of the guests amused the party by skillfully walking on a slackwire strung between two trees. Another delivered a perfect rendition of the 'I've always relied on the kindness of strangers' speech from *Streetcar*.

Stockley, shirt open now and rubbing his scarred, nascent beer paunch, whispered to hungry ears, 'We were on the good ship *Venus* / By Christ you should have seen us / The figurehead was a nude in bed / Sucking the Captain's *et cetera*, *et cetera* ...'

As puerile and profane as this ditty is, his co-conspirators were delighted at his subversion of the showcase culture of the other entertainers. In his smile, sometimes furtive and wicked, sometimes broad and debauched, they recognised the real thing.

As the party continued, Stockley turned to poetry and then politics. By the end he had won over the party.

And he was full of Mill Valley. This fairytale town, all sunlit and sylvan, was his dream made real.

'Just a small house on the side of the great mountain-bosom. That's all I want, mate. It's not much to ask, is it?' he asked on the drive home, his besotted head leaning affectionately on my shoulder. 'And a couple of bars nestled in the cleavage?'

When we finished the record, we were going to be confronted by the great American dilemma: where to move. We could live anywhere we wanted. But Stockley became doggedly insistent that we move to Mill Valley.

'It's fantastic, I reckon. It's got everything there. It's the most beautiful place I've ever seen. We oughta live there when the record's finished. Just think how the wives will like it. They'd die, I reckon, in a place like New York. We oughta tell Rudge when 'e comes next week.'

Kerryn's, Chris's and Broderick's wives were due to arrive any day. Stockley's pitch of serene domesticity was appealing, and, without experience of alternatives, winning.

This decision seemed very important to him. More important, perhaps, than what he was doing on the album. Mill Valley was, in its airy brightness and affluence, the antithesis of his dreer and rainy Coventry boyhood, and it represented the fulfilment of his rock'n'roll career. So Stockley coveted Mill Valley and was losing his focus on the thing that might get it for him permanently, namely, the record. He started to leave the studio earlier than the rest of us. He seemed unimpressed with any sounds going on the record. With each playback his demeanour became more dour. I couldn't tell if he was paralysed by lack of confidence or if he was merely disengaging. It seemed at the time that this was even affecting his playing. But to make a fuss over it now would threaten the myth-that-was-to-be of The Dingoes. The show must go on.

Then came the vocals. Kerryn looked at Broderick as a plain, smart girl looks at a dull beauty who is nevertheless attractive to every man who sees her: he wished he had a singer's voice. So some of Kerryn's instructions to Brod through the headphones (that most intimate of communication devices) could betray irritation. Kerryn wished he could sing. He had an idea of how the songs should be sung but he was not quite capable of expressing it to Brod. And Brod, like any singer, sometimes resented taking directions.

'Can you just give it something that'll make it believable.'

'Like what, mate? New words?'

'Put the emphasis on the *right* words and don't shout it as much. Do it like this ...' Kerryn sang what he meant, and Brod listened with good-natured patience to begin with, and, later, with irritation.

Isolated in a soundproofed booth, Brod screamed the song in just the same way but with a vengeance. After the take he waited for a comment from the control booth, but none was forthcoming. '*Mya kanuka meah mahukah*,' he spoke the ancient Cherokee oath which means, 'Spare me the wisdom of idiots.'

Meanwhile, in the conspiratorial control room, Elliot and Kerryn were saying it was a waste of time trying to get this take now.

Kerryn said softly into Brod's phones, 'That's okay for now, Brod.'

Brod, of course, understood that records are not *for now* but forever, and that what Kerryn was really saying was, *Gee, is that really the best you can do? I guess we'll have to live with it if we can't do better tomorrow.* Brod stepped out of the vocal booth and sat down on the couch in the studio. He lit up a cigarette and waited until he was called upon to perform again.

'We're ready for you, Mr Smith,' said Elliot.

Brod stubbed out the smoke and shuffled into the vocal booth.

'How's the voice, Brod?' said Kerryn.

'She's alright, mate.'

'Wanna try a new one ... a new song, I mean?'

'Righto, mate.'

In a sane world, Kerryn's and Brod's strengths and weaknesses should have jigsawed with each other to form the perfect combination. Brod could sing intuitively but was not a prolific songwriter. Kerryn could write better than he could sing. But at times you could see they would have loved to really go at it. No, the stakes were too high. They both understood the need for at least a cohesive front. So a healthy repression overlaid their relationship and the vocals got finished without any bloodshed.

Second to the vocals, mixing was the most tedious process. By the time this culminating activity was reached, I had heard the same performance of a song at least one hundred times. The musical bit that I liked for its stark simplicity the first forty times around now sounded naked and infantile. The slight shifts in time and intonation that gave it a human authenticity now sounded amatuerish and grating. The song whose arrangement seemed so well constucted now sounded contrived. I often wished I could walk in and hear it for the first time, fresh. Instead, it was heavily draped with my own mental constructions, many of which had nothing to do with the thing itself. My destiny was absurdly tied up with those three minutes of magnetic tape, and I vested it with all my hopes and anxieties: the neat lick that would cement my place in the annals of Australian bass-player history; the timeshift caused by my playing too far in front of the beat that would expose me for all time as a charlatan; the nice arrangement idea that was not as spectacular as when I first thought of it, but which was still alright and would qualify me as an important contributor to the record.

I had no objectivity left. This made the next fifty listenings of each song a punishing exercise in aesthetic speculation. Was this blend of guitars better than this other blend? Was the snare drum too woody or should it be sharper in its attack? How could any reasonable person say that one sound was better than the other? It depended purely on our social context. And we didn't have one of those. Should the vocals be louder in relation to the instruments, or should Brod's voice be buried? I could hardly hear the bass. Should it be featured more? Questions. Questions only true artists or fools could answer. Not I! I didn't know and was beginning not to care. It had become so important to me that I could not think of it without anxiety. I wanted the thing finished.

Elliot's job was to keep a sense of objectivity, and this he did. The record was finished and delivered to the record company. He did a great job — I think!

As soon as the record was finished, Rudge met with us about our living arrangements. He wanted us to move to New York or Connecticut. But Stockley got to him early and convinced him to let us stay in California — Mill Valley, to be exact. This happened just as Kerryn and I were forming a resolve to live near Rudge. But the pace of events was picking up. Rudge observed that Stockley was passionate about this and the rest of us were still undecided. The rest of us, that is, except for J.L., whose only comment about our move to Mill Valley was, 'It's a wank!'

But we moved there anyway.

5

Los Angeles

I awoke, up on Stockley Mountain. Stockley and his wife, Jenny, were in the kitchen cooking bacon and eggs. I tried to slip back into a blissfully erotic dream. If only such control were possible.

'Morning, mate,' said Stockley, walking in with a cup of coffee. 'Sleep well?'

'Yes, thanks, mate,' I said, rubbing my eyes and scratching my head.

I had slept on the couch and woke up feeling intensely satisfied in spite of not consummating my dream.

'I feel good,' I said, and I stretched like a cat.

'Well, why wouldn't you, mate? Coffee, breakfast in bed, sunshine, not too much of a fuckin' hangover?'

'I should feel worse than I do. What the fuck is the matter with me!'

'When you drink good grog, you don't get much of a hangover. Didn't you know that, mate?'

'Of course. We had a couple of Foster's ...'

'Those don't count.'

'Some Napa red ...'

'If it cost over ten dollars a bottle, then that doesn't count either. Go on.'

'A couple of shots of tequila ...'

'Yes.'

'And three bottles of Brut.'

'Champagne definitely doesn't count. So that was a very moderate night. No wonder you feel so good, John.'

Cool and clear Pacific air moderated the warm morning Mill Valley sun. As I took a sip of coffee, Stockley said, 'I think we solved the problems of the world last night, didn't we, Boisy?'

'My fuckin' oath we did! Err, what was it we decided on again, mate?' I reached for my jeans on the floor, and rooted around in the pockets for my cigarettes.

Down in the valley a dog's bark reverberated among the redwoods and came in through an open window on the pine-scented air. The sound of a woodsman's axe bounced around the hills. Jen came out of the kitchen looking like Loretta Young. She carried a breakfast tray with orange juice, napkins, salt and pepper, and bacon and eggs.

'Des oeufs! Mmm. Thanks, Jen. That looks delicious!'

'It's what she does second best,' said Stockley. Jenny thumped him on the shoulder.

Stockley esquire radiated satisfaction. Both Jen and he had the essential quality of good hosts: they loved to be the agent of your happiness.

Jen got ready and called a taxi. She was going down the mountain to do some shopping.

'See you in about an hour, mate,' she said to Stockley. 'See you later, John.'

It had taken only three weeks to become established in Mill Valley. Brod and his wife, Kerryn and his wife, J.L. and I, all had houses in the valley. Stockley's Pub was up one of the winding roads on the side of the mountain. Whether or not it was a wise decision to live this far from New York, it was difficult to complain. Rudge had set us up royally. Our rent and utilities were paid from New York. We didn't even see the bills. We had enough of a wage to wine and dine three nights a week. The rest of the time, I ate at Stockley's Pub or subsisted on mashed potatoes and hamburger.

Meanwhile, in LA and New York, preparations were being made for the release of our record. We had already shot the front cover on the coastal foothills of Mount Tamalpais. In a couple of weeks we were supposed to go to LA to meet the folks at A&M Records. After that, the plan was to tour all the way to New York by road and to time the release of the record with our arrival there.

Stockley and I took out our acoustic guitars and went out on the sundeck. This was the pretext for my visit. Built on a steep incline, the deck was on fifteen-foot-high stilts. Redwood forest stretched out due south as far as you could see. Stockley was content. He was working on a song called *High Livin'*. Like all of his songs, this one had a clearly working class attitude:

I don't deny times are gettin' tough
And things between us weren't the same.
I lost my job and you took it rough,
Though heaven knows I'm not to blame.

We needed money but it didn't seem right
You helpin' out by workin' at night.
Walkin' 'round half-dressed down at the Rainbow's End,
Servin' drinks 'til three.

It hurts my pride to know you're makin' friends,
When you should be home in bed with me.
Imagination is drivin' me wild.
I lay here cryin' like some motherless child.

High Livin's gonna get you.
Your reputation's all over town.
High Livin's gonna get you.
Forever I'll be livin' it down.

It had a great R&B feel to it and I said, 'Stockley. It's a fuckin' winner. You ought to send this one right to Bobby "Blue" Bland. It sounds like it was written just for him.'

'Cheers, mate,' he said, justifiably pleased with himself. And we both had a sip of Napa Valley cabernet sauvignon and a bite of camembert cheese. 'Look. Here comes the wife.' We could see the taxi winding back up the valley. Stockley put down his guitar. 'Come on. Let's help Jen up with the shopping.'

We went down the path, which was bordered on both sides with rhododendrons. Jen was still talking to the taxi driver. As we carried the bags up the hill, Jenny said, 'His business had been good lately thanks to us Aussies in town.'

Jenny started cooking immediately and I was told I was staying for dinner again. They always made me feel welcome. I loved them as a couple. And Stockley's Pub had been enhanced by its trans-Pacific relocation. It was a relief to see that he had re-established himself this way. This was the life. He didn't seem concerned that his days of serenity and privilege were certain to be bracketed within turmoil. He was content to take them on face value; to take all the unearned perquisites as if they were his due. He would often look back on this time as the best weeks of his life.

I could not exist at this level. Except for my aberrant good feelings of that morning, I was very unhappy. I felt the calmness of the days but it seemed more like the calmness of a river just before it reaches the waterfall. I could not enjoy it. I still sweated over the band's quality or lack of it. And now I started to fret about my mother back in Australia. Since we hadn't been given any idea of how long we would be away, I had estimated that we would be gone about three to five months. We had now been gone six months and had only just got settled. My mother suffered from schizophrenia and I had left her invalided in my apartment. I had trusted her care to her mother. But all of Mum's paranoid delusions were directed almost exclusively towards her mother. And, to my eternal shame, I had not found a way to send back money. Too shy to demand or ask Rudge for an extra amount for this situation, not conservative enough to put some aside from my weekly allowance, selfish enough to forget the problem for days at a time (here I plead a childhood training where it was essential for my survival to forget the problems at home), and finally, too lazy to act even when I sensed the enormity of what I was not doing, I lost myself in the potential bigness of my burgeoning career. *When I hit it big,* I thought, *I would treat her like a queen.* Yet in not one of her letters did she ask for a penny. I allowed myself to think things were somehow alright with her. She was never alright. How could she be alright now?

If you cross the Golden Gate Bridge at eight o'clock in the morning, you speed through a tunnel with a rainbow drawn around its entrance. You are entering a putative fairy-land where peace and love are official doctrine. The first town you come to is Sausalito. The second town, closer to the mountain than the bay, is Mill Valley. Now, if you leave Mill Valley at eight in the morning you will get caught up in so much traffic you will wish you had stayed. It is a bedroom community — a town without a population. A town's character is defined by its people. Mill Valley had few people.

If the town did have character, we would never have known it anyway. We were rolling stones, gathering neither moss, nor knowledge, nor understanding of the towns we passed through. We had no kids in its schools and no families in its churches. And the chances of us staying here were small. We would either move up, down, away, or back to Australia. But Stockley bought a dog. He was digging in. He called it *Box.* Actually, Jenny had been looking at the Animal Control Center for a cat. But she fell in love with this five-year-old chocolate labrador. In the beginning, none of us could solve the mystery of how a dog with such a beautiful nature could have been abandoned by its owners. But after a while Box left some clues — and you didn't have to be Sherlock Holmes to decipher them. One night at dinner, she tried to mount my leg. Every day after that, whenever I came to their house, Box ran to greet me in the same familiar way.

'She's really *taken* with you, isn't she, Boisy?' said Jen.

Later, during the same dinner, Box let go of some formidable gas.

Stockley screwed up his nose. 'Phew! Better an empty house than a bad tenant, eh, Boxxy. Ha, ha. No worries, mate.'

I slept at Stockley's Pub again that night. But this time, instead of waking to the breakfast smells of bacon and eggs, my eyes, ears and nose were assaulted by the sights, sounds and smells of Box eating the turds she had laid in the middle of the living-room floor. Then she tried to mount me and lick my face.

Jenny came out of the bedroom and admonished Box like a beloved relative who, after years of devotion, had lost control of her bodily functions.

'Oh, mate. What have you done? Come on, Boxxy. You couldn't help it, could you, girl.'

I kept it to myself, but to my mind Box had done enough to get sent back to Animal Control for that one last regulatory act.

We were all itching to start playing again except for Stockley, who, like a soldier on leave, was savouring every second of his privileged existence. But before we toured we had to go through a show of privilege the like of which we had never seen. We went to LA and employees from A&M had been told: Make John What's-His-Name, Kerryn What's-His-Name, Brod What's-His-Name, What's-His-Name Stockley and the other What's-His-Name feel like they're Bosses of the World. Curse me if this didn't spoil the fun. The man given specific responsibility for our happiness was Luther LaMott. Like an overfed grouper emerging from the cool, grotto-like depths of the A&M limo, Luther, Vice President of the Department of Faint Praise of A&M Records, greeted us.

'It's The Dingoes. Cor blimey!'

One of the things we routinely suffered was people mimicking our accents. But, at that time, Australia was so exotic that no-one knew the accent. Like Luther, they fell into Cockney or, more commonly, a Beatles-like Liverpudlian accent.

'Watcha! Fair cop, Guv. At last! We thought we would never see you.'

'We were hoping,' I muttered to Kerryn.

'We've all heard so much about you. Welcome to LA, lads.'

'I bet you say that to all the bands,' I said.

'The boys from Down Under. I've always wanted to go Down Under.'

'I bet you did. You're a bloody horse's hoof, aren't you then,' whispered J.L. in my ear.

'Down under what?' asked Kerryn.

He wore a cravat, a shirt with a flower print, and white slacks. His bearded face was crowded into a very small area as if pinched in by his encroaching flesh. Luther's buffoonish veneer cracked almost immediately. He was actually very sophisticated, had hobnobbed with the greatest, and he couldn't, or it didn't mean enough to him to, disguise his true feelings about us — we were ersatz country bumpkins, uncouth and boorish. He didn't say this. Rather it was evident in his quickly fading smiles, his forced laughter and his undisguised yawns. What is it about human nature that, when one is assigned an unfair, unfavourable first impression, one is tempted or driven to grossly confirm it?

This wasn't the first time someone from A&M had been ostentatiously unimpressed by us. Biff Epstein, too, was loath to engage his sycophancy to the level of believability. It seemed to us that every time we came into contact with someone from the record company, they quickly developed a snitty little attitude. Was it us or them? I couldn't help but think that A&M Records was like a wicked stepmother. They accepted us as a regrettable consequence of their courtship of the very desirable Peter Rudge.

The first night in LA we were taken to a Moroccan restaurant. Biff Epstein and Luther Lamott were detailed to entertain us. Biff brought his wife, a woman whom he had married before his involvement with rock'n'roll and who seemed to despise that association. The restaurant was set up to imitate the real Moroccan experience. In the lobby a squirting fountain all but drowned out the sound of Arabian music. Huge goldfish patrolled the bottom of the peacock-blue tiled pool. The motif was continued in the restaurant with oasis vegetation.

'This desert country is making me feel a little parched. How about you, mate?' said Stockley as we waited for our table.

Guests ate in private cubicles. Food was placed on a low table and diners lounged on overstuffed cushions. This was awkward for Luther because he had to invest so much energy to keep himself organised. All his clothes started riding up and, before long, patches of bare flesh were exposed. Bearded, and looking like an inflated Brutus from Popeye, Luther gorged himself. He tried to hide his voluminous cheeks and jowls with facial hair. But beneath the worn-velvet prickle of his beard, however well maintained, existed a tumultuous celebration of fat and flesh that would not be denied. Between courses he pulled down on his shirt and pants. But, after a while, he succumbed to their insistent creeping and to the attentions of the waiters, every one of which was on the road to somewhere else and exhibited as much of their talent as possible. Talent, that is, for something other than waiting — they thought this was their show, not ours! They had two motives for this. Firstly, it was a hangout for film and record types and it was always possible that they would be discovered. Secondly, they were trying to charm us to drink more and so inflate their tip. But they were too thick to realise they didn't have to worry on that account. They should have spent less time amusing us and more time bringing our wine and beer. Inevitably they fell behind on the grog supply. Stockley, looking disgruntled, wickedly whispered to Luther, 'Who do you have to fuck around here to get a drink?'

J.L. was sipping a glass of wine as he overheard him. Laughing, he involuntarily spat it out.

Luther took a dim view of this. But he snapped for a waiter, anyway.

I was nauseated by the lie of having to appear to enjoy myself with the likes of Biff, Luther and those parading waiters. But Luther was completely enamoured with them. With a drumstick in one hand and a glass of wine in the other, he laughed hysterically at their grandstanding and clowning. Biff and his wife were both uncomfortable and disengaged. They stared longingly towards the door. He often looked at his watch as if wishing it were time to go would make it so.

Two things made me drink too fast: I was feeling awkward and nervous; and, being accustomed to the pace of beer, I drank wine at the same rate and suffered because of it. Looking at Biff, I started to feel even more sick. He was snazzily dressed and had a little button on his lapel. The button had a battery and a flashing light. It said, *Yes!*

My nausea increased until I had a sudden urge to vomit. I said to myself, *No!* Biff's button said, *Yes! Yes! Yes! Yes!*

I stood up, took the bottle of champagne out of its bucket, and threw up discreetly in the ice bucket. 'Anyone for champers?' I said, and poured some into Biff's glass. I was gone.

Just then the most flamboyant waiter came up and said, 'Can I help you, sir?'

'Yes. Thank you. Mr Lamott has finished with this,' I whispered, handing him the bucket. 'Be a good chappy and take it away.' I fumbled for a dollar.

'Let me help you sit down,' he said. And I plunked down next to the hairy belly of Luther Lamott.

I had to be retold the rest of the story by Kerryn the next morning. 'Then,' he related, 'you started telling Luther that you knew he was a homo.'

'What?'

'John, you were telling him he should be comfortable with his sexuality. But I don't think he ever admitted that he was homosexual.'

'Stop!'

'You were saying that people were either born straight or homosexual and that you were suspicious of men who didn't discover that they liked men until they were forty. You nearly closed us down when you pretended to have a big penis in your mouth and, in between breaths, said, like it was a major revelation, "This is fantastic."'

'Oh no,' I groaned.

'Luther got up, but I don't think you realised. Biff's wife, who had, thank God, missed the penis bit, came back and sat down. With Luther gone, she was next to you. Without looking at her (I think you still thought it was Luther sitting next to you) you said, just when you could've heard a pin drop, "Personally, I prefer vaginal juices." She thought you were, in your own special way, trying to make a play for her. She got up in disgust and she and Biff left. She was sobbing.'

Biff said to all of us, 'You're a pathetic bunch.'

A knife of embarrassment drove into my heart. I thought I had seriously damaged the band's chances and I was deeply ashamed.

'Stockley and Brod are in at A&M right now trying to smooth things over.'

'Oh, Jesus!'

'It was a good one, John.'

'I've gotta ring them. I've gotta go over there.'

'No, mate. The less they see of you just now, the better. They're telling Biff and Luther you had taken some pain medication for a toothache.'

'That's right. Good.'

Stockley and Brod returned at about six that night.

They both had the attitude of bemusement toward me. Stockley said, 'John, when we get back to Mill Valley I'm taking you and Box to the Animal Control.'

Brod just looked at me, shook his head, and ejaculated incredulously, 'Boisy!'

Because we were having dinner that night with Rudge, Emmett Grogan and Jerry Moss (the M from A&M), we called an emergency band meeting to discuss the situation. We speculated that the whole ugly nature of the incident had not been told to the M from A&M. This was my analysis. I argued that he was of such an ascetic nature (he had a life-size bust of Gandhi in his office) that his flunkies wouldn't report the details of my grande faux pas for fear of being soiled themselves by the mere telling of it. I said they may have reported their distaste for me (or us) but it would not have gone much further than that. Furthermore, I said, Rudge would not get wind of it. We should pretend it didn't happen. My friends may have been appalled by my behaviour last night, but now they were reporting to me, like a co-general on how best to deal with the problem. Desperately hungover, harbouring my shame and deeply touched by the undeserved soft treatment from my friends, I found a private place and quietly wept.

That night we were again chauffeured with Luther, this time to an Italian restaurant.

'Sorry 'bout last night, Guv'na,' I said. Luther acted like he had no idea what I was talking about.

The restaurant was notorious as a place where some of the biggest movie and record deals were cut. The waiters here were all part of one family, and they disdained talk with the customers. We arrived first and were seated at a large table. Then came Rudge, bubbly and small — an open book. Emmett Grogan, with his sparkling eyes, rye expression and poetic talk came in and sat down next to Rudge. The M from A&M, austere, inscrutable, serious and impressive, came in and sat on the other side of Rudge. Luther was at the end of the table where he could command the logistics of ordering food. And The Dingoes, except for J.L. who was next to the M from A&M, sat opposite this triumvirate.

We started out with some small talk.

'How did you like the El Morocco?' asked Rudge. 'Really good food, isn't it?'

Several of The Dingoes mumbled in assent.

Luther, who had skillfully ordered the first round of drinks and appetisers, said, 'Look who just sat down over there.' A group of ten men and women were being seated. They were being made a big fuss of by the previously unimpressed waiters.

'It's the head of the Corleone crime family, Don Vito Corleone,' added Luther. This of course was not exactly what Luther said, but you will understand that in the retelling of this story, names have been changed to protect the innocent.

You could instantly see whom he was talking about. Don Corleone embraced the maître d' and laughed loudly. He walked in a way that showed he feared no-one. The man was healthy, about forty-five, and wore a fist full of rings.

'He looks like a nice man. I'd hate to see anything happen to him,' said Stockley. 'But if he looks at me sideways, I'm gonna glass the cunt.'

'I just saw him look at you,' I said. 'He was saying what an idiot you are. What are you going to do about it, mate?'

'I'm afraid of what I might do to 'im. Here, mate. Hold me back. Hold me fuckin' back.'

Don Corleone ordered food and wine, oblivious to the menacing Stockley was giving him a mere table's length away.

The M from A&M smiled serenely, inscrutably, at our foolishness. Emmett, holding a finger to his mouth, hushed us up for our own safety.

Rudge swizzled his VO and said, 'Now, now, boys. You're too young to die. At least let's get some touring done first. Heh, heh.'

I started to feel kindly towards the world. I wished to invite everyone into my International Brotherhood of Man, an organisation that thrived after a few beers. The food kept coming and so did the wine and beer. Emmett and the M from A&M were engaged in a conversation. Normally, I would have contributed to this fascinating topic: goodness. But I was befuddled by the drink and my point of view was so esoteric that it required a small course in biology before it could be understood. I listened.

'Goodness is a state you achieve after doing many good things.'

'No, Jerry. I think you're born good. Society screws you up and you fall from your state of grace because of what it does to you.'

'So you think that, given the perfect society, Man would be perfectly good.'

'That's it,' I said.

'What about Don Corleone over there? He works so hard to damage society. Is that society's fault? Shouldn't he be responsible in some way for his behavior?'

'No. Go back to his childhood. If ya brought him up in a fine home, why, he'd be saint. Don't you think, Jerry?'

'Not necessarily. You can bring two people up in the same house. One will be a good kid and the other a terror.'

'Don Corleone,' I chimed in, 'is probably a very good man to his family.'

The M from A&M looked as if he would like to savage me for my opinion. I pressed on.

'There is no such thing as goodness. We all act in our self-interest. Luther is good to us because his job depends on it. You're good to us because you believe society will reward you for bringing five genuine artists to its notice. A man is good to his children because ...'

'Be a good man and pass me the wine,' said Stockley, trying to shut me up.

'... because, because, inasmuch as his genes for behaving good get passed on to the next generation, so does he, in a biological way.'

'Good genes?'

'Yes. And—'

'Wait. Are you saying there are genes for social behaviour? What do genes have to do with it?'

I wasn't sure. I thought I knew earlier that week, when I was reading a *Time* magazine article on the subject. But now, for the life of me, I couldn't pick up that line of thought — and my whole argument depended on this point. I made a mental note never to be caught out on this intellectual limb again. But for now I must beat a retreat. I was fired with enthusiasm for the argument, but I was also fired with booze. I was losing it again.

'If you think Don Corleone isn't good, watch this!'

I went over to the crime-family table. I said, 'Mr Corleone! You are a good man. I know you are. And I believe you will take this gesture in the spirit with which it is given. I throw myself on your mercy. And I kiss your feet as a representative of the International Brotherhood of Man.'

And I went under the table and kissed his feet.

And I believe, looking down at my besotted eyes between his legs, he may have had mercy on me because he recognised the spirit of humanity that was at the heart of my gesture.

Emmett Grogan, an altruist's altruist, came over and dragged me out. The realisation hit me that my high-minded gesture of universal brotherhood was being misconstrued as the gesture of a drunken moron. Suddenly penitent, I followed him straight out of the restaurant. He led me to the limo in the parking lot and rode home with me in the back seat.

'Sonny. You just came to within one boot-lick of your life. I believe you're crazier than I am.'

'Everyone's good,' I slurred. 'You're good. I'm good.'

'Yes. And it's the good who die young,' he said. 'Be careful, mate.'

He was right. Emmett Grogan died at the age of thirty-nine, murdered, for reasons known only to his murderers, about ten years after that night.

The next day I chastised myself. How many times could I do this sort of thing and still be regarded by myself and others as a viable person? Yet, even in my hungover state, a secret pride validated the incident as a kind of rock'n'roll derring-do. I know this was foolish. What do you expect? I was foolish.

After a couple of days of hanging around the recording company we returned to Mill Valley. And, after a couple of months hanging around Mill Valley, even Stockley was ready to rock and roll. We struck out for the American highways. On tour, at last.

6

Juárez, Mexico

This was the south-western leg of the tour and our tour manager, Mike (Mad Dog) Lahey, was driving us in a rented burgundy Cordova towards Albuquerque, New Mexico. We had just driven through a dust storm, and for a thrill since it was going our way, Mad Dog was driving thirty miles an hour to keep just ahead of it. The storm was like a giant, rolling wave. We surfed into Alburqueque.

To stay right on the edge of the storm, Mad Dog kept making adjustments to his speed; he was oblivious to the danger of tractor-trailers looming suddenly through its opaque wall. Mad Dog always lived on the edge, and I was becoming as fatalistic as he was: an actual disaster would just be filling in the blank.

Hiring Mad Dog was a shrewd move by Rudge. This was the third week of the tour, and everyone's threshold of tolerance for each other had been reached. But with Mad Dog on our team, we set aside our grumbling for the more immediate concern of self-preservation. Shock value was Mad Dog's gold standard. As we became used to one level of fear he would up the ante. Now he was close to the limit.

He had an artificial leg. He lost the real one in a motorcycle accident.

'I was totally conscious,' he said. 'I crawled over to it and held it like a dying friend ... until it stopped kicking.'

That he had lost his leg didn't sink in until he weighed himself. He was fifteen pounds lighter.

We made it to Albuquerque, showered and shaved, and went to the job. Dick, our equipment man, had all the gear set up and ready for us to plug in. But a booking mistake had been made. The audience was Latino and they were expecting a Latin band. When we walked on stage, half the crowd left immediately. Brod said something about being from Australia and I suppose the rest were curious to see whether Australian gringos were any improvement on the US variety. We played across a cultural void so vast we ended up playing to ourselves — and to Mad Dog, who was grinning malevolently from the wings.

During the breaks we drank beer. Stockley saw me drinking a glass of the amber liquid.

'What's that you're drinking, mate?'

'I think they call it beer, mate.'

'What's it like, mate?'

'Not too bad.'

'Do you think it will catch on?'

'I dunno, mate. It's got an interesting flavour. Why don't you sample a glass,' I suggested, going on with this ritualistic, imbibing behaviour.

He ordered a beer and tasted it, rolling it around his tongue and sniffing the glass as if it held fine wine. Then he quaffed the glass and said, 'Yes, it has a nice flavour, but I'm not sure about the texture. I think I'd better try just one more.'

And after his second glass he said, 'I'm still not convinced. This needs a *thorough* inspection.'

After some more of this he went off to play raconteur with some Hispanic rock'n'roll enthusiasts. I was left to deal with my particular problem: what to do in the breaks?

Talking to people used to be fun, but by then I was severely jaded. How many times had I been told, 'I've always wanted to go to Australia.' People were so predictable that after a time they became, to me, mere units of population. 'What's Australia *really* like?' asked every second person. Did they want an answer in a manilla folder or a nutshell?

'Listen, mate,' a friend had advised, 'when the septics ask you about Australia, tell them about our cute, furry animals. Tell them about our cuddly koalas that hang in clumps of thirty in the tallest gum trees. And how, if a cow or a septic tank walks underneath, they fall on them and gouge them to death with their nasty little claws. The septics love it if you pull the piss out of them.'

But this wore thin. Sometimes I would dodge the Australian issue entirely by saying I was from New Zealand. Then they couldn't very well express an equal interest without making their initial interest in Australia seem dishonest. But sometimes people's eyes would light up as they said: 'Oh, I've always wanted to go to New Zealand.'

I was tired of human nature. Like gravediggers become blasé about death, or like doctors, sometimes, about life, I had met so many people lately I was becoming blasé about them. This is not a nice feeling. So I drank. I drank out of boredom. But mainly I drank to recover sentimentality. And between three to ten beers I was plenty sentimental.

That night I danced a bastardised tango with a pretty señorita. She was trying, in broken English, to tell me something. But I was too witty, gallant and destined-to-conquer to take any objections seriously. At the height of my success, her prior engagement turned up. I tried to welcome him to the Universal Brotherhood of Man.

'Buenos días,' I said. 'Señor, your señorita is the belle of the ball.'

He spat on my shoes. I took this as an invitation to fight. Just then, Mad Dog, who was sitting on the edge of the stage and savouring a potentially dangerous situation, intervened on my behalf. He had a hammer and, as he smiled at my rival, he pounded his artificial leg with it. The psychology behind this move (whatever it was) was sound.

'Pack up your butt, and get out of here, señor,' growled Mad Dog.

The disgruntled man, muttering a venomous oath — I only understood 'loco' and 'gringo' — turned around and, with my beautiful señorita, walked away and out of the club.

Nobody suffered any pain that night, but the next morning I bore all the pain, and the sins, and the disgrace of humanity in the form of a hangover. Back in the Cordova, on our way to El Paso, Texas, I passed in and out of wakefulness. I was desperate to sleep because whenever I woke up I would punish myself. Every avenue of contemplation led to guilt. Outside was the land of cowboy-and-Indian romance, Kit Carson, Geronimo and his ragged band of Apaches (before he was deported to Oklahoma), the complete cast of my childhood imagination. And all I sensed was glare — glare and guilt. And more guilt at sensing only glare and guilt. I shut my eyes and ignored one of the most distinctive landscapes in the world. I clung to the belief that eventually tomorrow would come, and my hangover would go.

So I kept my eyes shut and soon Mad Dog stopped at a town called Truth or Consequences. Over breakfast the established wits in the band (everyone) tried to make remarks about the town's name. I used the power of suggestion to keep my food down. My failure to do this would have been, I thought, an appropriate critique of my companions and myself.

I noticed a crop duster busily working a field in the distance. The biplane dived to twenty feet and levelled off just in time to swoop under some powerlines, dust the field and roll over gracefully. It repeated the manoeuvre over and over again. I wanted to swat it. Nothing bore contemplation.

Then I got something to think about — my old friend, the anxiety attack began to set in. My hangover was inducing a nameless fear to swell up from some primitive hinterland of my brain. My solar plexus tingled with pins and needles. My palms sweated. I felt I was in immediate danger of dying. Was this only an anxiety attack, or was this really it? No real way to tell. Just ride it out. The only antidotes I knew for an attack like this were sleep and sex. Later that day I was to discover a third. I put my money on the table, got up and went outside. As I sat on the hood of the Cordova, the modulating drone of the crop duster and a gently fluctuating warm breeze seemed to give me a toehold on reality, and relaxation. Maybe I would go to sleep in the back of the car.

On the way out of Truth or Consequences, Mad Dog decided to take on the eighteen-wheelers. Weaving in and out of the paths of the ponderous trucks, he was driving the Cordova like a spitfire harrying German bombers. After bothering the trucks he would break off contact, leaving the truckers spitting oaths into their CB mics.

And then he came upon a convoy of two trucks. He was being a pest. He would pass the two semis and slow down — causing them to slow down too. But he stayed with these two trucks. If one truck tried to overtake the other, Mad Dog would stay parallel with it so it couldn't re-enter the right lane. Then he slowed down and pulled behind the first truck. When it changed lanes he quickly accelerated and pulled ahead of both trucks, only to drop back again and gratuitously annoy them even more successfully.

We were beginning to plead with him. He only laughed.

'You guys. It's alright. I know what I'm doing. This makes the trip a little more interesting.'

'This guy is a maniac!' whispered Stockley.

'Cut it out,' I said. 'I'm too young to die.'

'Ha, ha, ha. It's alright! Trust me!' came the inspirational reply.

Mad Dog was so close to the edge every day that he couldn't perceive a special threat from the speeding behemoths. He kept up his suicidal behaviour for thirty miles. We had no CB so we couldn't hear what the drivers were saying about us (it didn't take much imagination). We probably should have pleaded harder, earlier. But Mad Dog would turn around and face the back seat to argue and, like a bad actor on a movie set, recklessly forget to look at the road.

'Look out!' I screamed as we headed for the median strip and the oncoming traffic beyond.

He kept on pestering the same two trucks. Finally we got angry.

'If you don't knock it off I'm gonna have you fired in El Paso,' said Brod.

'Yeah,' said Kerryn. 'I know a guy called Homer (the Snail) Smith.'

Mad Dog, taking Kerryn's joke as a licence to continue (how could we be serious, he reasoned, if we were joking), became even more daring. Now he pulled up ahead of the lead truck and jammed on his brakes. The trucks, with high beams flashing and horns blaring, tried to slow down. Mad Dog, carefully gauging their speed, accelerated at the last second and left them behind to work through the fifteen gears required to get them back up to cruising speed. He held at a conservative fifty-five and our two friends began edging up on us (a fact only he was aware of until they pulled level). They were out for blood! The huge wheels inched past the left-side window as close as they could be without touching. Mad Dog, barely keeping off the shoulder, blew a kiss to the guy riding shotgun, and sped off at ninety. This time he maintained his speed.

'Mad Dog!' said Stockley, in a tone that reminded me of a black-box recording of a doomed pilot–copilot conversation. 'You do see those trucks up ahead, don't you?'

'You fuckin' guys,' remonstrated Mad Dog.

But he had badly misjudged the rate of closure. Two different trucks were side by side and doing only twenty — there was no way around them. They had been radioed by the trucks behind us: we were being taught a lesson.

'You moron!' screamed Stockley as we all saw we were coming up on the trucks way too fast. Mad Dog furiously pumped the brakes and then jammed them on. We were going to hit — hard. At the last second he pulled the wheel hard to the left. The Cordova spun all over the road. We didn't hit the trucks, but we had come to a stop in the middle of the road — facing the wrong way!

'Yeah!' said Mad Dog.

'Christ!' said Stockley.

'Look!' said Brod as our old friends bore down on us at top speed. At the last instant they peeled off, one to either side. We were left rocking in their slipstream.

'Whoa! That was great!' said Mad Dog.

The passenger-side rear-vision mirror was gone. So was my anxiety attack.

Mad Dog, relaxed now and possessed of a kind of post-coital glow, lit up a cigarette and drove toward El Paso at a sedate eighty. The arid countryside made me think of snow.

The Balwyn Baptist Church took us Sunday School kids on an excursion to Mount Buller to see the snow. Not one of us had seen the stuff before, and we were all between seven and eleven years old. After the long drive in a converted moving van with seats and windows along its side walls, after exhausting the *My Fair Lady* songbook, we came to the foothills of Mount Buller. The van lurched to the side of the road and the tailgate was dropped. We all jumped out. On the side of the road, in small clumps, was snow. It was all but melted away and was more like crushed ice than snow, but we picked it up and marvelled at it as if it were fairy spoor. We drove further up the mountain but the quality didn't improve much. I couldn't make the connection between this stuff and what I had seen on Christmas cards and in the movies. There must be some mistake, I thought, as a rock-hard snowball shattered in my face, stunning away all sensation.

Night was coming on and the El Paso lights were glimmering in the dusk ahead. As we came closer we noticed the presence of another civilisation. On our right side, across the Rio Grande (surely the name was a joke — you could jump across it in places), was Juárez, Mexico. It was enveloped by dusk and was completely dark except for a rare car headlight making its way through the mass of humanity like an occasional bubble in a slowly simmering soup.

Juárez was an ironic marvel of the modern world — a city without electricity. Its dark presence, said Stockley, was like a tumor growing on the fat underbelly of the US.

'Crap,' said Mad Dog. 'They're only fuckin' Mexicans.'

In El Paso, Rudge was waiting with a photographer and a writer for *New York* magazine. The writer, whom Rudge called 'The Major', was an English chap who had been slumming toward Hollywood. The photographer, who called herself 'McGillicutty', was beautiful and unanimously desired. But she had already succumbed to the bounteous charm of The Major. I figured Rudge had offered him decent money to do a story on us — that, and a chance at McGillicutty. Anyway, here he was: a step down from novel writing; a step down from screenplay writing; a step down from feature writing; writing about a rock'n'roll band — an Australian one, at that! How low could he go? He seemed to be disguising with all his might that his own awareness was infinitely beyond our ken. But his belief in that, and his class, stuck out like dog's balls — the emperor was playing scribe to the peasants.

El Paso was one long pose. Everywhere we turned, McGillicutty's motor-driven camera whirred in our faces. And just as we prepared our faces for her camera, we also prepared our personalities for the slumming Englishman. The Major's ho-hum appreciation of our existence (albeit appropriate) induced in us an inhibiting self-consciousness. Five aliens were answering his questions. And, just as you can't recognise some people from their posed photos, I'm sure none of our intimates could have recognised us from that article. It was never published, in any case.

We had been photographed in Tex-Mex restaurants; bars with pool tables, peeling walls and bouffant-topped waitresses who called us 'Hon'; on stage; in the desert; in the bath; shaving; looking pensive, jubilant, brooding, wistful, wry and puckish. But Rudge thought it was all too dry so he arranged for a trip into Juárez. He rented a large shark-nosed vehicle with a toilet and a bar. Stockley dubbed this mobile home 'The Enterprise'. Mad Dog, who was desperately trying to convince us that he would never pull such a stupid trick again, was beside himself with joy. He promised that, if we would keep him, he would persuade Rudge to let us use The Enterprise until the end of our tour.

We said, 'No ... it's over.'

Like a fly into a Venus Flytrap, we drove into exotic Juárez.

Just over the Rio Grande, Rudge saw the Juárez Hilton, and he and The Major were dropped off there, to be picked up on the way out. With McGillicutty we drove into the central market district. As The Enterprise nosed its way along the narrow, crowded streets, the Juárez people dropped whatever they were doing and stared at us as if an aircraft carrier were sailing through their town. A few young men leapt up to the tinted windows, trying to peer in at its fabulously wealthy passengers. But, seeing only their own reflections, they fell back to follow us to our destination.

McGillicutty saw a photogenic place with lots of waifs and peasant women selling fruit. Mad Dog parked. As if to prove that charisma is manufactured, I stepped out and received an audible gasp from the crowd — whatever that shark-nosed thing coughed up would have been appreciated. Stockley followed my Hawaiian-shirted eminence in a body shirt opened to reveal his scars. Then came J.L.: Champagne Charlie today with silver-streaked hair, festive shirt and his impenetrable shades over his inscrutable face, carrying a glass in one hand and a champagne bottle in the other. Kerryn disappointed in denim. Broderick, in World War II British army-issue shorts, boots and shirt (you never knew when Rommel might turn up) was a puzzlement. But when Mad Dog stepped out looking this way and that like a security agent, they knew whose side we were on.

Down we went into the core of the Flytrap. The deeper we went, the more McGillicutty egged us on, 'This is so funky. Oh, I just love it!'

The crowd was growing. People were leaning out of windows and yelling in Spanish. Then, as our circus passed, they joined the crowd. The five musicians crammed themselves into a jade-green doorway.

'J.L., I can't quite see you. Can you rest your head on John's shoulder?' shouted McGillicutty.

The lives in progress behind these doorways were being reduced by us to mere backdrops, photographic collectibles for the white-hunter. Maybe the crowd sensed the assumed superiority implicit in having our pictures taken among poor people, for when we emerged from the alleys it had become angry. Groups of young men were gathering and talking in heated tones. Mad Dog went up to McGillicutty and told her to wrap it up. But she was far too involved with the shoot to stop.

'Good! Okay. Yeah! That's great, Brod. Hold it. Now do it smiling. Say cheese. Ha! Wunderbar! Now, everyone, arm in arm, walk down the middle of the street towards me.'

We smiled as we walked, arm in arm, into a light shower of peppers.

We smiled bravely as the pepper-shower got heavier. It escalated to bananas and oranges. A tomato hit Stockley in the chest.

'Eh! Gringo!' yelled someone.

'We not gringo. We *Dingo*,' retorted Brod, and for his trouble a small boy zapped him from behind with an electric cattle prod.

We started walking back to The Enterprise, when two coconuts smashed at our feet, splashing us with milk. We broke into a run. The crowd chased us. Mad Dog was doing a hobbling sprint about fifty yards ahead of us. I couldn't believe he was being a coward! Then, before I knew it, he had opened The Enterprise's doors and ran back past us to face the mob alone. Well, not quite alone — he had a pearl-handled .38. The crowd stopped as a unit.

'Start it up!' he yelled, as he passed us.

Inside The Enterprise, McGillicutty was trying to take the shot that would make her career.

'Por favor!' Mad Dog yelled, as he pointed the gun right into the crowd. 'Make my fuckin' días, señors!' he challenged the crowd.

A couple of the more bellicose men edged forward. Mad Dog was going to have to do more than yell. He put his own peculiar brand of psychology to work again. He pointed the gun at his own foot and shot. The mob was impressed by this and backed off, except for one man who glowered and unsheathed a knife. Mad Dog raised the pistol to his knee and shot again. Then he pointed the pistol at his own forehead and acted as if he were going to pull the trigger. As if suddenly getting a better idea, he walked with an exaggerated limp to the man, turned the gun on him and cocked the hammer. Mad Dog had a look of such murderous intent that the man immediately fell to his knees. He was wearing a broad tie, and as Mad Dog held the gun to the man's forehead he turned his backside toward the man and wiped it with the man's tie.

'Shit. I can't use that!' cried McGillicutty from the bedroom. 'Shoot the son of a bitch!'

Mad Dog calmly walked back to The Enterprise, climbed into the driver's seat and drove off. We applauded as sticks, stones, names and produce rained down on our roof. Mad Dog, relaxed now, lit up a cigarette.

We drove into the Hilton and Mad Dog ran in. He came back out in five minutes and said: 'The Major is finishing up his cognac and will be joining us presently. In the meantime, he is most amused by our adventure.'

'That pompous twerp,' said Stockley.

In five minutes Rudge and The Major came out. Rudge was beaming with pride.

'Had a little adventure, did we, boys? Heh, heh, heh.'

'How on Earth did you get the natives so active?' said The Major.

'They thought we were gringos,' I offered.

'No. That can't be it,' he replied. 'The peasants tolerate the gringos. They live off their alms. You did tip them, didn't you? I mean for having their photos taken with you.'

No-one replied.

'Aha!' concluded The Major. 'That's it, I expect. Got to tip, mate.'

It was so kind of him to educate us in this manner. He turned to the crestfallen Rudge.

'Australians. Notoriously bad tippers.'

Rudge, who was usually good at hiding embarrassment, turned around and busied himself making a drink.

'Yeah,' said Kerryn. 'If we don't tip it's because we pay our workers a fair bloody wage and don't send our children up chimneys and such so our bloody upper classes can enjoy their cognacs and can stick their fingers up their arses in peace.'

Rudge perked up. But The Major would not bloody his hands in an argument with an Australian, and we were coming up to the border.

The US border guards inevitably saw in us a chance at promotion. They never thought to ask themselves who in their right mind would give a rock'n'roll band millions of dollars worth of cocaine and heroin to bring across the border. As we were being strip-searched, conservative-looking ladies and gentlemen with false-bottomed suitcases were streaming across the border to supply America's addicts.

At the El Paso border they found a joint in a seat crevice. Mad Dog voluntarily took the wrap for that and got a hundred-dollar fine (we would have been deported), which Rudge paid.

That night Rudge, The Major and McGillicutty flew out of El Paso for New York. We stayed. The next day we were bound for San Antonio. I wish I could say I went to bed early to rest up for the trip, but we played three wild sets and drank a lot. And at eight in the morning, as Mad Dog gunned The Enterprise to merge it onto the interstate, I remembered that last night it was with profound gratitude for his selfless heroism that we went against our better judgment and succumbed to Mad Dog's pleas to stay with us.

What manner of forgotten memories lay present but unobserved in our minds. As I reclined in the mobile motel room, waiting for an anxiety attack, a previously unremembered memory, undoubtedly jogged to consciousness by the Juárez experience, came to mind.

When I was seven I visited, in Australia, a foreign culture. The gold rushes of the mid-nineteenth century brought and left a Chinese population in several places. One of these was Bendigo. Alan O'Hoy was a long-time boyfriend of my mother's and his parents were the head of a well-respected Chinese family in Bendigo's Chinatown. The history of European–Chinese relations was marked by little contact, and Alan's father, although he was second-generation Australian, could speak very little English. Day after torpid summer day, he would smile at me and say 'Hot day, Johnny' as I went outside, and again 'Hot day, Johnny' when I came back in.

But what he couldn't tell me with words, he told me with a loving smile. I knew that if my mother's relationship with Alan flourished I would gain a doting grandfather. Alan's mother was more pragmatic and tried to teach me Chinese — the first three words I learned, and the last three I remember, were *yi*, *er*, *san* ('one', 'two', 'three').

On our first visit I explored their house. It was a shop that, as far as I could tell, was unused except for the living section behind the store itself. A seldom-used door led to the dark storefront. I went in. It was a large space with only a couple of pencil-thin beams of light streaming through small holes in the thick drapes. As my eyes adjusted I became aware of a large shape around the walls. Like a blind boy I reached out to feel it. I felt cloth, and as I walked around the store I felt more cloth, and then a stick — like a wooden rib. As I walked along its length, each new rib was taller than the last. When I reached the final rib I was staring at a large, seemingly amorphous shape. I could not fathom the mystery so I pulled back the drapes. A dragon was coiled around the room and it was ready to strike.

I ran out of the room screaming. 'Mum! Mum! It's a dragon! It's a dragon!'

'Johnny. What are you saying? For God's sake, calm down.'

'In the shop ... there's a big dragon.'

'Oh, don't be absurd, Johnny. There are no such things as dragons,' she said.

By this time, Alan and his parents had come in and they were laughing. They led me back into the dragon's den. The old man switched on the light as Alan explained, 'Johnny, this is the Chinese New Year's dragon. Every year we take it out onto the streets. Look, men go under here ... and hold on to these ... that lifts up the dragon's head, and this opens its mouth.'

The dragon was transformed immediately from an object of fear to an object of pride — I was familiar with the keepers of the New Year's dragon.

That New Year, the Year of the Rooster, I was in the parade supporting the last and smallest section of the dragon's tail as it wound its way through the streets and alleys of exotic Bendigo.

Just as a stone sculpture is defined by chips flying from a slab of rock, my image of self was formed by observing what I was not. In the village celebration of the Chinese dragon, in the instant communal support of the recently urbanised Juárez peasants, and in the culture-laden idiosyncracies of Queen Ida's music, I saw something that I and my culture — the mass culture — had lost: tradition. *I am,* I thought, *the inheritor of a traditionless culture.* But I was wrong! Just listen ...

7

Austin to Chicago

It was the inauguration of a grand new tradition. Stockley had conceived it. Stockley had procured it. And Stockley was its keeper — The Keeper of the Keg. While I was away wooing a young lady outside of Austin, Stockley had complained to the others that we were only catching a 'fleeting glimpse' of the local society and colour. What we needed was a more *thorough inspection*, a way to really get to know the flavour of the environs we were touring through. What better way of steeping ourselves in local traditions could there be than to carry a keg of beer from whatever state we happened to be in. But this was not a selfish act; it was an act of giving on our part, a tribute to our serial hosts. As The Enterprise pulled out of Austin, veritably nurtured along the streets by Mad Dog, Stockley drew the first of many Lone Star beers from our own private Texas keg.

Apart from games of chess, draughts and Five Hundred, we killed time either shooting flies with a suction-disc gun or making palaver. Like travellers to Canterbury, or an ancient community thrown together for a television-less winter, we had to amuse ourselves. And isolated in our little bubble of Australian culture, we had developed an oral tradition of relating stories in high-blown style, as if we were Emily Brontë reading from our work — in a thick Australian accent.

Brod was fond of observing. For example, 'Look, mate! The moon, like a fingernail thrown on high, sheds its meagre light across the frosted and icy landscape.'

Being one of the only two unmarried members, and the others staying true, by and large, to their vows, I was a primary source of a particular genre of stories: sex stories. Last night, I had been whisked away after our Austin job by a sweet thing. And I had just returned at 8.15 the next evening, fifteen minutes after we were supposed to leave for Memphis.

With my favourite audience of Brod, Kerryn and Stockley (J.L. was in the back bedroom reading a *Rolling Stone* magazine) in the air-conditioned Enterprise, sipping the suds off the first beer of the day and feeling the privilege of our very special class, I began my narrative: 'Earlier today, on a farm, thirty minutes' drive from Austin, my horse trotted across a flooded plain.'

I took a sip of Lone Star and proceeded with my tale:

> Waves of pain shot through my nether regions as I tried desperately to remember how to post. They, my nether regions, were choked with semen that the girl on the chestnut mare in front of me should have liberated last night. Margaret almost could have, but she had reasons why she could not. She wanted to. She was sorry. But she could not. I felt sure she would be mine before the end of this day.

'*Arr*!' said Stockley, as he poured himself another beer. 'And well she should be.'

> We broke into a more comfortable canter and, even as her horse kicked mud and water in my face, I scanned the distance for a patch of high ground, a place where I could tenderly convince her to make love.'

'You mean,' said Stockley, 'a place where you could perform the deed of darkness on her.'

> With a click of her tongue and a nudge of her knee, she urged the chestnut into a gallop. We pursued her, my horse and I. *Ti yi yippee ki yay*!

'John, you're an idiot,' said Stockley.

> Just then, her horse stumbled in a ditch we couldn't see because it was covered with water. With Margaret still on its back, the mare somersaulted. Instinctively, as my horse leapt over the flying water and cartwheeling horse's legs, I pulled my feet out of the stirrups. I couldn't see Margaret. Her horse had landed on its back on top of her. I reined in my horse and, with terrible anticipation, trotted back to the disaster.
>
> Good God! She was unhurt. As it landed, her horse must have caused a wave that, in that instant, flushed Margaret out from a certain death. She stood holding the reins of her jittery chestnut who was also, miraculously, uninjured.
>
> 'What was that?' she was stunned.
>
> 'Are you alright?' I asked, as I slid down from my horse. I held her head on my shoulder and stroked her hair. But she was giggly with relief. We walked a while between our horses until she became composed. Then we remounted and trotted to some high ground. Margaret's jeans and T-shirt were soaking wet. We got off the horses and walked, looking for a nice patch of ground to rest and eat the sandwiches we had packed in the saddlebags.

'Wait a second here,' said Stockley. 'Is this true? You're not to tell any lies, mate, or you won't get any of my bloody beer.'

'If it isn't, it should be. If it is, I'm glad it's me tellin' it,' I replied.

I continued:

> She was the kind of girl you would regret for a lifetime that you had come as close as I had last night, but had never prevailed. And with the danger gone, my primary goal regained its prominence in my consciousness. She was fair-haired, five-four, and almost willing to let her moral standards lapse out of desire. But she had not yet decided to sleep with me and was battling herself all the way. She should not have come up to me with a wiggle in her walk

and a giggle in her talk and an expression that said, *I am your gift.* She should not have gone for my line of talk — 'Shall I compare thee to a summer's day?' sez I. 'You're not quite as hot, and you're prettier too. The bloody flies are a bastard in summer, and the sun can give you third-degree burns. All in all,' sez I, 'I'd rather have you than a summer's day, any day.'

Her boyfriend had been away at college for three years, but still she should not have impulsively, secretly, grabbed my hand as I joined her for a beer. Her parents were vacationing in Florida, but still she should not have brought me home from the bar last night. We walked on between the horses. I stopped her. Looking in her eyes, I said, 'I'm going to regret it for a lifetime if we don't make love today.'

She pushed me away, and then, as if surrendering to a force stronger than her, roughly pulled me close. We kissed. I was befuddled with desire.

Then she broke away. 'I shouldn't be doing this.'

But she, too, was dizzy and I felt her denial lacked the conviction it had last night. We tied up the horses. To my astonishment she took off her T-shirt and asked me to help her off with her boots. Then she wiggled out of her jeans. 'I'm only drying my clothes,' she said as she lay them on a warm rock.

'Pig's ass!' said Stockley. 'She's a bad girl, mate. You've got to watch out for her kind. 'Struth. She probably likes it!'

'I think I should at least be able to kiss your breasts. I won that territory last night — fair and square.'

Last night I had kissed and fondled her breasts. I had nudged them and felt their precious weight with my nose. I had moved my head from side to side and let her erect nipples flick me in the eye. 'Not too big and not too small,' I had said. 'In fact, they are just right.'

'Ha!' said Stockley as he drew me another Lone Star. 'That's the fuckin' problem, isn't it, then? They're all just right. Can I get a witness?'

He chortled like a dirty old man, like Harold Steptoe, as I went on.

Last night she ground her pelvis into my genitals, but when I tried to manoeuvre her jeans off, she whispered a desperate, 'No!'

I believed she meant it, last night at least.

'Then, please,' I begged, 'let's get some sleep, before I explode. Ah! My balls! I hope you know I am the last true gentleman.'

'Thank you,' she said.

'And tomorrow I'll get my reward?'

'Never!' And she hit me with her pillow.

We talked quietly. And then we slept with my hand on her breast and my penis halfway up her back. She rose before I did and brought me coffee in bed. She would not return to my arms.

But now, here she was, after our ride, the supreme object of my desire, standing before me, naked, but for a flimsy pair of cotton panties.

'Margaret, let me kiss your breasts and I promise I will go no further.'

'You *are* befuddled with desire, aren't you.'

She forgave me my line of talk and grasped hold of a branch above her head with both hands and gave me a look that said, *Yours is the penis I want.*

She clutched the branch as I kissed her cheek and then the nape of her neck. I walked behind her and kissed the two dimples on either side, just below the small of her back. She writhed her hips and still she clung to the branch. I stood up and kissed her cheek from behind. I held her breasts with my hands and her nipples hardened between the lower joints of my fingers. She gently pinched my head between her head and her shoulder.

Kissing my way down her spine, my hands also moved down, stroking the front of her thighs. I pulled down one side of her panties and tenderly bit her beautiful left buttock. Still, she grasped the branch and gave a little moan. I artfully made to pull down her panties.

'Uh-uh!'

I pulled them back up and ran my hand quickly, like a butterfly, over her cotton-covered vagina. As I did this she grabbed my hand and lay it to rest — on her vagina. It was plump with arousal.

'See. What'd I tell ya,' shouted Stockley. 'She likes it. Oh, she's a very bad girl. And you, Mr Murray, are a fuckin' ratbag.'

As fast as you could say 'Jack Robinson' I gathered in the flimsy cotton protection and my fingers glided into her wetness. I moved back around to her front and kissed her deeply. I brought my juice-covered fingers to our sex-hungry mouths. She ground her crotch into mine with a vengeance. We were both beside ourselves, and she said, 'I want you inside me.'

With a sly expression, she put her hand in my front pocket. She held my granite penis through the cotton lining of my jean pocket. Excalibur cried to be unsheathed.

'That's a funny name for your piece of cutlery, isn't it, mate,' hypothesised Stockley.

'Undo my pants,' I whispered.

She did it.

My penis popped out ...

'Hello!' said Stockley.

'... and she allowed me to take off her panties.'

'So there you were,' said Kerryn.

'And there I was. What was a poor boy to do? As I took off my shirt she levered off my jeans till they draped my ankles. She stroked my penis and balls. The latter drew close to me in anticipation of an imminent event—'

'Not an eminent event,' said Kerryn.

'Come on,' said Brod. 'There you stood with your boots and your pants ...'

> ... and my penis. She grabbed onto the branch and gave me a look of exquisite longing. We kissed passionately and, almost without trying, my artful navigator found and entered her vagina. She leaned into it as if it were satisfying an eternal craving.
>
> She wrapped her legs and arms around me, and though she was no longer supported by the branch, she was so lithe I was unaware that she had any weight at all.
>
> 'Oh,' I said. 'Isn't that a perfect fit.'
>
> Her deep kiss drew me in completely to her sexuality. Her utter transformation from a demure, wicked little thing, into a sexual animal was as shocking and arousing as the aphrodisiacal scent steaming off our sexual organs.
>
> I took her, *in extremis*, to a patch of soft grass and, as I lay on top of her, she whispered softly into my ear the words that women have whispered since time immemorial: 'Fuck me, John. Fuck me!' Then she added, 'Fuck me! Now. Yes! Come into me, my darling. Oh, yes. Yes!' she said.
>
> I came out of control and she squealed. She had muscles which seemed to control the extraction of my semen — as if it belonged to her. And even when I thought I had finished, she twitched her vagina to drag out a couple of extra paroxysms. We lay, utterly silent, me feeling the warming sun and cooling breeze on my back, and her fingers walking with idyllic distraction along my spine. I stayed inside her. And we did it again in a few minutes. God! She was unbelievable.

I clutched my genital area involuntarily.

As the summer light faded outside, I lay down in the back room of The Enterprise. I was practically delirious with pride and satiation, and still redolent with sex. I began to long for Margaret. But I knew very well that our relationship existed only in the past. It was the very recent past, to be sure, but the past nevertheless. While I could always recall it in an auto-erotic episode (it would feed my sexual imagination for weeks to come), its essence was gone. That was the way it should be. Margaret understood the recreational nature of an affair with a musician visiting her town from Australia. I was sure that the anonymity of this (romantic as it was) was what had sparked her desire. Only a traveller could have been considered for such special favour. I took advantage of that. But now I must bear the hurt that came with it. In this sense, the something gained must become something lost. For, even though I emphasised the animalistic and naughty side of the affair to my friends and was smug in its telling, the dimensions of my loss were greater than sexual. In relating my sex story, I had participated in the timeless and amoral tradition of bragging and sharing among men of sexual exploits. But I felt guilty, not for revealing secrets embarrassing to the lady, but for not having the wit to relate the greater dimension of my feeling for Margaret. By being content to tell only what I was able to tell, I had cheapened it.

So little of daily life is worth the telling. Yet all of it is impossible to describe as it truly exists. Then why bother? We do it because we must. We are storytelling animals, entities who have been created by God or Nature to relate experience and even to make up stories. As a biologist, I later came to believe our brains evolved to their gigantic size, not only to build tools, but to build, cement and comment on our relationships — and even to amuse each other. The most complex thing we do, and the most difficult thing to copy with machines, is to manipulate the symbols of language with human complexity. Rocked in the swinging rear section of The Enterprise, I lay awake with my nose buried in the clothes I had worn that day, trying — succeeding — to evoke Margaret with her smells. I could hear Brod, Kerryn and Stockley rattling on about this band and that girlfriend. I berated them, to myself, as gossips. But I envied their sociality. I climbed out of bed. I had to be a part of it.

Stockley, still with the keg between his knees, was now talking about the Australian bands that had been burned trying to make it overseas, particularly The Easybeats and Daddy Cool.

'Daddy Cool were fuckin' great,' he was saying. 'Jesus, if they couldn't make it ... Hello, John. Have a beer, mate? Or would you rather suck my dick, you animal!'

'They got Phar Lapped,' said Brod.

'What's that, mate?' said Stockley distractedly as he pulled me a beer.

Kerryn, Brod and I understood what it was to get Phar Lapped. But growing up as he did in England, Stockley had missed this bit of Australian lore. Brod told the tragic story of Phar Lap, the racehorse, the big Red Terror.

> It all happened in the thirties. Phar Lap was his racin' name. But this big chestnut colt was called Bobby by his trainer. The racing public called him Big Red. He was big for sure. When he died, they weighed his heart and it was fourteen pounds and as big as a bloody watermelon. And he won everything there was to win in Australia — Caulfield, Randwick, the Melbourne Cup — until, at last, the race officials put so much weight on him, his owners were forced to race him somewhere else. They took him to the States.
>
> South of LA, south of the Mexican border, a syndicate of big-time hustlers grabbed the idea of using the Aussie nag to create a market for their new racetrack/casino/prohibition-free zone. They hyped him from tabloid headline to newsreel. He got more names — 'The Red Terror', 'The Antipodean Antelope', 'The Red Kangaroo'. And in a place and a time that fathered the great superheroes, Phar Lap was dubbed 'Super Horse'! His name was connected to Joe Kennedy, Will Rogers. Ingenues and bona fide stars scrambled to be photographed with this phenom of the turf, this wonder from Down Under.
>
> But still, Big Red had not run a race. All of this hype was for his first race, a really big one, against the best horses in the US, the Agua Caliente Handicap. Everything was new to Phar Lap. The track was dirt, not turf. The starting stalls were newfangled and foreign to him. He carried a gnawing injury that only he knew about until he sprang a blood leak from his hoof in the final stretch.

> For most of the race he was out wide and dead last. But then he crept up and went around the whole bloody pack and when he rounded the turn he moved into the front. Down the straight he was pulling away. Suddenly he faltered. Blood from the long-lodged pebble splattered from his hoof up his flanks. He slowed down. The champion, Reveille Boy, gained on him.

Brod took a sip of beer.

> Then … Phar Lap took off! Pulling away, and then easing up on the finish line, he won.'

We sat in reverence of this well-known story. Brod made a gesture with his hands to indicate banner headlines:

> *Australian wonder horse beats the world! Phar Lap Wins*, crackled the Melbourne *Herald*. The nation cheered. The Prime Minister cried for joy in front of the reporters, saying, 'I'm taking the day off, gents.' King George, himself a fan of Big Red, telegrammed his congratulations.
>
> Phar Lap could beat any horse there was. But he couldn't beat the system. By just trying to be his best, he had made some deadly enemies. The last thing gambling concerns in the US wanted was a horse that comes in from the outside, wins everything — and who can't be bought. His first race was his last as well. Sixteen days after Agua Caliente, Big Red got a bad case of something in his gut. He died suddenly. After the investigation, they said: 'We will never know what killed Phar Lap.' Bullshit! We know what killed Phar Lap. From Gallipoli, to Les Darcy (the boxing champ who went to the US and died just as suddenly), to Phar Lap, to Daddy Cool: Australians must get screwed! That's all. That's because they don't know, can't know, what they're walking into.

Just about every Melbourne school boy and girl has seen Phar

Lap standing prominently, pre-eminently, in the centre floor of the Melbourne Museum. He has been stuffed for many years, but he looks alive. His veins are, it seems, inflated with blood and his eye, showing a rim of white, is apparently ready to flinch at the bridle. He was a Great Australian Hope: something home-grown that could take on and beat the spirited Americans. He would show the Bleedin' Poms that the Yanks were not the only colonials to be reckoned with. But we were thwarted by the American ethic, foreign to the self-image of Australians, that winning was everything — even if it meant cheating. From Galipolli, where Anzac soldiers selflessly threw themselves at German and Turkish machine guns simply because it was the right thing to do, to Phar Lap, Australians had travelled for international honour, naively believing their good faith and sheer ability would carry the day. If only because of their colonial naivety, The Easybeats and Daddy Cool were definitely in the tradition of lambs-to-the-slaughter and cannon-fodder. Unlike Phar Lap, they had no outright ill-wishers; unlike the troops at Galipolli, they had no overlords who were inured to loss of life; but they were innocents in a savvy world. This implies no inferiority. It is caused by the bane and salvation of the Australian character: isolation.

'Daddy Cool should have been as big as The Beatles,' I said.

'It ain't gonna happen,' said Brod. 'Not to us. Not to any Australian band. You wait. We're gonna get Phar Lapped.'

Kerryn rolled his eyes. But I felt uneasy whenever Brod engaged this mystical side of his personality. He didn't waffle on about UFOs, Big Foot or the Loch Ness monster. His mysticism was based, though sometimes very loosely, in reality. He liked to relate the legend of the Aztecs that predicted the coming of a bearded white man (Cortés took advantage of their open-armed welcome to enter what is now Mexico City). Rasputin, the mad monk who controlled waning Imperial Russia through his influence with the tsar, was another topic Brod sometimes talked about. Rasputin had almost magically survived poisoning, knifing and shooting. Who needed bogus works like *Chariots of the Gods* and *A Separate Reality* when the fantastic was faithfully recorded in legitimate history books. Brod was a romantic. He believed Phar Lap, the Anzacs at Galipolli, Daddy Cool and The Easybeats were merely victims of a mystical, romantic but real historical principle: Australians must get screwed when they try to make it overseas.

'Now he tells us,' said Kerryn. 'Why did we bother coming over? We should have just stayed home.'

'Too right, Brod.' And I made a toast, 'Here's to the Anzacs, Phar Lap and The bloody Dingoes.'

'I'm not saying that. We gotta make a go of it. But if we don't crack it we'll know why. That's all.' Then he stood up, 'I'm gonna get get me some shut-eye.' He walked into the swinging rear-end of The Enterprise.

Kerryn and Stockley made a cuckoo sign to each other. Stockley suggested buying an Uncle Sam doll to stick pins into to try and defeat the spirit that defeated Phar Lap.

The plan was to drive all night. With The Enterprise, theoretically at least, we could sleep all night and wake refreshed at our next job. Leaving Austin at eight that evening, we should hit Memphis fourteen hours later at ten in the morning.

We passed Houston around midnight. From the perspective of Route 59, this appears to be a city that everyone deserts at five o' clock. But they forget to turn out the lights. This made a perfect contrast with Juárez — a city with people but no lights. And Stockley eagerly pointed that out.

'I read this article,' I said, 'by this architect who worked on designing one of those skyscrapers. She had only ever seen a model of it. So when she was in Houston visiting someone, she thought she would try and find it. She drove up and down all the downtown streets. But she couldn't find it! Actually she passed it several times but didn't recognise it. It wasn't until she was leaving that she saw it — from her plane!'

'So?' said Stockley.

'Well, she makes the point that in designing these buildings, modern architects forget the human scale. They're not designed for people on the ground but, instead, they make these models to sell the corporate types. They're more likely to get the job if they stroke the egos of the suits.'

'So?' said Stockley.

'So, you're a fuckin' ratbag.'

We played Memphis that night. We were the warm-up band for a fusion-jazz band called The Dixie Dregs. The crowd was there for them. They didn't care for us. Because they didn't care, we didn't rock.

'Thank you, Memphis!' screamed Brod, as Stockley flailed his last power chord. 'Remember Phar Lap!'

'What's 'e on about?' asked J.L. as we hurried off the stage trying to beat the failing applause.

The audience was wondering the same thing.

On to Nashville.

Coming into these famous music cities was always like arriving at a party after everyone had gone home. We loved good country music. So the trip to Nashville, especially since we weren't playing there, was something of a pilgrimage. But it was hard to believe that from this tacky town emanated that organic and most human of genres. Nashville looked more like Luna Park or Disneyland. Once upon a time rural pickers traded licks and songs on these street corners. Now tourists traded kitsch mementos under neon cowboy boots, neon guitars and neon ten-gallon hats as they flashed on and off in a tawdry display. Of course they were just the glitzy remnants of what had passed. The essence of the thing, the commercial king-harvest and processing of rural traditions of the thirties, forties, fifties and sixties was forever gone, and the rural traditions themselves were going the same way.

I was a jilted tourist. But I was like any traveller trying to recapture the flavour of a music style, a famous person, a battle or an era. Short of cash; perhaps fighting off a cold, and regretting the bad company of his wife, child or former best friend; desperately taking snapshots, like a dog peeing on a tree just to say he was there, the tourist, even if things are going well, eventually has to confront the deflating reality: you're there — *it* has gone.

On to Louisville where, since we weren't going to make it to St. Louis, Stockley directed the acquisition of Budweiser in the place of Lone Star.

If this needed a justification, Stockley had one, 'It is only fitting that the King of Beers should be served to us, the King of Beer Drinkers.'

Chris Stockley, King of Beer Drinkers, held court through Cincinnati, Columbus, and Cleveland.

In Cleveland we played at an outdoor festival. On a hot and humid summer day, July the fourth, we waited at the side of the stage for a thundershower to pass. When it finally stopped and fans began yelling 'Rock and Roll!' it was time to do just that. But the stage had treacherous puddles and Stockley, lest he be forced into mortal combat with the evil electrickery, would not go on until the stage was squeegeed. Kerryn had a great idea for a stage entrance: we took the buckets, mops, hoods, parkas and squeegees from the stage crew and, in this disguise, started readying the stage. This was a signal for the fans that the next act, some band from Australia called The Dingoes, was about to come on. After five minutes' labour, we put down the cleaning tools, took off the disguises and, to the crowd's disbelief, picked up the guitars. Immediately we launched into a raunchy *Smooth Sailin'*. And the crowd went wild. Under the cover of the noise, Brod yelled to me, 'Look at me! Playing! In America, Johnny!'

And later that same set, Stockley cried, 'I think they really like us! What's their fuckin' problem?'

Everything was going very well. I went up to the microphone to sing a harmony and *ZAP!* I was thrown back ten feet into my amp. I stopped playing, completely stunned and tried to figure out who and where I was. The band played on. In just ten seconds I recovered enough to play. I felt light-headed and had a sense of wellbeing that was foreign to me. The feeling lasted on into the night.

That night we stayed in a hotel right on Lake Erie, at a place called Sandusky. Mad Dog acquired a stash of fireworks. He called us all out to the pier at about two in the morning. A thunderstorm was in progress out in the middle of the lake. In the Michigan and Ohio skies, lightning crackled and boomed with a power we were not used to.

Stockley eyed it with deep suspicion. 'Thy foul electrickery. Thy spirit is restless. Thou fiend spark, vile crackling entity. Hast thou not had thy sacrifice already today? Must thou torment?'

'I feel like I've had a dose of electroshock therapy, Stockley. I feel good.'

'Back! Thou'st possessed!'

Mad Dog lit a nice quiet firework. Out it went in a beautiful arc over the lake. And another. The hotel behind us was quiet and dark except for the flashes of our fireworks. I felt good.

Later that night, as I tuned into The Weather Channel on the TV, the announcer said, '... cloudy with patches of sunlight'.

The shock therapy allowed me to become coolly analytical. Here we were, toward the end of this tour. How were we doing? The weatherman called it 'cloudy with patches of sunlight'. We were still not connecting with audiences. Why not? We used to blame the audiences for that. But the question was becoming academic. If we didn't, it didn't matter why not.

But this need not be a disaster. We were still in the preparation phase of our onslaught on America. We were not expected to set the world on fire on this tour. When we hit New York, the record would be released, reviews would come out, radio would play us (we had received word that this very week reviewers were writing their copy). Reaction to the record would be telling. Then we would tour with Lynyrd Skynyrd at bigger concert halls and maybe, perish the thought, stadiums. How we did on that tour would tell all. *Don't panic,* I told myself. *We should just relax and enjoy this tour.*

We played at a club in suburban Chicago. Being a big and important hub for the great Midwest market, Chicago was a place that was needed. So Rudge and A&M set up a little after-the-job backstage party. And it was lousy with record-company and radio-station types eager to hobnob with future celebrities, and even more eager to drink their beer.

Stockley had to be dragged on stage because it meant leaving behind the huge tub of blue Foster's 'neck oil' cans that the ever-resourceful Peter Rudge had somehow acquired. Stockley could not bear the thought of these types drinking the Australian holy water.

'Pearls before the swine,' he griped.

By the time we came off stage — sweating, animated and thirsty — the party was in full swing. Everyone stood holding a big blue can. It was a cold biological fact that even if you had lots of resources, if you also had a big population, those resources would be depleted fast.

Stockley was no biologist but he understood this principle very well. He barged through the crowd making his way to the tub of ice and Foster's. Just as he got there, a man in a suit and tie pulled out a can from the ice, held it up like the Statue of Liberty and said, 'Look, everybody. I think I found the last can! Ha, ha!'

Mad Dog quickly led the exultant gentleman outside. A minute later they both returned, Mad Dog with the beer, the man with the look of someone who had just seen his life flash before him. Mad Dog went over and gave the beer to Stockley. Then he took off his baseball cap and went around the party *accepting* money for a beer run. This was more of a demand than a request, more a punishment than a solution. And the record and radio leeches left, almost immediately.

When the last person left, Stockley said to Mad Dog, 'You're number one in my book, Mr Murray. Number one.'

'Those people are fuckin' ratbags,' replied Mad Dog.

Stockley had completely won over Mad Dog. Apart from his official duties, which he performed perfectly well, his most sacred task was to ensure the happiness of Chris Stockley. The King of Beer Drinkers appointed him Royal Procurer. Mad Dog also spent a great deal of time sparing Stockley from persecution by the evil electrickery. He could be seen before every job with electrical tape and a flashlight making Stockley's equipment ready. This influence also extended to Mad Dog's eating habits. Stockley, the connoisseur, had by sheer force of personality, led Mad Dog to emulate him. And after twenty-seven years of cheesesteak subs, cheeseburgers, fried chicken and french fries, he had a lot of ground to make up.

The more Mad Dog tried to class himself up, the more Stockley enjoyed a joke at his expense. Back on board The Enterprise, at last heading east on the Ohio Turnpike towards New York City, Stockley related an incident that happened in Chicago.

'Bad Dog and I stopped at this Italian place for a quick little something. I said, "I'll have a capucinno, please." Bad Dog says, "Make that two cups of chino."'

Stockley shouted to Mad Dog who was at the wheel, 'Bad Dog, you're a fuckin' imbecile.'

Mad Dog turned around beaming, privileged to be the brunt of Stockley's humour.

He had yet another change in his lifestyle. Through the agency of the CB radio, he had become, in spirit at least, a trucker. His handle was ... Mad Dog.

'Breaker 1-9. Ah, yeah! Good, buddy! This is the Mad Dawg, pedal-to-the-metal on the eastbound side. Rubber Ducky, I'm, ah, watchin' yer back door in the, ah, Enterprise, and, ah, let's have another Smoky-free day out here, ah, come on back, 10-4.'

'That's a big 10-4, Enterprise,' came the reply from Dick, our equipment man. He was in a yellow Rider van (The Rubber Ducky) about five miles ahead.

By this time we all had handles. Mine was Tasmanian Devil, in honour of my birthplace. The rest were: The Desert Fox, Maury, Rastafar-I and The Bomber.

Late that night, a hundred miles past Youngstown, Brod and I were in the front seat with Mad Dog, playing with the CB. Brod was casting out on the airwaves for a late-night conversation.

'Breaker 1-9. G'day, good 10-4 buddies. This is the Desert Fox. Is there anybody out there who's not asleep at the wheel? Come back on, y'all.'

A trucker replied, and before we knew it he and Brod were engaged in a conversation. It turned out that the trucker had been released from prison only about a month ago. He had a story to tell. I hoped we would hear it all. You see, he was on the westbound side somewhere ahead of us. Soon we would pass each other and we would be out of range. He told us to move over to a side channel so as not to clutter emergency radio traffic. He related his tale:

> I was at this bar. A man thought I was hittin' on his chick (but I weren't). He started talkin' fight.
>
> 'Shit,' I said. 'You wanna fight. Then let's get to 't.'
>
> Man, I seen some mean types in my time, but this one ... he smashes his beer glass on the bar, and jammed that thing right in my face!

> It cut the whole side of my mouth and my lip is hangin' right down beneath my chin. Well, that jus' made me downright mad. I remembered what I learned in the army. I made this karate move and pulled out his eye with my two fingers; pulled his eye right out of his head. I put it on the bar and squashed it with my beer glass.
>
> Well, that jus' made *him* downright mad ...

But we went out of range.

Out of range, discontinuous; coming late for the party; visting towns, experiencing nightclubs; on a tour that didn't count; conversations true and untrue, important and irrelevant; people seeing us not knowing what to think, thinking nothing; meeting strangers, leaving strangers; checking in, checking out; reviews being written, opinions formed; my mother abandoned; the wives installed in Mill Valley, the husbands jealous, horny and celibate in Pennsylvania, Illinois, Ohio, Kentucky, Tennessee, Texas, New Mexico.

America, Johnny!

8

New York City

Babel, Mecca, Quetzalcoatl, Machu Picchu, Paris, Rome, Troy, London, Melbourne. All these cities can be imagined. New York City cannot. Nothing — no photos, no films, no books, no traveller's tales, prepared me for the reality of Gotham. Driving down one of its avenues in torrential rain, gaping as if before one of Nature's own wonders, the five of us pressed our faces into the windshield of The Enterprise. Yet here was a place that was unnatural, a place that apparently fulfilled the human wish to at last have dominion over Nature. Above, sheer lines etched in concrete, glass and steel met at points above the rainclouds. Ahead, on both sides of the Avenue, the artificial landscape, the most massive of its kind, merged to an ever-distant, nonexistent point, just as it had on the perspective drawings of its planners. For miles it continued. Within its strict geometry, taxis, trucks, cars, buses and suicidally-pushy bicyclists vied for advantage and choked at intersections like mad rats in a linear maze. This mid-afternoon mercantile hubbub carried on regardless of the summer downpour. Pedestrians dashed here and there, some with umbrellas, some without, and some buying them at corner vendors that had sprung up in the rain like instant mushrooms.

And look at the faces of these New Yorkers: light, dark, mulatto, Watsons, O'Connors, Schultzs, Zabromnys, Jeffersons, McKenzies, Verdiers, Ngobes, Anastasioses, Minervinis, Fuenteses, Singhs,

Goldsteins, Bogdasians, Horsbolses, Neusses, Washingtons and Muftis. This surely was a modern Babylon, a place to which people of all races and cultures were drawn by the universal magnet of commercial opportunity.

And liberty, too. We had seen one of the New York trains. It was completely covered with graffiti.

'Look at that,' I said. 'Isn't it great?'

'What's so great about it?' said Mad Dog.

'That they give over the trains to the kids to paint like that. What a great idea!'

I am embarrassed to say I wasn't joking.

Mad Dog laughed hysterically.

'It's a bleedin' joke, mate,' I lied, as they all laughed at my ignorance. But mine was still a more reasonable explanation than the facts of the matter — that is, until one became accustomed to the insanity of New York.

The traffic slowed and our attention was quickly refocused: on the women of New York.

'Heaven, thy name is diversity,' I said.

Slavic women with flushed cheeks, medallion cheekbones, determined faces and supple bodies; Jewish women with wilful eyes, olive skin and hair-trigger sexuality (or so I liked to imagine); black women — Africa, the source of humanity; African women, the source of human sexuality — since seeing The Raelettes when I was fourteen I was compelled to find this source, in the USA if not Africa; Connecticut women (Stockley put on his dirty-old-man face and said: 'Their clothes say no, but they fuckin' go, mate'); business women, party women, secretary women, doctor women, nurse women, ballet-dancer women, women students — all of them in the realm of the possible for the Walter Mitty nature of these visiting males' libidos.

Mad Dog turned onto Broadway. Neon signs flashed on either side of the road, competing for our attention, and were reflected by the shiny, wet road surface and in the raindrops landing between strokes of the wiper blades. But Mad Dog seemed to be focused directly ahead, peering into the rain for the biggest neon sign of them all — Times Square. Suddenly he lost control of himself. He banged his hands like a chimpanzee on the steering wheel and dashboard.

'Yes! Un-fucking-believable! Look at that! Whooh! I don't believe it!'

Then we all saw it. Like a vision, its brilliant lights were visible even before the building they were mounted on and, appearing to be suspended high in the sky directly in front of us, the huge neon sign said: *New York City Welcomes* ... and then a new screen ... *The Dingoes.*

Stockley blew softly on his ring finger and whispered, as if witnessing a miracle, 'Fuck ... me ... dead, Mr Murray!'

Mad Dog yelled at passersby, 'Hey! Look up there. *The Dingoes*. They're right here. That's us! Wave, boys! Ha, ha! New York City, man! *New York City Welcomes The Dingoes*. Look at that!'

'That's alright,' said Kerryn, pleased but unflappable as always.

Just then, the tough and electrifying (if I do say so myself) start of *Smooth Sailin'* came on the radio. Mad Dog jacked it up full bore. I stepped back out of the front seat and mimed my part in the bar section of The Enterprise. The others joined me and soon The Enterprise was rocking on its suspension amid the New York afternoon mayhem. Mad Dog opened the windows so that all of New York could hear us. With his arm out the side window, he slapped the panel of The Enterprise in time to our rocking band.

'We fuckin' *own* this town,' he yelled.

From here we went back uptown to West 57th Street to visit Rudge in his office. Taking up three floors of a thirties Art Deco building, Sir Productions carried on business and had been thriving for five or so years. We went inside and were greeted like stars by the office staff of four ladies and Bill Szisblatt.

'It's begun,' Bill said, reminding us of his extravagant promises in Unionville. 'I wasn't lying, was I?'

When we had gone through the receiving line, Bill took us into his own office. Once inside, he opened the curtained double doors that led to a balcony. The balcony overlooked Rudge's office. He was working at his desk across on the other side, next to the window. We waved down to him like the royals and he beckoned to us to descend the black wrought-iron spiral staircase.

'Look ...' he was saying into the telephone, '... I don't care if it's Godzilla making the threats, I'm not going to let a couple of nut cases stop a whole show. But tell them, if they try anything, I'll take care of them. Alright? ... Alright.' And he slammed the phone into its cradle.

'It's the fuckin' Hell's Angels. They're trying to get me to cancel a Rolling Stones concert. Fuck 'em! Well, how do you like New York, boys? Did you see Times Square? Eh? Heh, heh, heh.'

We took in his office. His windows looked down on fashionable and bustling 57th Street. Gold records hung from the walls. A basketball hoop hung from the balcony and a picture of Rudge's archrival, the promoter Bill Graham, was on a dartboard mounted on a wall next to the fireplace. In front of the fireplace was a living room set. 'Got some good reading for you, boys. Heh, heh.'

And he read from the *Rolling Stone* magazine. They had reviewed our record:

> For its American debut, this Australian quintet comes on like a cross between the Band and Steely Dan. *Five Times The Sun* is a provocative mixture of rural remembrance, burly rock and plaintive balladry. The result is a sort of populist rock and roll that very few since John Fogerty have done convincingly.
>
> Above all else, The Dingoes convince.

'So far so good,' said Kerryn.

> The band tends to set up tidy melodies and terse narratives and then rip through them with careful intensity. Most of this tension is provided by guitarists Chris Stockley and Kerryn Tolhurst, but lead singer Broderick Smith adds his own sort of ragged power, sounding on the slow songs like an adolescent Neil Young and on the fast ones like an apoplectic Roger Daltrey.

'Apo-fuckin'-what?' said Stockley.

'I had to look up that one myself,' said Rudge. 'It means he likes you, Broderick. Heh, heh heh.'

'Say no more,' said J.L.

> All this rawness gives the group an ironic edge. The lyrics of such tunes as 'Smooth Sailing' and 'Shine a Light' are just clever cruise-and-booze sagas, but the cracks in Smith's voice and Stockley's and Tolhurst's livid, now-or-never guitar playing lift these jaunts into harrowing journeys through their past. Songs like 'Way out West' and 'Waiting for the Tide to Turn' present visions of white, working-class existence which, if they are meant to be representative of Australia, could just as easily be set in the American Midwest.

I breathed a huge sigh of relief. I had convinced myself that this was going to be a killing review. It wasn't bad! Kerryn seemed a little miffed at the 'cruise-and-booze' comment, but Rudge and Stockley were thrilled. Rudge went on with the good news, 'We've got *Smooth Sailin'* on hourly rotation on seven of the top twenty stations in the country. The jocks love it. This is just the beginning, boys. It should be a good one tonight. Are you ready for the Bottom Line?'

The Bottom Line was a club in Greenwhich Village. It was small and intimate and used to showcase new acts to the New York rock press, and record and radio types. We were the warm-up band for another unknown group called Tom Petty and the Heartbreakers.

As we played that night we looked at each other with the now-familiar expression that said, *How come we don't sound so good tonight?* We were trying so hard to be good. We looked like we were trying hard! But we knew we only sounded good when we weren't trying. And Rudge was in the audience, right on the edge of the stage, urging us to do our best. But even in the best of times, at the Station in Melbourne, we were famous for having good and bad nights. At home, when we had a good night people would talk about it for weeks. If they were there on a bad night they behaved like patient animal breeders. 'Oh well,' they said. 'We'll come again tomorrow night. They'll hit it soon and, boy, won't it be worth the wait.' But we had no idea what conditions made the difference between a good and a bad night. To be sure they were not those of this showcase job. And with anxious and eager eyes at the edge of the stage, Rudge was no patient animal breeder. He looked more like a disappointed zoo official who had wasted his prestige and spent a ton of money to bring together The Dingoes and New York City, only to find the chemistry was all wrong and that this was all a horrible mistake.

We finished and gracious Tom Petty came backstage and told us how much he liked us. Then they went on. He was natural, confident and bigger than life. They were everything we weren't. Petty looked as if he were born to be a rock star. That baffled me. So many things in America seemed to come ready-made, packaged, perfect, bigger than life. I sat in the audience and foolishly compared the names of Australian and American footballers: 'Bluey' Adams and 'Froggy' Crompton with Roger Starbuck and Joe Montana. Even in nature the US was bigger. I thought of the flat and worn ancient Australian countryside and compared it to the grand scale of the Rockies. I compared the Yarra River with the mighty Hudson and Mississippi. I thought of the giants of US country music, blues, rock and soul, and I compared them with … I came up with a harsh judgment. We tried hard. But, try as we might, we were nothing more than little Aussie battlers: brave but pathetic.

After the show, as I sat beating back negative thoughts, two Hell's Angels backed their motorcycles into the club and revved their engines into the red. The club filled up with noxious exhaust fumes and the patrons left quickly. Whether this giant motorcycle fart was a prank, an opinion (on Petty or us?) or an insult to Rudge, we didn't know.

Mad Dog dropped us at a bar at about 2am and said to call him if we wanted a ride back to our hotel, the Gramercy Park. We told him not to worry, we'd get a taxi if we needed to. We drank a couple of pitchers celebrating and mourning our success and failure. As I brought another pitcher to our table, I bumped the table of a well-built gentleman. This jarred his pitcher off the table and into his lap. He stood up and was ready to punch me. Trying a Mad Dog strategy, I poured my pitcher over my own head. He laughed and forgave me. But the staff of the bar had their eye on us after that.

Later, near closing time, we sat at the bar draining the last precious drops of our beers. Drunk, almost to the point of stupidity, I tried to make small talk with the ageing bartender. She may have been interested about ten thousand drunks ago but now she yawned widely, revealing a geographic tongue and a gruesome hole with brown, grey and gold things in it.

'Geez,' I said. 'Do you mind covering your mouth when you do that? I could almost see what you had for breakfast.'

'You know,' she countered, 'people always say they have trouble telling Australians from the English. "It's easy," I tell them. "The English are the ones with class."'

'You're a bit of a classless broad yourself. Aren't you, then,' snapped Kerryn.

A male bartender came up just then and said, 'Gentlemen, it's past your bedtime. I'm asking you to leave.'

'Yeah?' said Kerryn. 'Askin' ain't gettin'. Come over to this side of the bar. I'm gonna put *you* to bed.'

Quickly, four bouncers surrounded us. We got up to leave but one of them had to get a lick in. He threw Kerryn into the door and broke one of his teeth. Kerryn turned around to battle them to the death. But we held him back and made a strategic withdrawal. We walked back to the Gramercy. As Kerryn got ready for bed, I walked out on the ledge of our eleventh-floor room. I sang '*O Sole Mio* to the building across the street — the Salvation Army Hostel for Young Women.

Full of sexual longing, yet feeling that my hopes of fulfilment were in some way less than at the start of this day, I lay in bed with the room spinning around. Kerryn was snoring. I sat up and pulled the *Rolling Stone* out of my satchel. I comforted myself with our review. It's not every mother's son who gets a good review in the *Rolling Stone* magazine.

Above all else, the Dingoes convince.

So ended my first day in New York City, a town filled with

opportunity, but open only to those who have what it wants. I knew we were ignorant of what that was. Was it important to know? Surely we should be able to stand on our own without reference to what was 'happening' in New York. Maybe it would have been smart to slow down and look around outside our Dingo bubble. As it turned out there was plenty happening in New York's underground clubs like CBGBs and Max's Kansas City. But we were geographically and culturally isolated from its underground scene since we were never in New York. And when we were there, nobody told us about it. Anyway, Rudge, I knew, wanted us to make it on our own terms. Like the troops of Gallipoli, we were here, now, primed and ready to rock. We must take our chances with an open assault.

We played with Tom Petty again the next night. I believe we played and were received better than the night before. Rudge was complementary. We broke a record for the Bottom Line: not crowds, not the number of standing ovations, but the amount of beer consumed for a performing act. After surrendering our pay to the bar tab, we still owed the Bottom Line four hundred dollars.

After the second night we went to a club called the Lone Star Café. Here the staff were amused by their Australian patrons. In fact, they had just began stocking the big blue Foster's cans. The bartender didn't believe anyone could drink such big helpings of beer.

'I think he's right, don't you, John?' said Stockley.

Like five Br'er Rabbits, we pretended to be impressed and dubious as to whether or not we were up to this task. The bartender said for every can we drank he would give us one free. The next thing I knew, Stockley and Kerryn were using the empty cans as ten pins. Drunk and foolish again, we were getting into more trouble. Stockley went up to the mezzanine floor and poured beer from a Foster's can down to Kerryn and I who were trying to catch it in a shot glass below. The staff were becoming irate. They came out from behind the bar and asked us to leave. I knelt down behind one of them and beckoned to Kerryn to push him. I was caught and we were ejected again.

Was this good clean fun or pathological behaviour? Probably the latter. Anyway, we got Mad Dog who was in a restaurant next door. He drove us to Fifth Avenue. Stockley was on a mission to improve our public relations with the good people of New York. We helped him roll the keg out onto the pavement. He set up a little stand and, at four in the morning, distributed free beer to passersby. Two derelicts, astounded at this soup kitchen with a difference, eyed us suspiciously. Then, still looking for the catch, they joined us for a quiet beer. Before long, Stockley's winning conviviality had attracted a small group of loiterers. The party was in full swing by the time the cops came. Hearing our quaint accents, and recognising us as Australians, puppy-dogs-of-the-world, they had a quiet beer and a chat before asking us to move on.

Back at the Gramercy, we got on the elevator. J.L. pressed every button up to the eleventh floor. We pulled down our pants. Harmless enough at 5am.

With time to kill and money to burn, and now nowhere to play, we ran amok in New York City. We returned to the Lone Star for another night of shenanigans. That night I developed a comedic device that, though it lives in infamy, was purely for the amusement of my friends The Dingoes. And, though I was its most artistic practitioner, others also perpetrated the same comedic device on me. They are not blameless. However, I do blame myself and take full responsibility for having conceived it. Though I never behaved in such a way before I met The Dingoes, I in no way hold them accountable. And even though when I did it they responded not by admonishing me, not by threatening me, and not by sending me to a psychiatrist, but by laughing, I don't blame them for encouraging me, one bit. Anybody that happened to be in my shoes could have thought of it as easily as I did. And I didn't have to think of this particular comedic device. I could have thought of a less controversial one. For example, I could just as well have gone up to the lads and said something like, 'Have you read the book *Underneath The Grandstands* by I. Seymour Butts?'

They may have laughed — they may have not laughed. And then they would have thought nothing more of it. But this is a random world and the comedic device that did occur to me, they will never let me forget. Whether it was a harmless and playful way of working through my anxiety, an act of pure comic genius, or a surface ripple of a deep disturbance in my psyche, I must confront It. It was known as *bum bothering* or, more familiarly, bothering.

Kerryn was the first person to be bothered — my first victim. He was standing, talking to a curious New Yorker. I was sitting at the bar, alone, with a beer. Something came over me, Yer Honour; I crept up behind Kerryn, about five feet away, and came charging in. I grabbed him around his chest, pinning his arms, and pumped him vigorously from behind with pelvic thrusts. Like a shark striking a stationary victim, my momentum carried him about five yards from his original spot. The victim was held in such a way that he could do nothing about it, and it was over in a second. I casually walked back to the bar as if nothing happened.

Kerryn, violated, tried to explain it to a horrified sophisticate. 'He had a difficult childhood.'

Later that same night, Kerryn sought retribution. I was talking to a girl when suddenly I got bothered. After a good bothering, it was impossible to return to normal conversation. After this bizarre in-joke one had to give an explanation. Yet there was no explaining such a senseless act. In our inebriated state the enormous negative potential of bothering infatuated the whole band. Like a machete introduced into a pre-technological society, the novel power of bothering swept through The Dingoes that night at the Lone Star. You would think that the Lone Star would have been grateful to us for this invention. Perhaps you would expect to go there today and find a plaque on the wall proclaiming itself the birthplace of bothering. But like all true inventors, those in the vanguard who bring new ideas to a society that is not quite ready for them, we were persecuted. That night we were banned for life from the Lone Star Café.

This got back to Rudge. Two days later the wives arrived with the explicit purpose of bringing us to heel. We were moved to a cheaper hotel in the theatre district. Each couple had a room. I watched a lot of TV. and listened discontentedly to beds banging on walls, grunts and little squeels of delight from band members' rooms on either side of me.

I had been deprived of my friends by their wives. After two days of self-pity I snapped out of it. I went to the Statue of Liberty. I took a grafitti train down to Battery Park and stood in a half-hour line to get a ticket. Then I stood in an hour line to get on the ferry. On the ferry I looked back to New York City and up the Hudson towards the George Washington Bridge.

A man behind me was saying to some strangers, 'Yup. They wanted to get funded for the forward-looking radar system. The DOD closed down the GW and brought out some twenty congressmen to see it in action. I flew my F-111 straight up the Hudson. Just before I reached the bridge I turned her upside down and flew her right under.'

Eavesdropping was always a favourite pastime, but here I was getting more than I bargained for. I turned around to see who was talking. He was about thirty years old with thick glasses. He wore a T-shirt with an American flag and a pair of jeans hiked up beyond his belly button. He was licking a double-headed ice-cream cone and smiling serenely.

'I hurt my eyes flying up the Ho Chi Minh trail. We had to take out a bridge and the canyon was so narrow I had to turn my bird on its side. A tree hit the canopy and knocked it off. Some branches came right through my visor. It happened so fast and I stayed right on my mission. I took out that bridge and it wasn't until later that day that the doctor told me I was legally blind.'

On Governor's Island I walked quickly off the ferry to put some distance between myself and this confabulator.

It was hot and humid, and not even a breath of air moved off the Atlantic to cool down Liberty's island. The crowds were thick and garish, bedecked with Liberty paraphenalia. Unhappy children, appreciative of neither the size nor the history of Liberty, screamed for immediate gratification. Tourists from Nebraska, England and India jostled among native New Yorkers on a day trip. An Australian wearing a hat with corks dangling from it, an Australian flag draped around his knapsack and a stuffed koala bear attached to his shoulder strap, walked about ten yards ahead of me. He was walking with a friend. Like a penguin who can distinguish its chick's call in a flock of thousands, I could pick out an Australian accent in a polyglottal confusion.

'She's a beauty, isn't she, mate?'

I put distance between myself and that gentleman, also.

Towering above, Liberty was truly impressive. Stretching before me was an even more impressive line disappearing beneath her robes. A sign said this was a two-hour line. I had already invested a lot of time and I decided to see it through. I had been standing in the line for about fifteen minutes.

'Yes, this newsprint has a carbon base. They're changing over in two months to a type that doesn't rub off.'

'No. No. Not the *Washington Times*.'

'*The New York Times*.'

'Well. I used to work for *The Times*.'

He spoke so loudly, and the stranger he was speaking to spoke so softly, that you had to infer the gist, like with a telephone conversation.

'I was working for the CIA down in Venezuala. A Sandinista operative was trailing me. I had to take him out with my army-issue knife. I wanted to take him back to Langley for an ID, so I cut off his head and wrapped it in a *New York Times* I was reading. But they caught up with me at Dulles. I had to race out of there. I gave the head to the Customs Officer and said, "Jack Pringle, CIA. You deal with it."'

The line inched forward. Six people separated myself and Jack. But then a group of four bailed out of the line.

'Oh, yeah! I know the New York cops real well. One time I was coming home from the movies when I came on a hostage situation. Two men had botched a drugstore robbery. I went up to the captain and introduced myself. He shouted to his marksmen, "Hey. It's Jack Pringle. Bill, throw him your rifle." I took out both perps with one shot.'

At last we were inside Liberty. Foot by foot, inch by inch, we crossed the large foyer, moved up a wide staircase and, finally, reached the foot of the one-person-wide spiral stairway leading to the crown of the Statue of Liberty. Beneath the hot, dark and dusty copper folds of Liberty's robe, with a horde of tourists below zigzagging down to the base and a silent mass somewhere above us spiralling up to the crown, the last two people decided it was all too much and they left too.

'DNA. Linus Pauling got his idea for the structure of DNA from this staircase. I was his grad student in the sixties before I went to the Bell labs to work on inertial guidance systems. I told him he was wrong. The backbone was on the outside, not the inside.'

The spiral staircase was built around a thick pole and carried both the stairway going up and down. We moved one step every five minutes and sat down between moves. Jack was on the stair below me and was now talking directly at me.

'The first guided missile we made took off and got away from us right there in the lab. It flew around the lab at a thousand miles an hour, making sharp turns whenever it came to a wall.

'Where are you from?' he asked.

'I live around here,' I said, desperately trying to hide my accent.

'You're from Australia, aren't you?' he said. 'The best fighters in the world. But crazy. We used to party with you Aussies in 'Nam. Did you see that other Australian guy, with the hat and the koala?'

'No,' I lied.

'Oh yeah. He's just a few people back. G'day, mate!' he shouted, trying to raise my fellow countryman.

'Hello?' yelled back the Australian from somewhere a few base-pairs below us.

'We've got another man from Down Under up here, mate.'

'Fair dinkum?' came the incredulous reply. 'Grouse, mate. What's yer name, mate?'

'Frank,' I said.

'Can't hear ya, mate. Speak up! Whereabouts you from?'

'Melbourne.'

'Where?'

'Melbourne!'

'Me too, mate. Whereabouts?'

'East Melbourne.'

'Unreal. Where you staying?'

'I'm going home tonight.'

'How do you like it here? It's alright, I reckon.'

'Good. I like it.'

The people above us who were up until now assiduously ignoring everything going on below them, discovering not just one, but two puppy-dogs-of-the-world, chimed in.

'I've always wanted to go to Australia. What brought you over here?'

This was a sane woman and I felt she deserved an honest answer.

'I came over with a rock'n'roll band.'

'What's the name of your band?' asked Jack.

'The Dingoes,' I said softly.

'Hey, mate,' he yelled. 'Ever heard of The Dingoes?'

'Who? The Monkeys?'

'No. The Dingoes!'

'The Dingoes! Unreal! I saw youse guys at the Croydon Arms. Youse guys are grouse, I reckon. How come youse got to come to the States?'

'It's a long story.'

'Did ya bring yer guitar, mate? Give us a song while we wait.'

Nasal Australian laughter reverberated in Liberty's chest. I shrugged my shoulders and gave a look of such agony that the people above me kept to themselves after that. We all sat on steps or haunches as we waited to move up to the next step. Every now and then the Australian called up: 'Are ya there yet, mate? Can ya see the crown? We're still stuck in her armpit. It's worse than Werribee down here.'

I was stuck in Liberty's throat now, and unable to move up or down to escape this dingy, claustrophobic nightmare. We were, I thought, the answer to Liberty's hyper-altruistic plea: *Give me your huddled masses.*

'Three people died when they filmed *Vertigo*. Hitchcock always picked the big monuments for his American films. This and Niagara Falls, Mount Rushmore. He had a real thing for heights. I used to be terrified, too. But I got over my own fear when I trained with the Green Berets. I had to drop into Cambodia in '69.'

I nodded, carefully balancing between humouring and encouraging the man. But I needn't have bothered. What I did had nothing to do with his actions.

'When I got back out they put me into F-111s. One time I was testing forward-looking radar. It was so secret the agency didn't want the Air

Force to know about it. So it had one of its own fly it. I took it down a canyon so narrow I had to fly it sideways. I took out a bridge and the gooks didn't know what hit 'em.'

At last we reached the crown. I glanced at the Atlantic and headed straight down the stairs.

'Vertigo,' I said to explain my quick exit. I made my way to the ferry and, in true cloak-and-dagger fashion, skulked around in its passageways trying to avoid the Australian and Jack Pringle.

Then I heard them.

'... Jack Pringle, CIA. You deal with it.'

'That's unreal, mate!'

This is what passed for existence in those weeks. Save for the patrons of a few bars, we had no social existence at all. We were languishing in hotel rooms in New York City. In this stifling environment, the married Dingoes were as suffocated within their four walls by female companionship as I was starved by the lack of it. For, lacking the instant credential of performing on stage, I had nothing whatever to recommend myself to the women of New York (handsome features and striking physique, it seems, were not enough). And, unlike foreign places in Australia — such as Perth, where the local populace welcomed us into their society — New Yorkers behaved like subtle bees, guarding their social groups against outsiders. I could understand this.

Bee sociality, and their fervently cooperative behavior, is said to have evolved because of intense predation and other environmental vicissitudes. Surely, there was no more competitive place than New York. There was a constant flow of people coming in to make it and an equal number of those who couldn't make it or who were fed up with trying, leaving town. The highly desirable status of making it drove up property prices and rents. And people either paid the prices or bailed out of the city. In this unforgiving environment, people formed groups to protect and aid each other. They stuck tenaciously to them and jealously guarded admittance. To qualify for this or that group you had to have succeeded at this or that thing. We had not. We were, and would remain, outsiders. It had little or nothing to do with talent.

Or so I told myself, feebly, as I watched the gifted and talented, the rich and the stylish, on the streets of Manhattan and in the medium of my vicarious social life — TV. But surely this must not be my destiny. Had I come this far merely to experience envy, and then to return home with my dingo tail between my legs? My number had come up on the great wheel of fortune before, in Australia. An impossible dream was realised. But the correct denouement was not forthcoming. After our triumph over stagnation and lawyers in Australia, despite our sticking together through thick and thin in the US, it seemed very possible that success could elude us completely. Our record was still being played on radio. But sales were slow. Stockley pined for his mountain-bosom home. I was in solitary confinement and yearning for fulfilment of any kind. Mad Dog was assigned to another band. Kerryn was trying to act level-headed while his marriage was breaking up. Brod waited for the inevitable Phar Lapisation of The Dingoes. J.L. formed strange alliances with strange people. Then we were liberated to the road.

9

Woodstock

We kissed off the wives. They returned to Mill Valley. Back in The Enterprise, Mad Dog — recalled from another band — and The Dingoes cruised full-speed-ahead up Highway 87 North. Stockley sat straddling our keg representing the great state of New York, Genesee Ale. Singing an African American work song, he slowly worked its pump.

'Some bastard's got to do this job,' he said.

'Is it a good drop, mate?' I asked.

He took a sip and rolled the beer around his tongue. Then he sniffed the glass.

'It has an unusual flavour. I'm not sure if it will catch on. Here, see what you think. Kerryn, have a glass of Genocide, mate?'

The glasses he poured for me and Kerryn were half beer and half a rich, creamy foam.

'A frothy, energetic little beer,' I said. 'Not a poofter's beer. Not exactly a man's beer either.'

'More like a dog's beer,' said Kerryn.

Lynyrd Skynyrd were leasing this propeller-driven Convair 240. On a flight from Miami to Greenville, The band's sound man saw six-foot flames coming out of its right engine. He wondered if it was some mechanic's screw-up. Probably the mechanic was worried about troubles at home. Or was the plane just too damned old? Anyway, they decided to get rid of it in Baton Rouge the next day.

I took my frenzied dog beer and went to sit at the panoramic window in the back room of The Enterprise. Kerryn came with me. I wanted to see the geography of this town we were approaching, this town that occupied an overly and badly defined place in the consciousness of my generation: Woodstock, New York.

The road was cut through the Saugerties mountains, exposing miles of rock layers formed by sediment on ancient ocean floors. I would have loved to have stopped. I would have loved to shout, 'Hey! Bad Dog! Stop The Enterprise and let's look at fossils! What d'ya say, huh?'

I pointed the strata out to Kerryn and said, 'What do you think of this idea, mate?'

'Wait a minute,' he said, as he readied himself to ponder some very big question or other. 'Okay, mate. Let her rip.'

'If you believe in evolution, you have to also believe that your existence depended on a fight between two fish in the Devonian sea.'

'Where's Devonia? What are you talking about?' Kerryn was bemused.

'The Devonian was an era or an epoch millions of years ago. I mean a fight between two fish back then, you know, affects whether we, John and Kerryn, were born or not.'

'What do the fish have to do with us?'

'Man is a mammal. Mammals came from reptiles. Reptiles from amphibians. And amphibians came from ...' And I put my hand out in a gesture which prompted Kerryn for the word.

'Tadpoles,' he said, quizzically.

'No, no, no, my good man. Amphibians evolved from fish! Imagine you're a fish and you're that one fish carrying the genetic how's-your-father that led to the evolution of land-living animals.'

'Like lungs?'

'Or skin that didn't dry in the air. Well, if you've been eaten, evolution would have turned out differently. Even if that fish weren't eaten. Even if any fish was eaten. Like in a football game, how every little bounce of the ball changes whatever happens after. You know what I mean? Like I used to wonder if, when I went to see Melbourne play, if I called out to Ron Barassi — you know, "G'day, Ron!" — if he even heard me at all wouldn't it change everything that happened in the match. Maybe Melbourne was going to lose but my "G'day, Ron!" changed the result.'

'You're saying that every little thing changes everything else forever. Alright, but back to the sea: the fish that survived was the better fish. Aren't we the fry of that struggle? Don't we deserve to be here because we are the best?'

'You sound like Adolf Hitler. He said that the German people had the right to dominate the world because evolution had put them on the top — they were only fulfilling the destiny of nature.'

'It's the Genocide talking,' Kerryn explained, and we both had another sip.

'Think about the night you were conceived,' I said.

'Just for you, John.'

'It was pure chance that you, your particular genetic self, exist. The sperm in your father's how's-your-father were being shaken around like a cocktail mixer. What determined which sperm came out first?'

Kerryn started to answer but I got in first.

'Chance is all. That you exist is sheer luck. It has nothing to do with the best.'

'Hey. Hold on. How do you know? How do you know the sperm that made me wasn't the strongest, best sperm? It could've started out at the back of the pack and swam up into first place. Isn't that survival of the fittest? In the how's-your-father epoch, the best fish won and we're at the end of a long line of winners. We deserve to be here. It's genetic justice.'

'It doesn't work according to some plan,' I said. 'If some evolutionary events had not happened, there may not have even been such a thing as humans. In evolution, where you get to depends on what road you take. All I'm saying is that small irrelevant things affect everything that follows. Every time we meet someone we change the bounce of the ball.

Every thought anyone ever had. This conversation. Every fish being eaten. Every bounce of every ball. Every jiggle in the nuptial bedroom.'

Kerryn nodded and gyrated his toes. 'You make it sound like a huge fluke that any of us is here, at all.'

'Think of the odds against your or my existence. Is it thirty million sperm in one how's-your-father? Thousands of how's-your-fathers in your father's life ...'

'... Not to mention the eggs ...'

'Getting to be alive is like winning the lottery! It's like winning a fucking lottery. What they say is true: we are lucky to be alive.'

And for a moment, in the company of my good friend Kerryn, speeding through the picturesque Saugerties on the way to the hallowed ground of Woodstock and feeling the sensation of wellbeing imparted by the first beer on a lunchless stomach, I believed the fundamental wisdom of my words: I was lucky to be alive!

High above, vapour trails, ephemeral, like man, crisscrossed and decayed in the afternoon sky. Some were from planes descending into New York a hundred miles to the south. Other trails were from planes flying to or from Toronto, Washington, Philadelphia, Montreal, or any of the many other choke points in the vast swathe of population on the eastern seaboard.

At some places on the Saugerties road the rock strata formed lines as mesmerising as telegraph wires seen from a train. I started to daydream about home. Sometimes I thought about friends I had left behind. Sometimes, in homesick reveries, I would even think of certain intersections and follow the course of a particular street through suburbs of my childhood. Strangely, these prosaic images evoked intense nostalgia. Straying farther afield, I followed the Princess Highway through Geelong and down to the Great Ocean Road. The powerful swell of Bass Strait erodes the southern edge of the Otway Ranges. And the Great Ocean Road makes a tentative connection between sparse resort towns. They are built on small estuaries formed where the Otway's creeks fall to sea level. Sometimes the road runs on a shelf blasted into the sheer cliffs. I travelled past Torquay and Anglesea, dodging rosellas and trying to evoke the smell of eucalyptus smoke from a distant bushfire. My mind wandered to an incident that happened when I was fifteen.

Summering at Airey's Inlet on the Great Ocean Road, I was the guest of the family of a sexy classmate. She was a classmate who had, after our high school dance, allowed me to express my admiration of her breasts by touching them. I was beside myself with joy when I contemplated this vacation. But I was foiled when her nineteen-year-old ex-boyfriend from last summer kept coming over. She had rediscovered his more sophisticated charm. I was sure he was expressing his admiration of her more profoundly than I had those months ago.

Though he had bested me sexually, he liked me and, I think, felt bad about it. His way of making amends was to take me walking and, in an avuncular way, educate me as to where the action truly was. The hypersocial adolescent craves party action. I became a reluctant protégé and I fell into listening to his tales of the legendary parties at Lorne, the next resort to the west. Here, he said, every Saturday night, groups of revellers burst out of bars and private homes and formed a drunken sexual procession down the main street. He made it sound as if all the girls were hungry for sex — even with a juvenile like me. At this orgiastic parade, this sexual El Dorado, all one had to do was be there. But I didn't get there until two or three years later. By then the sexual procession had moved on to some other place I was not.

The subconscious mind directs the subject matter of daydreams. My subconscious had unerringly singled out the importance of Woodstock to me: it was a sexual El Dorado.

While I was prepared for a letdown, I believed the promise of sex was greater here than in Airey's Inlet or Lorne. After all, in Woodstock people didn't have sex just for its own sake. Seven years ago, in 1969, sexual freedom had been vaunted at the Woodstock Festival as part of a more romantic whole. The reproductive act was even tied to your geo-political view in the slogan, *Make love, not war*. At Woodstock, it seemed, you could enjoy the pleasures of the flesh while contributing to world peace. For a while, that naive generation accepted on face value the idea that, armed with only good intentions, good karma, good vibes, good drugs and good sex, *we* could magically transform societies at home and abroad.

But if contributing to world peace did not convince women to relax their stingy attitude to sex, there were even more convincing reasons. Two generations of psychoanalysts, sociologists and anthropologists had fuelled the development of feminist doctrine and the sexual revolution. They said that the behaviour of Western women was repressed. Cultures in the natural state, say in Samoa, enjoyed sexual freedoms that were good for the psyche. In those cultures women were said to be very relaxed about sexual relations. The feminist doctrine said: *There is no reason to be prudish. With the pill you may be as promiscuous as men are.* To be a virgin, since virginity's only purpose was to assuage the prospective husband's ego and assure his paternity, was to admit women's status as second-class citizens — as the property of men. Women should control their own reproductivity! They should have sex when, where and with whomever they wanted. Virginity and even monogamy were relics of the Victorian age — they were old-fashioned ideas. And most women of that time felt social pressure from their peers to indulge in free love to some degree. I was very supportive of this platform.

Seven years ago at this place, the magical hippie promise of peace, love, harmony, understanding and, most importantly, lots of sex seemed possible. But, as we craned our necks for evidence of these sacred non sequiturs, we saw that the great sexual procession had moved on. The legendary party sought by we delayed adolescents was elsewhere. Without awareness or gratitude that my generation and I were even then experiencing a glorious window of opportunity — after the pill and before HIV — I felt only disgruntled. We docked The Enterprise and, while the others went to make arrangements for that night's job, Kerryn and I went for a walk.

'Not a naked breast in sight,' I said.

'Look,' said Kerryn. 'Let's check out some of these shops.'

The spirit of hippie mercantilism had survived. Shaggy proprietors of leather-craft stalls, sceptical of a sale, eyed their clientele with disdain. Health-food store workers, their cheeks flushed with piety and joy in the knowledge that their next bowel movement would turn out well, performed their duties like androids. Head shops sold hookahs, bongs, pipes and cigarette papers — paraphernalia for the generation's drug, marijuana. But remnants of the counterculture were interspersed among straight shops with credit card decals emblazoned in their front windows. Flashy grandmothers with white slacks, gold-chained handbags and pursed lips sought the legendary bargain in dozens of pricey knick-knack stores.

The town was still a strong, sad magnet for a generation looking for the great hippie promises. While the generation's numbers were being felt around the world, its attitudes seemed to crystallise at Woodstock. The festival was an outbreak of pastoral yearning, a long weekend back to the garden of feebly imagined pre-technology. This, from a generation that was raised on, and would be forever open to, the seduction of *high*-technology. Even the icons of Woodstock, its musicians, were the avatars of a new technological age. As fetishistic operators of Stratocasters, Precision Basses, synthesisers, multi-track studios and megawatt amplifiers, part of their allure was their command of the very latest technology.

By sheer force of numbers, it seemed self-evident that at Woodstock, the generation was ushering in a new set of pre-industrial values. There, for all the world to see, was ostentatious kindness, artistic transport, peace and love — the messianic fruition of a generation's goodwill dawning in the Age of Aquarius. I'm talking 'bout my generation. We were the Baby Boom generation. We were defined by our peer-group media as *We*, the helping/caring generation, the counterculture. Initially, we were described in a bemused way by the adult straight press as a curious, quirky, but fond phenomenon. But after we crossed the threshold into adulthood, we were seen merely as a bulge of population moving through time as a digesting rat moves through a python.

Truthfully, if Woodstock were observed by another intelligent species, it would be seen as a biological event — a massing of sexually mature organisms at a stage in their life cycle that was sensitive to cultural influence. Like millions of horseshoe crabs responding to mysterious signals to gather on a single night on a preordained beach on Cape Cod, this generation responded to the call to come to Woodstock. And then, like the crabs, as soon as the biological function had been served the crowd dissipated. But, unlike the crabs, the Woodstock organisms and all the other organisms of the same age (including the organism writing this) had to suffer constant re-evaluation of their lives using the event as the standard of measurement.

Woodstock should have been like a song — beautiful, but sung. Over and done. But it was filmed. Commentators saw the event and its idealism as defining our generation. And ever since, when the rat moving through the python passed through child-rearing stage, when the rat had to earn a living, when the rat started to get old and need more health care, we were seen as confronting a new dream-eroding reality. But as far as I could see, that dream existed only in popular analysis. The dream of Woodstock was naive but it was dreamt at a youthful, wide-eyed age. It was dreamt when dreams should be dreamt. The perception of failed promise was caused by the media who kept saying, in effect, *Don't you remember what you said when you were nineteen?*

As Kerryn and I walked we talked.

I spoke first. 'I think the whole Woodstock hippie thing was a broad expression of what many of us felt, you know, that it didn't have to be this way. I mean poverty, war, prejudice, that whole plasticness ...'

'... of the Elvis and Frank Sinatra–loving generations ...'

'... that came before us.'

'It's pathetic how it fizzled out.'

'But some good things did come of it,' I said, as if defending a culprit.

'Fiber.'

'Jimi Hendrix.'

'Communes.'

'How are they good?' I asked.

'They were supposed to be a return to a more natural way of life.'

'But they mostly all fizzled 'cause people just can't resist the creature comforts of TV and fridges. They come home. I used to swear I would throw away my TV. I know I would've been happier, done more things like reading and honing my conversational skills ...'

'... a lost art ...'

'... present company excepted. But, anyway, I couldn't. It's all too fuckin' seductive.'

'You could return to your rural roots like Thomas Hardy did,' said Kerryn. He and I had been in bands together for years and we had read many of the same books.

'God! Wouldn't I love to live in a town like Casterbridge, the way he describes it, anyway,' I said.

'Or Woodstock?'

'But this is more like a theme park. "Good morning, campers."'

We stared at a hippie family as if they were a soon-to-be-extinct species. The man was big. He wore a big beard and a Grateful Dead T-shirt. The woman was the Earth Mother–type with thick leather sandals, braids and a long flowing dress. They had two children, and the smell of patchouli oil, in tow. Just then a group of Japanese tourists started to take their photographs. One of them, in a gesture meant in friendship and recognition, gave the two-fingered peace sign.

The hippie man gave them a single-fingered gesture in reply.

'They always hassle you, man,' he said to his woman.

'Be cool, man. You're too paranoid. They're not putting you down,' she replied.

I was reminded of a photograph I had seen of an Amish family visiting their local town and being surrounded by tourists.

As we walked past the Japanese tourists we heard them pondering the meaning of The Grateful Dead.

'Grayful Deh?'

'Kamikaze?'

And they nodded to each other in tentative acceptance of this familiar idea. We told Brod about this incident. Later that night, playing to a packed, small club in Woodstock, he opened our set as if we were a Japanese band. In a stereotypically guttural Japanese accent he introduced us.

'We, ah, come from, ah ... Japan! We come to Woodstock to, ah, rock and roll! We love The Grayful Deh! We listen to, ah, Beatle. We first band from ... ah ... Japan to ... to ... to ... ah ... visit United State of America. Thank you. You are welcome. Rock and roll! Take it away, boys.'

And we launched into *Boy on the Run*, a song of nostalgia written by Stockley and Brod.

He was runnin' like a native across a creek,
Singin' in the field, in the wind, in the sun.
There he goes racin' down the street:
Just like a boy on the run.

He takes a stone and throws it in the water,
And watches the circles as they slowly fade.
He fills the air with sudden laughter,
As he thinks of all the plans that he made.

Well, he's scared of the future. In need of the past.
Just sittin' here watchin' his hourglass.

Down the street the accordions are calling:
'Stay away, boy. There's nothin' for you here.'
And he can hear the buildings falling
As they're strippin' away all of his years.

The words are Broderick's. They held a plea, not for conserving a rural way of life, but for stopping the desecration of Brod's traditional seat: the suburbs. I loved that about The Dingoes. We were writing about ourselves. And, anyway, that song has the best bass part that ...

'We are unworthy. But we thank you,' shouted Brod, after the song had finished.

We struck into *Smooth Sailin'*.

Our hard-edged rock'n'roll was not what Woodstock was looking for. They were polite, but by the end of the night a large portion of the crowd had gone home.

At twelve the next day, Mad Dog let me take the helm of The Enterprise. We were booked to open for Southside Johnny and the Asbury Dukes, the next night in Oneonta, New York. The sun was directly overhead but on board the air conditioner kept the temperature artificially low. Cars seemed insignificant and the size and sturdiness of The Enterprise made me feel secure. Brod was sitting in the passenger seat. With only my little finger on the steering wheel, I puffed myself up and said in an arrogant tone, 'Herr Von Rommel, I feel that ve are destined to be victorious.'

'God has preordained it, Herr Kapitan. And the Bismarck is in ... des ... tructible.'

'It is ridiculous to think that there are those ...' and here I raised my voice so that Kerryn could hear me, '... who deny the justice of the position of der Master Race at the very top of all peoples — it is Charles Darwin himself who says ve haf der right.'

'Piss off, John,' shouted Kerryn. 'Or I'll tie you up with piano wire.'

Twenty minutes out of Woodstock, back on 87 North, I got a jolt of anxiety. In Australia I had had to pull off the road a couple of times. Behind the wheel, my primary and overwhelming fear was of losing consciousness. The more I studied my state of mind, the dizzier I imagined I became (here is one instance that imagination can quickly create its own reality). This happened enough times so that I finally realised I would not actually faint. That realisation taught me that if I persevered it would eventually go away. I persevered in The Enterprise. I counted the yellow lines to distract myself. But the anxiety kept building, and after a while I said to myself, *Who needs this.*

I decided to pull in at the next rest stop. I would hand the wheel over to Mr Security, Mad Dog.

I didn't notice it at first, and I couldn't have told you what it was, but there was something unrealistic about my surroundings. Something was out of whack. I looked behind me and back into the cool recesses of The Enterprise at the lounging Dingoes. Everything was normal. Then I saw it. It was the road itself. The road surface was made of reptile scales — yellow stripes on glossy, dry, ebony-black scales. I blinked and it returned for a second to its regular macadam texture. But then it was a reptile again. And now the cars were multicoloured beetles crawling along its back. And then, in the distance, the road bends became kinetic and the big black reptile slithered into the distance. It was moving faster than we were. We began to slide off its back. I glanced at Brod. He was not reacting. I pulled over to the side of the road.

'I'm sick,' I said, and I went to the back room to lie down.

Mad Dog drove on.

I knew what was happening to me. Ever since I was fourteen and read that schizophrenia runs in families, I was on guard for its symptoms. For thirteen years, now, I had been listening for the voices. I sobbed out of control as fear and the enormity of my own destroyed promise hit me. Kerryn came back and sat on the bed. He put his hand on my back and stroked.

'What's the matter, mate?'

In fear for my future, remembering the paranoia that destroyed every single one of my mother's friendships, and knowing this insidious disease would do the same for me, I clutched Kerryn and wept in his lap.

'Hey. Hey. What is it, John?'

I looked up at him. His beard became a mass of fine, seething worms.

'The voices,' I stammered. 'The hallucinations are here. Schizophrenia.'

'Come on, mate. It's just anxiety. Try to relax. I'll get you a glass of water.'

He reminded me of my own pathetic attempts at treating my mother's delusions and hallucinations. He left the room.

'Jesus! Mad Dog!'

'You fuckin' *idiot*!'

I heard shouting and recriminations. I wished Mad Dog would finally take us into culvert. I began to list my suicide options.

Then I saw all of The Dingoes come back to witness my horror. Kerryn said, 'John. There were some biscuits in a brown paper bag next to the sink. Did you take one?'

'Yes,' I whimpered.

'Mate,' he laughed. 'You're tripping. They had LSD in them.'

'Sit back and enjoy the ride,' said Stockley.

'Boisy!' said Brod as his head melted on his shoulders.

Mad Dog had accepted the LSD-spiked cookies last night from a mind-altering hippie. He clumsily left them lying around. It served me right.

'Do you think you'll be alright?'

'I th-think so,' I said. My voice reverberated inside my head like it was the Grand Canyon.

> The Convair 240 taxied down the runway. It shuddered once or twice as if labouring under the band's load. Everything was on board. All the equipment — heavy, heavy equipment. All the band and its roadies. Twenty-six people. Jack Daniel's was brought out. The band celebrated their recent success and recalled some of the funnier moments from the last gig. But mostly they celebrated because they were getting a new plane when they reached Baton Rouge. The lead singer lay down on the floor and went to sleep.

I had freaked out. But now, accepting the fact of my LSD trip, I tried to enjoy the journey. The others left me to hallucinate in peace. I lay in the supine position, my hands clasped behind my head, and let her rip. My waking dream lasted almost all the way into Oneonta.

> The keyboard player noticed that the right engine of the old Convair was spluttering. The pilot was dealing with what he thought was a routine problem.
>
> 'Everything's okay,' he said. 'I'm only transferring oil from one engine to the other.'
>
> The keyboard player went back to his seat.

Twenty minutes out of Oneonta, the hallucinations had diminished to the extent that I could stumble up into the bow of The Enterprise. I could even make an attempt at a joke.

'Okay, Bad Dog. I'm ready to drive again you son of a bitch. Quick. Give me the wheel, you bastard, before you crash into those newspaper taxis.'

> The drummer and keyboard player heard the engine die. Together, they ran to the cockpit. The pilot said: 'Oh my God, strap in!'
>
> They woke up the lead singer. He was cross at them but they forced him to strap in anyway. They only had to wait a minute.

The drug left me feeling clammy and spent. The other Dingoes had a full head of Genesee and were laughing hysterically at things which, in my emotionally flat state, seemed unfunny.

> They braced themselves as the trees kept getting bigger and bigger. The pilot was eight miles short of the McComb Mississippi airport — not Baton Rouge. The Convair went in and suffered strikes from what the keyboard player said sounded like hundreds of baseball bats. Something loose in the back of the plane flew forward and killed the lead singer instantly. The top of the plane was peeled off. But still, twenty of the twenty-six people onboard were alive. But not the lead singer, nor the lead guitarist, nor his sister, a backup singer, nor the pilot, nor the copilot, nor the band's assistant road manager.

10

Boston

The next morning I stood ready to board The Enterprise. I took one last, fond look at the motel parking lot in Oneonta. It was eleven o'clock and already the air was damp with humidity. I had a small, clammy hangover. I couldn't tell if the moisture on my skin came from me or the air. I could see lightning flashing in the distance — too far away for the thunder to reach us. Mad Dog had been running The Enterprise for twenty minutes. Heavy, cold air poured down its steps and onto my sockless wingtips.

'Look out, mate,' said Mad Dog as he stepped out of The Enterprise. The motel manager was calling him in to take a telephone call. I boarded.

A few minutes later Mad Dog returned looking very concerned. 'That was Sir Productions,' he said. 'Lynyrd Skynyrd has had a plane crash. Ronnie Van Zant and Steve Gaines are dead.' We were stunned. We had met them a few times. For a number of minutes we were absorbed by their tragedy and blind to our own.

Brod was the first to see it. 'We're fucked,' he said. 'We're fucked, too.'

This was no Phar Lap theory. Brod's realisation derived from hard economics. Lynyrd Skynyrd was managed by Rudge. They were his main moneymaker and the basis of our support. From them came the houses in Mill Valley, The Enterprise and the whole touring apparatus. Rudge also managed The Rolling Stones, who hardly ever toured, and a band called 38 Special. But, like us, 38 Special were a cash calf.

As if a killer comet had crashed on the other side of the Earth, we carried on as normal as we waited for the pall to reach us. Mad Dog steered The Enterprise towards Massachusetts, towards Boston.

With the bad news we got into a grumpy little conversation.

'I hate to say it but I think you're right, Broderick. We're fuckin' pist'ry,' said Stockley.

'Wait a second,' I said. 'We just released our record. Give us a chance.'

'It's just a matter of time,' said Brod. 'There's no way he can keep us now. I'll give it three months.'

' 'E's cocked it up from the beginning, anyway,' said Stockley. 'Rudge 'as.'

'Alright. Let's blame everyone but ourselves,' said Kerryn angrily. 'If anyone's "cocked it up", it's us.'

'How has he done that, Chris?' I said ignoring Kerryn's comment.

'Number one: he should never had brought us to Boronto, nor left us there,' replied Stockley. 'Number two: we should have recorded a lot sooner. Okay, he does have some good ideas but he doesn't know how to put them into action.'

'I don't see how it's his fault,' I answered not emotionally but too quickly. 'We recorded, we toured. What else could he do? Can he force the audiences to jump up and down for us? Jesus, how many other bands would give anything to have our chances. He's not God, for Christ's sake.'

'He's our fuckin' manager. He's supposed to be God! The most successful bands had great managers. That's why they were successful. And we're pist'ry because we don't have one. That's all.'

'We're crazy if we don't give it everything now,' I said.

'We had our shot. We just shot it,' said Stockley.

' 'K'n oath, mate. That's the attitude.' I felt the futility of my exhortations. 'So, what now?'

'We're fucked for the US. But we should keep going, I reckon,' said Stockley. 'And when the shit eventually hits the fan we should start up again back home. Maybe we're better off trying to make it our own way — from Australia.'

I nearly fell off my seat. Brod, Kerryn and I looked at each other as if to say, *No fuckin' way!* J.L. smiled behind his sunglasses. I always forgot how much Stockley loved The Dingoes — enough even to begin again in Australia. I could not see going back in shame to Australia.

We all stared into space, pondering our separate futures. I went alone into the back room and lay down. The Enterprise's rear end shimmied and shook. It was comforting for me to surrender my own movement to its greater forces. To complete the metaphor I assumed the fetal position. Here in the belly of The Enterprise I was protected against the storm that was now raging outside. Of course I must surrender, too, to the events of my personal history. But The Dingoes and I were not a part of US society. We were not in its belly. We were peripheral. Bouncing from one town to the next, we could be flicked off its back at a moment's notice. With this strange combination of comfort and fear, I escaped into sleep and dreamed this dream.

I stood on top of the geological column. A theoretical structure, this is made up of existing strata from around the world whose layers are in order of their believed deposition. The most recent layers are at the top. Like the pages of a book, I peeled away layer after layer. After the third leaf I saw some fossils. It was the hippie family of yesterday. They came to life and the layer became a neolithic landscape. The family of four walked off, leaving the tracks of their bare feet in the cooling volcanic ash.

I turned the next geological page and revealed pop-up-book dinosaurs. Then they came to life. Kerryn was standing under a monstrous titanosaur. He was pointing up and gesturing like an extra in a Japanese monster movie.

'Look!' he said. As if I could miss it.

What an idiot, I thought.

The titanosaur peed on Kerryn and he was washed away in waterfalls and rapids of urine.

'You're right,' he mocked. 'Even a single dinosaur pee is changing my life forever ...'

I became a feather and floated down through the rock, seeing untold species of plants and animals. The deeper I floated, the more primitive and bizarre they were becoming.

Finally, I was a fish, a human fish, trying to escape a Devonian shark. I beat it by being able to crawl out of the water. Kerryn was on the shore casually towel-drying himself.

'That was a close one,' I said.

'Nearly curtains,' he said. 'But you did it! *You* did it!' And he pinched my cheek like you would encourage a baby.

Then I was playing a song for Paul McCartney and Mick Jagger. They were going to be our replacement singers for Brod (Brod had left because of his certainty that we were doomed). They both loved the song and Paul said, 'You write much better songs than the others. That's a hit single if ever I heard one. Let's get in the studio. Tomorrow, mate!'

A deep wellspring of pleasure poured concentrated self-esteem into a hungry, empty space in my mind.

I woke up steeped in satisfaction with my songwriting coup. *Man,* I thought, *that chorus was the greatest. If I could just remember how it went.* I strained to remember. Then I got it. It was to the tune of *Amazing Grace*. The words were about finding my car keys in my coat pocket.

Looking out the back window I noticed that all the licence plates of the cars were from Massachusetts. We were driving through the Berkshire mountains. I walked out to the front and said, 'What a coincidence that all the licence plates are Massachusetts and we just happen to be in Massachusetts. That's really cosmic, isn't it, Brod?'

'Too right, mate. It makes you think, doesn't it.'

'God! Look at this storm. It's transmogrifying the landscape, isn't it, Broddles?'

'Truly, mate. The water, in rivulets and torrents, is flashing down gullies that are bidding farewell to their sediment as the tender, gentle, inexorable, ineluctable tug of the rain tears them asunder.'

Thwack! went a rubber suction-cup dart fired by Stockley.

We drove into Boston. Driving alongside the Charles River with its low-arched bridges, you could swear you were in Melbourne. Scullers from Harvard leaned into their spring-loaded shells — fresh-faced young men, their heads filled with ideas that I would never even hear — or would I? I was so tired of the sensation of envy — envy for those with knowledge, envy for those with love, envy for those with sane mothers and fathers, envy for those at home, envy for those who ...

We drove to do a sound check at a club called The Paradise. We were to open for a band called New Riders of the Purple Sage. On stage that night we were subdued. I was shy and full of self-doubt. I felt I was not worth the price of admission. I envied the audience and wished I could step out of my life and into theirs. As I played I imagined a conversation between two patrons as they left:

> 'That first band — who were they? The Dingoes? What the fuck is a dingo?'
>
> 'Who the fuck cares, man. They sucked. Shit. I could play better than them.'

I would have been glad to have been the inspiration for someone learning to play. Sort of like when I saw Ray Charles when I was fourteen.

One of the New Riders came back to compliment us on our sound. But he confided in me, 'You guys are great. But you don't look like you enjoy playing.'

As I have said, we staunchly resisted any extra-musical gimmicks like glitz, glam, masks and big stadium-rock poses. We were snobs. We wanted the focus to be on our music. As strange as this was for musicians, we regarded all the posing of seventies bands as boorish and trendy. Not that we didn't like to entertain. When Brod was in top form and the audience was eating out of our hands — those were our favourite nights. We were thrilled to be entertaining. But the audience had to have some idea who we were or what we were about: our stage style, dependent as it was on natural personality, was so understated that many audiences missed it altogether. This was especially true in the US since we played to a new crowd every night (generally one who came to see the band we were opening for). Since we had no masks, we had nothing to hide behind; we were what we felt. The human face is a social tool. At The Paradise ours expressed not joy in self-appreciation, not even righteous loathing of a crowd weaned on the pretentious mannerisms of stadium megastars, but defeat, self-consciousness and inferiority. The New Rider was right. We didn't enjoy playing.

After a couple of weeks of touring around New Hampshire and Vermont, we drove back to New York City. Rudge summoned us in to Sir Productions for a meeting.

'I know you've heard the news. About Skynyrd. I've been really fucked up. I don't know what I'm doing half the time.'

His bounciness had left him. Instead, an Alka-Seltzer-popping jitteriness had taken over. He looked drawn — as if a close family member had passed away. We tried to look sympathetic. But we were eager to hear our fate. I had one thought: *Let's have done with it, then.*

'I've taken a hit right to the balls,' he said. 'It's going to be hard. But I'm going to keep you on. I'm dropping 38 Special. I think we'll be okay. A&M still wants to keep going — at least they want another record.'

Curse me if part of me wasn't disappointed.

'But,' he said, 'we're going to have to do it on the cheap. I'm afraid that means no more Mill Valley, Stockley.'

'What about the wives, Peter?' asked Stockley.

'You can fly them out here for a couple of weeks. Then you're off on tour again. Maybe it's best if they go home, back to Australia, at least until we do the next album. I'm sorry.'

'You can't help it, mate,' said Stockley.

I did my best to look appreciative. I wanted to say, *For Christ's sake, Peter. Put us out of our misery!* Instead I said, 'What's happening with the record, Peter? Is it selling?'

'No, it's not. You had a few guys in a few towns who wore the grooves out on the thing. But it didn't catch. But that's okay for a first album. We need to get you on a good tour. Get your faces out there. I wanted to put you on with Skynyrd. But ...'

Mad Dog was reassigned. The wives came back to New York after closing everything up in Mill Valley. Their attitude was the same as ours.

We were not being reprieved; we were being sent back to war. They were very sweet, and then they were gone. The tour didn't materialise. Instead, we were warehoused in a hotel on the west side of Central Park — the Empire. This was a cruel blow because, although the hotel wasn't swish, it was opposite the Lincoln Center. A horde of privileged people came nightly to see their favourite ballet or opera. Drawn by the beauty of serious art, they swept by us cultural no-accounts holed up in this hotel of well-decayed respectability.

From my window on the fourteenth floor I had a split view. Across the inert piece of space between two wings of the hotel was a communal bathroom. On these hot nights, its frosted window was open about four inches — right about at the level of an average genital. During peak hours, every thirty minutes a new set of genitals appeared about ten feet away. If I craned my neck to look beyond this wing, I could see the second view: the backstage door of the Lincoln Center.

That's entertainment! I thought, as every night sacred ballerinas and profane genitals went by on their way to work.

We were still being paid an allowance. But it was much smaller than the Mill Valley sum. Now we could afford only one night of loose spending a week. For the rest of each week I went to the local deli. Usually I bought a plastic container of chopped liver, some lemon juice (so I wouldn't get scurvy) and a bag of tortilla chips that I used as a spoon to gouge the stuff out.

We were rejected by the majority of society. We were confined to cramped, inhumane quarters. The Dingoes could have earned a better living and been more psychologically rewarded if we could have banded together for the purposes of crime.

CRIME WAVE ROCKS GOTHAM

New York City. A rash of petty crime has struck the Upper West Side. The victims of these crimes seem to have one thing in common — they love opera and ballet. Five men carrying guitar cases, which they said contained weapons, demanded money and jewellery from their well-heeled victims.

'They were as cute as puppy dogs,' said Maid Marion, of Manhattan. 'I liked the one with curly hair and freckles.'

Her escort, the Sheriff of Nottingham, also of Manhattan, said: 'They were ugly customers. They were squabbling and fighting among themselves over the money. One of them, the curly-haired one, kept talking about the needs of the poor. The little one had scars on his belly and said he would "glass" the curly-haired one. "This is beer-money," he said.'

We waited for our fate to be delivered. Kerryn moved out of the Empire and into the apartment of his future new bride. J.L. spent time down in Virginia. Stockley, Brod and I went quietly insane. My sleep–wake cycle worked itself about twenty minutes later each day so that, before long, I was going to sleep at 5am and waking up at three in the afternoon. The maids were supposed to clean at ten. I asked them to stop coming in. My room became choked with newspapers and laundry — but, please, no rotting food.

We often ran out of cash a day or so before payday. With only a couple of dollars left, the dilemma for Brod and me was whether to keep the food or the cigarette-monkey off our backs. But we found a good supply of tobacco. No smoking is allowed on elevators in New York City. Ashtrays were next to the doors of each floor. At the Empire these ashtrays were filled with sand and this had the good effect of putting the cigarette out immediately, leaving a wholesome butt for Brod and me. Late at night we rode the elevator to every floor and harvested these ashtrays. We carried the butts back to Brod's room, snipped off the filters along with an eighth-of-an-inch of the most tar-soaked tobacco, and combined the remaining pure leaf from several butts by rolling it into one fresh cigarette. Of course our craving had to be strong before we degraded ourselves this way. Yet this, in turn, made these recycled smokes highly satisfying.

Stockley said these enterprises were worthy of rats. But he had his own monkey to shake. He, however, suffered in noble, drape-drawn silence.

'I wonder if this hotel has a suicide-watch service?' I asked Brod.

The subtle bees of New York City denied us their society. They did this not because they were cruel, but because they were living things in a highly competitive place. We were without social context. This made others uncomfortable and it made me uncomfortable, too. The more I tried to relax, the less amusing I became. I knew intellectually that this was because of my situation. But emotionally I felt inferior and clumsy. I was a tension-riddled bore. So I contributed to the subtle bee behavior and became a hermit in my room. Again, my only society was the TV.

One week, I was out of money by Saturday and payday wasn't till Tuesday. Luckily we got an invitation from Kerryn to come over for Sunday dinner — lamb.

After we had finished, I eyed the leftovers. I shamelessly asked to take home what was left of the large joint of lamb. Kerryn wrapped it up in tinfoil.

Later that night, feeling angry and ... but why try to rationalise the irrational. What happened was this. We were walking home along West 57th Street. I was cradling the joint. We came upon a restaurant whose front window was tinted, like The Enterprise. We knew it was a swank place, and we knew that the patrons could see us though we couldn't see them. I stopped and unwrapped the bone. Peering into the window, I ripped pieces of flesh off it, like a barbarian. I passed it on. Stockley and Brod, normally more reserved than I, got into the spirit. They savagely gnawed at the bone and wiped their mouths with their sleeves. I rewrapped the joint and we started walking. As we passed the entrance we saw a sign: *Closed Sundays*.

I lay awake at five in the morning listening to the eighteen-wheelers banging down Eighth Avenue. At this hour they made much better time — and much more noise. Amid the clanging of metal reverberating around the empty streets and the towering stone structures, I contemplated my hard luck — and the nature of justice. Does cream always rise to the top? Do I deserve success? Beyond the context of The Dingoes I was not sure of the answer to that question. And even if The Dingoes deserved success, that didn't mean we would find it. In soccer, the beautiful kick doesn't always get the goal. In life, the protagonist (one's self) doesn't always get the girl. Justice, I thought, is not a thing to which everyone has access. With Rudge we had a powerful ally — we were, therefore, treated fairly. But without success that couldn't last. Our power was ebbing. We all knew it. For myself, I had no claim to anything. I made a brave play to leave my country and shoot for huge success. I had felt I was being dragged along by some fantastic destiny machine to my rightful place among the stars. My life would be spent half in the bosom of my beloved Australia, and half touring and creating in the glamorous world of international rock'n'roll. Now, I finally admitted to myself what I had argued in conversations for years: no such machine exists. And, as if it were an umbilical cord, I cut my connection to my destiny machine and became an adult.

11

Atlantic Studios, New York

Hark! The clarion call to purpose. The Dingoes were to try out Atlantic Studios with a view to recording their next album there. Growing up, we had learned our instruments by playing along with records. The records that I studied the most were Aretha Franklin's. Many of the songs of her heyday had been recorded right here, at Atlantic Studios. On our first day there, I snuck out of the control room and into the studio itself. I sat at the piano and played. I closed my eyes and tried to conjure the strings to vibrate like they had to Aretha's gospel touch. I wondered where the bass and drums had been set up and what those inspired players were thinking on those few trips away from their Memphis home. As with any great music, there is a rightness to the tracks laid down on those sessions — an illusory sense that they have always existed and only needed a medium to be expressed. I have read that the musicians on that session felt they were making history. I, too, have often felt as if I were making history. I have often been wrong.

We set up our amps. A technician miked us and plugged us in. The Dingoes looked strange. I wasn't used to seeing them behind their instruments.

'Stockley,' I said. 'Is it possible that we might catch some of Aretha's electrickery as we go down the same wires?'

'Dost thou have a spell?' he said distractedly. 'Fuck me! My amp won't even switch on. Excuse me,' he said to the technician with that uniquely

Australian upward inflection on the last syllable. The technician went on with what he was doing. 'Excuse me.' The little bird in the big forest. Still the technician worked on. Then J.L. started hitting his skins. 'Excuse me.' But now nothing could be heard. I waved to the technician to take care of Stockley. He came over.

'J.L. Just a minute, mate,' said Stockley. But J.L. didn't hear him. Stockley communicated his problem with gestures. The technician ripped the plug out of the wall, took out the fuse and held it up to the light.

'Here's your problem,' he yelled. Then he ran to a supply cabinet and brought out a replacement. He gave it to Stockley. Stockley screwed it in and switched on his amp. Nothing.

'Excuse me.'

But the technician was already busy and couldn't hear him because now Kerryn was fingering off a few licks.

'Excuse me.'

'Chris,' came a voice from the control room. 'We're not getting a signal from you. Could you turn it up, please?'

'It's not working,' he said with heavy sarcasm knowing they couldn't hear him. 'Here, look. I'm turning it all the way up to ten now. I'm strumming the guitar now. It's still not working. Are you getting a signal, yet?'

The technician came over again. He pointed to the plug.

'It's not plugged in.'

'What a fuckin' idiot I am,' said Stockley. He plugged it into the socket and wailed on the guitar. Unfortunately it was still on ten. Every VU meter in the studio pinned to the red. Engineers scrambled for faders. Stockley dusted himself off as if he had just won a fight.

'That's better.'

Then he tore into some screaming guitar passages. Again, the voice from the control room, 'Err, we got a signal now. Can you back it off — if it's on nine now, put it down to three. Okay?'

'This amp doesn't sound any good below eight.'

Being among the first wave of Australian rock'n'rollers, we grew up fighting the battle of volume. Everyone, except most of our audiences, who were in collusion with us wanted us to turn down.

But when we got big enough we told the clubs, 'This is the volume we play at.'

We were touchy about volume. Telling us to turn down was like saying we didn't know how to work our instruments. Stockley had said, 'Would you tell Michelangelo how much paint to put on his brush?'

We were really fairly moderate in our volume. We liked to think that the interplay between musicians counted for something. If you played too loud, the sound coming from your amplifier acted like a curtain: all you heard was yourself. This, of course, had natural ego appeal. For many bands the ethos was simply, *Build a louder amp and we'll use it*. The three-piece band immodestly named Cream was famous for its volume and ostentatious musicianship. They paved the way for decades of heavy metal bands for whom volume was everything, perhaps the only thing. But one night, Cream's guitarist, Eric Clapton, stopped playing in the middle of a song. The other two musicians didn't notice. Clapton left because of it.

At last Stockley backed it down to seven and a half. I said, 'This is only a demo. It doesn't matter if we get any bleed-through. If we do the album here, we'll get a different amp. Let's run down a song.'

We played five songs live. It sounded nothing like Aretha.

'Sounds more like *urethra*,' whispered Stockley during a playback.

Since Aretha's album, the studio had replaced the old machinery. The room sounded the same as it always had. But, unlike the great opera houses and symphony halls, which are famed for their ambient sound, the acoustics of the studio were practically irrelevant. The sound of a studio came from the technology in its control room (and the musicians). And, as much as I worshipped Aretha and her musicians, we shouldn't sound like her. No, we should sound like The Dingoes.

We wanted to finally take control of the music ourselves. In Australia, with the help of a brilliant engineer, John French, we produced our own album. If we could've done that it might have meant our rebirth. So we were actually auditioning the engineer and the studio. They both passed. 'Let's do it!' we said.

Rudge wanted to do it, too. But he had to get the record company's consensus. He took the quick Atlantic tapes — sketches as they were — to A&M. In a couple of days we were called back to Rudge's office for the verdict.

'What can I say? A&M doesn't like it. I do.' We sat in front of his desk. 'But it's A&M who's payin' for it. And they nixed the idea of The Dingoes producing their own record. Hey! You know what I feel. That Australian album, the one that you produced, it's fuckin' marvellous.'

A&M had a bad attitude about us. Having seen us at play in Los Angeles, how could A&M trust us at work? In reality, trying to enjoy ourselves with the likes of Luther and Biff, they had seen us at work. For us, recording was play. We were focused and sober in the studio. If we had come across as the able characters we were, maybe they would've given us this shot. I don't remember seeing the lesson in that for my own behavior.

It would have been nice to tell A&M to fuck off — like we had done to the low-volume-mongers in Australia. Perhaps, if instead of trying to get absurd percentages in our initial contract talks, we had fought for an artistic clause — but we didn't. A&M could dictate the who and the where of our recordings. This meant we were going to be warehoused again at the Empire. This was awful to contemplate. It felt like the end. As soon as we were outside Brod said, 'It is der Führer bunker all over again.'

'Look,' Kerryn said. 'It's raining outside too.'

'Who wants a post-mortem beer, and who's a poofter,' said Stockley.

We crossed busy 57th and dashed into a bar. In the late-afternoon rain, the bar was almost empty. We bought a round of beer. I said, 'Everyone tells you, "Oh, you know, you're going through the roof with success," — and, because it's you, and for no better reason than that, because it's just fuckin' *you*, there's no fuckin' way that you're going to ever get it.'

'It's not you, mate. It's me,' said Stockley. Then he pointed up to the heavens. 'He's got it in for me. This band should have been number one. I'll bet you that they'll still be playing The Dingoes in twenty years' time — I bet young bands will cover our songs and get to number one with 'em. We're leap years ahead of our time and history will show it!' Kerryn and I started humming 'Pomp and Circumstance.'

Brod rose to the occassion. He started to speak and he gradually assumed the personality of Hitler, 'Mozart, Vincent van Gogh, the list is long of those whose true genius was not recognised until after they had died. But Se Dingoes will live longer ... than any of them. Sey are se greatest failure of all time.'

Unimpressed, Stockley said, 'Just as well they serve beer here, or a bloke's likely to get bloody angry. We ought to go straight back to Australia and record there. This is crap, I reckon.'

'Chris,' said Kerryn. 'They'd eat us alive if we went back. We'd be the punchline of every cruel joke from Perth to Mooroopna.'

'We've got so fuckin' much ... too much to lose.'

'That opinion's not universally held,' I said. 'And besides, I don't think I could bear going home in ignominy.'

'Go back in a fuckin' plane then,' said Kerryn.

'What about you, Brod? What do you want to do?' I asked.

'I'll get me a little spread by the banks of the River Murray, mate. Then I'm gonna get about fifty 'ead of cattle. Me and the missus'll raise up some young blokes. They'll play in the wattles and the blue gum. That'll be bonzer, I reckon.'

'Unreal, mate.'

The rain kept coming down. It was late afternoon and the table was littered with empties. Couples were walking up the hill to Carnegie Hall. They were cuddling close under their umbrellas. I yearned for that kind of intimate companionship.

'It must be nice,' I said, pointing to one very attractive couple.

The other Dingoes, holding up their heads with their hands, nodded forlornly.

'Enough! This is pathetic,' said Kerryn. 'Let's up and down these beers.'

'Why don't you all leave the money,' I said. 'I'd like to just sit and think for a while.'

Always a dangerous prospect, each Dingo tallied up his contribution. The risk of coming up short was high. But today I didn't care. They left their money with me. We all shook hands.

'See ya tomorrow, mate.'

'Okay, mate.'

I sat for another beer and, feeling that ugly awareness of not thinking straight, I called for the bill. I was ten cents short and could pay no tip.

'Excuse me. I find I am just a little short — just ten cents, actually. Could you let me off and I'll come back later and make it good.'

'No. You pay. You pay now. We call police if you not pay.'

I sat back down at my table feeling wretched and evilly disposed toward the manager. Finally, after seeing another four or so couples walk by, deeply in love, I went up to the manager. He was behind the bar. I took off my rubber sandals and said:

'You see these. I was going to come back with a big tip. Instead, these cost me two dollars. I'll bet you could get ten cents for them at a yard sale. Take them.'

And with that I slapped them loudly on the bar and sprinted, barefoot like a native, out into the rain. The city is a place for walking. At a full sprint I felt like I was moving at superhuman speed. I was invincible. The manager chased after me but I left him for dead. I ran into Central Park and, by some miracle, passed no police on the way — *Stop or I'll shoot!* they would have said. Too drunk, embarrased and hateful, I would have run on. I would have felt the slug entering my chest from the back. I would have had a premonition of the headline in Melbourne's *Age: Australian Musician Shot Evading Ten-Cent Bill.* I would have become part of the lore of how Australians see New York. Then, over time, the legend would become more streamlined; the musician bit would get dropped:

> 'Did you ever know that guy, John Bois?'
>
> 'No.'
>
> 'Didn't you ever hear of the guy shot in New York for coming up ten cents short on a bill?'
>
> 'Oh, yeah!'

Fame at last.

12

The Hit Factory, New York

With A&M's refusal to let us do our own album, now began another search for a producer. Elliot Mazer wanted to record us again. And we should have gone for it. But we wanted a different sound — and we were still hankering for more control. Eventually we were assigned to A&M's staff producer, John Anthony. I don't think he liked our band, or saw any kind of future for us. But he seemed to like us as individuals, though — that's more than I could say for Biff and Luther.

After a couple of weeks of rehearsing with John, we began recording at a studio called The Hit Factory. This had the very latest in electronic technology. It also had a high-tech room. Its parquet floor was supported on flexible rubber blocks so that the studio was insulated from external vibrations. I walked into the empty control room. Green and red lights testified to the ability of twenty or so machines to shunt electrons this way and that to process ... The Dingoes. What other art form has enjoyed such technological advances? Do painters still use brushes? Do sculptors still chisel wood and chip stone? Do actors on the stage still strut on boards? Well, though they were heavily processed, I suppose we still played guitars and drums.

One night, as J.L. was getting drum sounds, Kerryn and I went downtown to a fashionable club. The audience's involvement, and the club's intimacy, reminded me of the Station Hotel back in Melbourne.

'Shit,' I said. 'Let's get ourselves booked in here.'

'It's alright, isn't it?' said Kerryn.

The crowd was fixated on the stage. An angry young band was performing. They were louder than I could bear. But I heard the words of one song:

I hate you,
You're a fuckin' drag.
I hate you,
You're a fuckin' fag.

The musicians could hardly play. Punk music. The singer wore a T-shirt that said, *I Spit on You.* And this was a recurring theme in their performance as he spat on the fans a foot below him. Seeing the poignancy of the statement, they bumped and pushed each other in a nihilistic dance. The band finished *I Hate You.* The singer chanted, 'Never gonna play no boon music!'

The crowd erupted. I asked a man with a ring in his nose what *boon music* was.

'Nigger shit — *ba*boon. Alright!' And he pumped his fist in the air.

I studied the audience. I could see two basic kinds of people: white, working-class young men with spiky hair, obscene tatoos, jackboots, safety-pin earrings and toxic manners; and critics. Uncomfortable in their schooled deportment, they too were absorbed and were noting things — things I read the next day:

> Mr Fuckeverything growled threats of violence. Screaming, mewling, and puking, he creates an image around himself. The effect is that of shock. In that it confronts society with an image of itself, the spectacle evokes the terrible imagery of William S. Burroughs, who once justified his work by saying: 'Look around. Just look around.' The music is unimportant. The instrumentalists can't play. And that's intentional. The point here is that while society is as it is — evil and unjust — music is trivial, even irrelevant!

Damned if they weren't *still* getting J.L.'s drum sounds as I sat in the control room reading this. I couldn't, for the life of me, figure out where The Dingoes fit in this cultural puzzle. At one end of the spectrum was this meticulous, almost obsessive attention to detail. Since perfection was now technologically possible, it drove engineers to superhuman lengths to achieve it. But this, in a way, was anti-musical. It nudged the focus away from the performance and towards the means of capturing and processing the performance. And so I now picked my toes and read reviews. I should have been playing — building musicality, which, like a good conversation, feeds on itself. There was a whole class of musicians who were very skilled at switching on skill. Precise, efficient and very inventive, these studio musicians lacked only one thing: the idiosyncrasy that comes from idle musical *conversation*. The Dingoes didn't fit in with this homogenous perfection. But we didn't fit at the other end of the spectrum, either. We would never make it in the punk scene: we could play! I wondered how I would have reviewed the punk band's show:

> The deadening tentacles of perverse modern art have finally putrefied that last bastion of natural cultural expression — popular music. We may no longer ask the once relevant question: Is it music? Now we must ask: Is it art? Kiss music goodbye as it disappears into the black hole of modern aesthetic discussion.

I felt old-fashioned, a ransacked soon-to-be-extinct creature, about to be gratefully dead. How could we have known what we were sailing into when we came to this shore? It was all wrong. We were *anti*-invaders. It should work the other way. The newcomers bring a new technology or ethos that bamboozles the natives. But it was *we* who were being bamboozled. Between the anti-musical *volume* of heavy metal, the anti-musical *attitude* of punk, and the anti-musical technical perfection of the modern studio, we didn't stand a chance. Was this, at last, the ghost of Phar Lap rearing up to say, 'You Australians don't know what you're letting yourselves in for. *Australians must get screwed.*' Or was it because of the mundane historical fact of our travelling around in The Dingo bubble that we were naive and isolated from the real world as it was? Then I remembered the other historical forces acting on us: the random falling out of the sky of Skynyrd, our soul-destroying lapses in limbo ...

'John! Wake up! Stop picking your toes, sailor,' said John Anthony, the producer. 'Plug in your bass guitar. Give us some sounds then, matey.'

But, as I picked up and plugged in my bass, I was thinking: *Historical forces! Shit, I could write a book about why we we're* not *going to make it. Reason number one: Bad Attitude.* I played a walking jazz-blues. It was good. Then we got guitar sounds and we were off and recording.

And then we were finished. The album's title, named after one of Kerryn's songs, expressed our state of mind: *Orphans of the Storm*.

13

New Paltz

Ice, expanding, chisels off huge sheets of rock from the towering cliffs of the Shawangunk Mountains. No-one I know has ever seen one fall. But there, up to a mile from the mountain's face, the rocks are stacked up where they came to rest after crashing and tumbling through the trees of the foothills below. They were always falling, I thought, just in a different time-scale from the one I was experiencing.

The farmhouse where I was staying faced the mountain and was about half a mile away from the leading edge of that rock fall. I had tired of the view and was lying down in long grass colonised by early autumn Queen Anne's Lace and Black-eyed Susan. Above, crows flew from tree line to tree line along a crooked aerial highway to a primeval gathering place. They flew, not in a murder, but in haphazard clusters. Overhead now, three crows cawed as they lazily made progress across my field of view. Behind them nothing, for a minute, and then ten crows flapped by complaining in single file. Then two crows flew over. This went on for two hours. Two ducks, heavy and fast, flying with squeaking wings in a straight line, intersected the crow airspace at right angles. The ducks veered off at the last second but nevertheless sent three crows cartwheeling around each other and voicing their discontent. Then the ducks and the crows flew on.

But I, at last, for the moment, was settled. After we finished recording, Rudge humanely put us in limbo in upstate New York while he and A&M figured out what to do with the tapes. We were still attacking America, but we were doing it on the cheap. We were billeted in the eighteenth-century farmhouse of the rock promoter Ron Heinrich. Ron was a strange package. He loved young women, gambling and rock'n'roll. But he had a monumental forehead, swept-back Germanic hair, and wore glasses that enlarged his eyes. This, combined with his modestly buckteeth and frumpy conservative clothing, gave him the appearance of an out-of-work structural engineer. On any given night he might be visited by an intellectual from the local college (the State University of New York at New Paltz), a New York City gambler looking to settle a debt, or a chess player — one night the Russian Grand Master, Anatoly Karpov, played Ron while we watched.

He had a lifelong interest in pop music. This fascination was like that of a horse fancier. He believed he could pick a winner. True to his gambling nature, it would have been a thrill to rise to wealth and power on the back of a horse — not just any horse, but a horse predicted by his acumen and native intelligence to win big. Like any compulsive gambler he had a ceaseless childish fascination with the fulfilment of trivial predictions. Holding up AC/DC's album he said, 'What did I tell you? The Kid knows what he's talking about. It went platinum. See.'

'Did you say it would, Ron?' I teased.

'Yeah! I said it would go platinum. You remember, Brod, don't you?'

This put him in a great mood even though he didn't gain personally from it. If, on the other hand, he had money riding on the success of some horse or team, he was manic: gleeful and hyper-generous if he won, morose and angry if he lost. I was amazed at the different agents of causation he invoked. If he won, it was because of his skill and intuition. If he lost, someone (a player or a friend who had given him a tip) had screwed up. Or fate was trying to get him.

If Ron had an insider tip, all the better. The Dingoes were his horse. The insider tip was the knowledge that Rudge was our manager. Everything was right for our ascendance. We were cute foreigners (like the Beatles). We sounded unique and, to his ears anyway, modern. We had the right connections. And, above all, we had Brod. In Brod's voice, zany stage persona and James Dean look, Ron saw the answer to his star-

fancier prayers. The rest didn't matter. The horse that would drag all of us to the big time was Broderick.

I came to learn that Ron's friendship did not depend on our ability to succeed. At that time, however, ours was a robustly mutualistic relationship. He worked like a dog for us and was the soul of generosity; we would bring him renown. He booked us into local Hudson Valley spots. He put us up in his own house. And he introduced us into the social milieu of New Paltz, New York. To an outside observer perhaps this would seem no great prize. New Paltz's social stature was hardly the commodity that acceptance into Manhattan society would have been. But it was a boon to us.

New Paltz was almost a casualty of its closeness to New York City. But, seventy-five miles to the north, it was just out of commuting distance — it was its own focus. Settling on the fertile floodplain of the Wallkill River against the advice of the indigenous peoples, the French Huguenots, way back in the 1600s, said this was a good place to build a town. The next year, after being flooded out, they moved to the high ground on the other side of the river. This, they said, was a better place. The first time I entered this town I came off 87 North and drove two miles west into New Paltz. I came to the high ground first. The narrow road is flanked closely on both sides by stores as it slopes directly to the river. It is the oldest main street in the United States. Across the bridge you accelerate to sixty and speed across the floodplain. All traces of the first settlement have been washed away by the annual flooding. Now, only a couple of historic markers remain to say something used to be here. Past farm stands, cornfields and a road that veers off to an exclusive resort on Mohonk Mountain, it takes only two minutes to reach the foothills of the Shawangunks. Ron's farmhouse was on the last of these foothills, just five miles from town.

The town had a long history and was something of a tourist attraction because of it. But the college had dominated its recent history. New Paltz had the reputation of being a party town and was famous for its lax academic standards. Finding it hard to ignore a dollar, the locals cashed in on student drinking and eating habits. Every third building on Main

Street was a bar or restaurant. And Ron and his friends owned them. Rudy Neuss owned The Thesis in partnership with Ron, and The Homestead across the street with Frank Giamascola. Rudy also owned Speakers, a rock'n'roll club a mile out of town where we were regulars. Rudy was at Cornell and Frank wanted to study medicine. Ron lured them both away from those enterprises, not so much as business partners, but as friends advising each other on how to make a killing. But all the advice emanated from Ron. Their friendships dissolved and coalesced with their fortunes, particularly Ron's gambling status.

We played at Joe's Place, at the Last Chance across the Hudson in Poughkeepsie, and at the Hudson Valley Wine Festival. We jammed on Monday nights at the Northern Lights restaurant with local party-band musicians terminally infected with blues and R&B.

Within two weeks of our moving there, we could each walk down Main Street and wave to ten acquaintances. This surely was what we had been searching for: a place where we could establish robust connections with our audience — a place like the Station Hotel. The analogue of The Station was Rudy's place, Speakers, out on Route 32. For two months, we played there every second Saturday night. Ron, Rudy and Frank stood at the back of the room and nodded appreciatively as crowds built up week from week. Beer sales skyrocketed (I know you're thinking, *The Dingoes were responsible for that.* But you are wrong: The Dingoes drank for free, just like at the Station).

What a thrill it was to arrive at the job and see a long line of, dare I say it, fans! We were not the warm-up act; they were here for us. And we gave them what they came for: a good, beer-drinking, social event. The Poughkeepsie radio station, at Ron's urging, had been saturating the Hudson Valley with our US record. People actually cheered when they heard the opening chords of several songs. They clapped after a Stockley solo. They whistled after Brod's harp solo at the end of *Sydney Ladies*. The audience parted like the Red Sea for Moses when we got off stage and headed for the bar. Attractive girls beckoned me to talk to them. One of them said she was coming back next time we played, without her friends, without underwear beneath her dress!

Brod became brilliant again. He was Johnny Weismuller, James Dean, Slim Dusty, Ned Seagoon — he was himself. Singing for real people, his voice carried the intensity and emotion it lacked in the studio. J.L. and I fell back into a relaxed groove as intense as it was unforced. Kerryn and Stockley, on either side of us, seemed to be trading off licks. We were enjoying ourselves.

We had been enjoying ourselves for two months. As the last griping crows flew by I stood up, picked the burrs off my clothes and walked back to the house. As I approached I could hear the forlorn whistle of a teakettle. It had been abandoned in the heat of a monstrous fight between Ron and his wife, Susan. Not wanting to intrude, I sat on the doorstep and listened.

'Ron! I love them. They're all nice boys. That's not the problem. There's too many of them. That's all.'

'Come on, Susie. It's not going to be like this forever. These guys are going to make it. But they can't make it unless they have a place to stay.'

'Why is that your problem,' she shrieked. 'Let them make it. Good luck to them in making it. I wish them well, honestly, Ron. But the New York guy, he's the one who should worry, not us.'

'Susie. They're gonna release their record. If that record does well, they'll go to the top. And that will help *us*, too.'

'How do you know they'll go to the top? And if they do, how do you know they'll take you with them? You don't have a contract or anything. The New York guy, he's the one with the contract!'

'Susie, I can't convince you of the things I know. You just have to trust me that I can do the work to make it happen for them.'

'I trust you, but *I'm* the one doing all the work. It's killing me, Ron.'

'Oh, Susie. No-one could cope with this as well as you have. I owe you everything. You know that. I promise you'll be glad we did this.'

'Ron, I love these guys just as much as you do. But I never see you alone anymore, except to have a fight — like this. I'm afraid of what it's doing to us.'

'C'mon, Susie! Nothing can touch that. Don't even think like that.'

Susan was always an unwitting participant in Ron's schemes. She had married him five years ago when she was eighteen and he was twenty-seven. She idolised him. For a long time Ron had maintained a very high standard of living from his winnings. He took her on trips, leased luxury cars and generally pampered her. So, despite a recent long losing streak, she suffered the vicissitudes of life with Ron with adamantine resolve.

Susan was Jewish and from Long Island (she pronounced the 'g' hard — like a Liverpudlian). She was a Jewish mother to all of us as individuals. But lately, especially when she was cooking for us, her manner was gathering perfunctoriness. She was beginning to resent what The Dingoes were doing to her life. Today the other Dingoes had gone to town and, in fighting, Susan and Ron had forgotten that I was still around. So I waited until they were finished, walked a distance away from the house, and strode in breathing heavily.

'Hello! Anybody home?' I cried for a warning.

Like two pill bugs exposed by lifting a rock, they greeted me and, after taking the kettle off the boil, quickly went their separate ways. I switched on the TV and sat down in the living room. Susan came in and vigorously dusted the furniture. She apologised for blocking the screen. I was embarrassed by that — it was I who should have apologised. I would have liked to have said, 'Susan, your generosity is giving us this one last chance. Rudge has lost his cash cow. He can't afford to put us up. If we make it, we will see you right. You can believe that. You and Ron. And Rudy. And Rudge. And my mother. And Mad Dog and all the other roadies who spent their youth helping us succeed. If you can just hang on for one more episode of your life, you may be glad. Probably not. But possibly. You never know. But believe me, I know having five men in your house is putting incredible stress on you. Really, Ron's expectations are outrageous.'

'So why don't you pack up and go back home?' she may have said in reply. 'Every time you leave the house, Ron and I have these soul-destroying arguments. You Dingoes are destroying my marriage. I'm sure you would pay back our kindness if you could. But you're right! Maybe you're not going to get the chance. You should just leave.'

'I can't! I can't just leave. I'm too proud. I can't go back to Australia without first making it here. At least while there's a chance.'

'That's stupid. You're a sweet man. There are sweethearts for you back home. There is family back home. At home you're not a stranger. Just go home. Give it up! Give me a break, here. What's the big deal? Just go home.'

'Susie, we came over here with such a big fanfare. People believed in us. My friends believed in us. For them we are the *Great Australian Hope*. I can't just *go home*. I can't!'

'What's that, nearly three years ago, now? Realistically, John, how many people spend how many minutes of their day thinking about you? You're a little more than proud. You're conceited. What you had, whatever it was, is gone! Nobody's going to care one way or the other if you make it or not. If they love you, they love you for you. And anyway, the love of someone who loves you just because you're famous is not worth having.'

'Geez. I wish you were right about that, Susie. But sweethearts love their sweethearts for lots of reasons. You can't deny that women find accomplishment in men attractive.'

'But you *are* accomplished, John. Nobody denies you that.'

'No, I'm not! How do you measure accomplishment in music? For a pilot, he lands the plane — that's it. He's accomplished. A doctor finds the tumour, takes it out — everyone's happy. He's accomplished. But I am accomplished only if millions of peons say I am. It almost has nothing to do with my art.'

'Well, go and be accomplished in Australia, then. I gotta live. I can't dream of the day when millions of peons are suddenly going to discover me — or you! Jesus, mate! Do something else then. But go home!' she may have shrieked.

Outside a car door slammed. The Dingoes were back. They trudged through the house. I was staring blankly at the TV where a soap opera was playing.

Stockley said, 'Hamlet, is it, mate? I told you. Too much Shakespeare will fuck you right up.'

I caught Susan observing the desecration of her newly polished hardwood floors. She disappeared. A minute later Ron came downstairs. He said, 'Susie wants you to take off your shoes when you come inside.' But the way he said it, he also expressed this: *You know how women are. But I suppose we should do as they say.*

Susan prepared dinner in the kitchen. I'm not sure if I imagined it or not, but it seemed that the saucepans hit the counter and the stove with a louder clang than usual. And when she served the dinner, Susan's voice betrayed barely suppressed anger. 'Who wants gravy?' she asked in a tone that, to me anyway, said, *Here, accept some more non-returnable favours.*

But witnessing the afternoon fight, I was in better possession of the facts than the other Dingoes. They didn't seem to notice. Stockley was jovial. For his part he had purchased a bottle of wine and was distributing it with magnanimity. Susan may have felt even more irritated in the face of this simple gesture of kindness — she may have felt guilty at her own sour feelings. She sat silently as Ron and five guests-who-wouldn't-leave laughed and caroused in the hearth of the domesticity that Susan had built.

In the shadow of the mountains, it became dark early at the farmhouse. But this was all the better for watching the basketball season on Ron's monster TV. He had money riding on every game. After the Boston–Los Angeles game, in which he won a little something, he put in a call to a bookie. He dumped all of his winnings on the outcome of the Chicago–New York game. He took Chicago to beat the ten-point spread. If they did it, Ron would be temporarily rich.

The afternoon had been chilly. But now it was so cold that a wet snowfall was sticking to the ground. Having no interest in basketball (whose rules seemed as arcane as they were arbitrarily enforced — a game I had steadfastly refused to play unless they would bring the net down to a reasonable height, a height at which I could at least slam dunk!), and since snow was still a novelty, I went outside for a walk. The weather was clearing. Above the clouds, and sometimes breaking through, a full moon doused the already chilled farmlands with its cold light. I took a silvery path through a small wooded area. I found an old wood pile and felt it to see if the frost had stolen the heat from its smokeless decay. But again, the wood was burning up in a different timescale than the one I was experiencing. After an hour or so I headed back. Just outside the house I heard something snort. Twenty yards from me, water vapour blowing from its nostrils, a doe stood staring right at me.

'YES! *Un-fucking-believable*!' I heard Ron screaming from the house.

The doe turned and ran flashing its white tail in the moonlight. Two relatives became suddenly visible because of their movement. The trio crashed into the woods.

'We're *rich*, Susie!'

I walked into the house.

'What did I miss?'

'Chicago *crushed* New York! *Crushed 'em*! Baby! I'm tellin' ya! The Kid is on a roll. We're *rollin'* here! It's time to hit the big time. Atlantic City, babeee! Tomorrow I'm taking us all to ... Atlantic City!'

The next afternoon we were headed south on the Palisades Parkway in a driving rainstorm. In Ron's leased Lincoln Town Car it scarcely seemed possible that we could come to any harm. Ron, Brod and Rudy were in the front seat. Susan, Stockley, Kerryn, and myself were in the back (J.L. was in Virginia). Ron told us of his days teaching history in Bedford Stuyvesant High School. And he talked for two hours as the rain beat down on the Lincoln, its spongy suspension squelching the effect of the weather and the world. The Manhattan skyline, barely visible in the rain, passed by on the left as Ron told us how Washington society drove out to see the first battle, the Battle of Bull Run; how the North buried their dead in Robert E. Lee's frontyard, now Arlington Cemetery; how brother fought brother; how the war framed everything that came after it.

Past Newark Airport, where the jets take off so close to the highway you can smell the kerosene; past the New Jersey Meadowlands with its wetland smell of sulphur bacteria; past the swathe of petroleum processing plants that wrap Route 95, their exhaust flames burning bright like beacons in the storm; past acres of storage tanks leaking their gasoline into the air; sweeping southward as if caught in a torrent of cars — a red ribbon of lights ahead, and a stream of white lights over to the left — toward the South Jersey Coast; finally, with the weather more foul by the minute, we drove into Atlantic City.

14

Atlantic City

A nor'easter was pounding the New Jersey coastline. Traffic lights were bouncing around like piñatas. We got out of the car. From the streets of Atlantic City you could hear the steady, dull roar of breakers smashing into the sandy beaches just beyond the hotels and the boardwalk. Ron opened an umbrella for Susan. He had to hold it horizontally to avoid getting wet. But then, the wind shifted, swinging them around and inverting its flimsy superstructure. With that, Ron, Susan, Rudy and The Dingoes sprinted into the chilling wind and rain toward the lobby of our hotel. Laughing and cursing, our thighs saturated, we blundered inside. The desk clerk looked at us askance — we were dripping on his marble floor. Ron identified himself. He was going to pay for everything on this trip. Before going upstairs he gave us each a hundred dollars' gambling money. We agreed to meet back in the lobby in twenty minutes. As we walked to the elevator I saw that the desk clerk had already summoned a worker to mop off the water from the lobby floor.

We went to our rooms. I was sharing with Stockley.

'Look, mate. Class, this is,' he said, pointing to the refrigerator stocked with beer.

'They knew you were coming, mate,' I said as I peeled off my wet jeans.

Up on the fourth floor I had a panoramic view of the Atlantic. The sea was raging. Yet, behind the thick glass of the hotel window, its sound was completely muted. I sat down with a beer and stared out into the stormy weather. I was still alive with Ron's tale of teaching and history. But I couldn't understand how someone with such an obvious love for the temporal expanse of history could abandon it for the strictly here-and-now activity of gambling. At least I was following my first love, music. I would never abandon that for anything less. But this was disingenuous. Surely the machinery of The Dingoes had long since ceased to be a creative music-maker. Now it was just cranking along playing the same old songs. And what were we doing other than waiting for some event beyond our control to occur — for millions of peons to say we were accomplished? How was this different from gambling? Ron and I were brothers in occupation. Both of us were surrendering our fate to forces beyond our control.

Stockley had a quick shower. We headed for the lobby where everyone was waiting; we walked into the casino.

I forget which species of goose it is that has this very effective genetic rule: *Roll the nearest, biggest round thing into my nest*. Usually this would be its egg. And this rule has served it well during its evolution. But if a devious scientist places a big round rock next to its nest, the foolish goose rolls that into its nest and expels its egg in the process. The bird then proceeds to incubate the rock! As far as the bird is concerned, the bigger the round thing, the better. The stimulus of the big round rock is called a supernormal stimulus. Advertisers and manufacturers know this term well. We respond to supernormal stimuli, too; for example, a ton of sugar in a soft drink can, pretty women selling us just about anything, flashing lights at a carnival, etc. In a sense, inasmuch as we spend our money on these stimuli, we are incubating these manufacturers instead of our own genetic stock. Walking into the casino, we are aware of the masterfully understated, but nevertheless seductive, supernormal stimuli: the discreet clatter of the roulette wheel, its little ball subservient to the impartial laws of physics; the cushioned thud of dice on felt at the craps table; the hoarse purr of the wheel — round and round it goes, where it stops nobody knows because it is obeying the laws of physics, laws that can favour you just as easily as the Prince of Monte Carlo; the brisk shuffling of cards at the Twenty-One table; and over there, in the commoners section, the not-so-understated supernormal stimulus of the brash poker machines. Still, the uncouth pokies are muted by the plushness of the decor. Felt, leather, thick-pile carpet, all redolent with the sort of opulence that could be yours if you should happen to be favoured by the laws of physics tonight. Your subconscious probably tells you that you could also win one of the many sexy waitresses. After all, as far as your subconscious is concerned, their upthrust breasts signal their readiness to mate. You call a waitress over and order a drink. As she writes down your order you enjoy the stimulus regardless of its counterfeit nature. You don't stop to think that her breasts are arranged that way to part you from your money. Do you? You silly goose.

I looked at the clientele. They had one thing in common: they all seemed to be having a thoroughly loathsome time! All of these losers were haunted by the same dread: if and when they quit, it would be just before a huge winning streak. Men softly pounded their fists on the green felt as they saw their fortune wasting away. Hopeful faces arriving fresh at the tables became miffed at early big losses. Obsession gave way to frustration, and finally to exasperation. Dishevelled men and women dragged themselves out of the casino still not convinced of the futility of their quest — Lady Luck, they believed, would be with them tomorrow! For, while the apparent neutrality of the machines was what led them to risk their money, the clientele would not have characterised their fate as being operated on by random forces. Each was being watched over by the Fates. Lucky charms were rubbed, rabbit's feet were stroked, dice were blown on, lucky words were spoken, a lover's hand was grasped and kissed as the roulette wheel spun, chips were handled like worry beads, the sign of the cross was made, eyes were closed in prayer beseeching The Creator to turn from His universal works for a teensy second to intercede with the most minor of miracles.

Ron was convinced he would have a big day for himself. He was animated with anticipation. 'Craps,' he said. 'The kid's got a system.' And he walked directly to the craps table.

Stockley and Brod went their own way; I wanted to see Ron in action. Rudy, Susan, Kerryn and I followed him. He placed a bet on a number. He won!

'Babee! I'm tellin' ya. The Kid is on another roll. Susie, roll this one for good luck. We're gonna ride on the same number.' Susan rolled the die. They won again. Then he won, lost, won, lost, lost, won, lost, lost. I gave a signal to Kerryn and we broke away from the table to do our own betting.

'I bet I can lose my money quicker than you can,' I said to Kerryn.

I went over to the big Wheel of Fortune.

I put thirty dollars on red. The wheel spun. It came up black. I put another thirty on black. It came up red. I stayed with another thirty on black. It came up red.

'That was easy,' I said. 'What's that? Ninety bucks down in under two minutes.'

'I'm rouletting it,' said Kerryn.

'Russian or French?'

'Thousand Islands.'

We watched the mundane motion of the little steel ball. Kerryn put ten dollars on the number thirty — his age. The wheel spun. The ball settled on number seven. Despite this instant loss, he liked the pay-off for this long-shot strategy. If he hit the number he would reap three hundred dollars from his ten-dollar bet. He rode on thirty. But the next spin came up number twenty-five, then fourteen, then fifteen, fifty-two, and so on until he too had just ten dollars left.

'You're right,' he said. 'There's nothing to it. Do you want to hit the pokies with our last ten dollars?'

'Oui, parce que les temps de merde rouler!'

At the poker machines you couldn't lose your money quite as fast. You had to work at it. But, despite a couple of time-wasting wins, we surrendered all our money to the casino. I wondered how Ron was doing and we walked over to the craps table. His mood had developed. Like all the other patrons he was intensely focused on the dice — on what they were doing to his destiny. I greeted him. He grunted. I asked him how it was going.

'We're still alive.'

But, whereas Kerryn and I were operating on ten- and thirty-dollar bets, Ron was dealing in hundreds. I wondered if he was obeying the first rule of gambling: *Set a limit and don't go beyond it.* Susan was supporting him. Rudy was giving him advice.

'Don't take such long shots,' he said.

'I've got a system. Leave me alone. Leave me the fuck alone, okay? Heh, heh.' He was trying to contain it, but he was angry in a way I had never seen before.

But I was bored with all this losing. I decided to escape that stifling atmosphere and see what the weather was doing outside.

As night fell, so did the temperature. The rain had turned to snow. I went upstairs, got my pea coat and gloves, and went out behind the casino. I was alone on the boardwalk. Waves were crashing right below my feet on the cement bulwarks that separated Atlantic City from Atlantic Ocean. They were gouging tons of fine sand and washing it out to sea. They sent plumes of water up on both sides of the boardwalk — on both sides of me. I felt it quiver with each boomer. But, I thought, this structure had survived many nor'easters, hadn't it? I walked out to the sand dunes — dunes that had persisted despite the casino construction. I went down the steps and climbed a dune. The snow mixed with the sand to form a creamy conglomerate. And all the while the wind was a blizzard of snow and sand. I couldn't look seaward because of its gritty load. But I was drawn down to the water's erratic edge.

My mother and I moved to New Zealand when I was eleven. We lived on top of some mighty cliffs at a place called Fort Rose. Here, on the south coast of the South Island, the Mataura River, after carrying its water from the Southern Alps through a wide and fertile estruary, debouches powerfully into the Foveaux Strait. Its mouth is a narrow, thirty-foot-wide channel bounded by sand dunes on one side and the same mighty cliffs on the other. I often stood at the river mouth and, even at that young age, sensed the awesome flux of nature: the constant movement of water from sea to sky to mountains and back to the sea. But not just of water; the flux of life, too. Dead, bloated cows floated as fast as speedboats through the channel, their legs stiff in the air, to become part of the grand natural solvency, their existence dissolving into the Mother Ocean for recombining or dissolution.

I imagined myself discorporating and becoming so many parts per billion of the grand whole. This was not an unattractive thought. Then (and I didn't tell my mother this) I made my way along the base of the cliffs. The foot of the cliffs consisted of alternating sandy beaches and rocky outcrops. I played chicken with the breaking swell of the Southern Ocean. I waited on an outcrop for a small break in the waves. Then I sprinted the thirty yards to the next outcrop, arriving just before the massive wave crashed ashore. If I were late I would have certainly become part of nature's solvency. But I accurately judged my ability to beat the wave. I was not gambling. I was not leaving my fate to another force. I was *in control* ...

Down to the sea I walked, smarting at the stinging wind. Back towards the casino I could hear the pummelling of the bulwarks by the pulverising waves. But here they spent their energy running up the dunes. I put my hands up to my face — like horse blinkers — and shielded my eyes from the sand-blasting. I looked laterally along the line of dunes. Every twenty yards a light post illuminated the white foam and white snow. The rest was violent, murky blackness and furious white noise. But by looking at two lights I could judge the timing of the waves. I could estimate how much time I had to dash from one light to another. I believed I could do it. But I had to get down to the first light. Each light post was anchored in rocks and concrete. The sand around them had been dredged out by the storm. But if I climbed up between waves I would be safe. I ran. I made it. And then the wave came in and below me was awash with tempestuous energy. A gull joined me (hoping I would throw it some fish entrails?) and flew motionless under the light. I got ready to race a wave to the next light. I climbed to the lowest safe point, and, when the spent wave slipped back into the sea, I sprinted. My boots sank deep into the loose sand, slowing me down. I ran closer to the sea to get a firmer footing. Midway, in complete blackness, I could hear the slipping wave sorting pebbles down the tidal zone. It sounded like a choir of randomly shaking maracas. Then, *whoomph*, it stopped, just as I made it to the rocks and the light. This time the wave came with such force that it crashed onto the concrete and sent a fine salty spray into my face. I was invigorated. I looked seaward and saw, not regular sets of waves, but a jostling crowd of wind-cropped peaks. And now one huge rogue wave mounted towards me at eye level. In studying the waves, I had given myself a big margin of error. But I had made an even bigger miscalculation — the tide was coming in. My margin was being eroded by the second. To play this game any longer would be risking my life! Gambling! Beyond control! I abandoned the light and ran up the beach towards the dune. The rogue wave landed. I sprinted in the loose sand. It hit me waste high and knocked me down. Pushing me forward, then pulling me back towards the solvency, it finally released me down the tidal zone amid the maracas. Then, *whoomph*, another wave broke right on top of me and swept me back up the beach.

'Let me go!' I seethed through gritted teeth as I spun in a ball. The water slowed down and my legs touched bottom. The water was waist-high. I snorted saltwater as I tried to move further uphill. But my legs were swept from under me by the retreating wave as it accelerated downhill. It pulled me back to the grand whole. Yet again I was released in the sorting pebbles. *Whoomph.* Back up I went, carried willy-nilly in the powerful surge. *They'll think it was suicide,* I thought. My legs touched bottom. I pumped them desperately. My exertion was futile and it left me struggling for air; this was difficult thanks to the cold and the restriction of my pea coat. But this time another wave surmounted the previous wave. Dragging on my clothes, it pulled me back. *What a silly way to die,* I thought. I was on all fours in the maracas waiting for the next wave to have its way with me. There was nothing I could do! There never was anything I could do. And, as the next wave swept me back up the tidal zone, it occurred to me that this was a fitting way to die for a man who never controlled his destiny. My head came out of the water. I saw the dune. My feet touched bottom ... back I went down to the pebbles again.

This time the water left me on my back. I cried from fear and sorrow that my life was probably ending.

Whoomph. Winded, I still flailed for air in the rushing whitewater. It slowed down but this time I couldn't even touch bottom before I was whisked back in the mighty tow. Dumped again in the hissing pebbles, breathing deeply now, I turned around and got up on all fours and again braced myself to receive the next wave. The maraccas shook. I wondered how many times I could do this. I waited. I waited. *Whoomph.* Back up I went. Back down I came. This time, instead of waiting for the wave, I stood up and dived into the wave. In that way I instantly found myself treading water thirty feet out into the Atlantic Ocean, in the solvency. I had to shed my pea coat and gloves — had to, but *fuck* it was cold. Riding up ten crests and down ten troughs I surveyed the onrushing waves. I spied the biggest, most evil, rogue wave. As it loomed I swam as fast as I could toward the shore. I struck forward even as it sucked me backwards into its immense power. It picked me up and threw me forward. I surfed in on it. Swimming in the foam I reached a higher point on the tidal zone than before, and when my legs touched bottom, I was just able to resist the backward pull. The wave fell back to sort pebbles, leaving me half-drowned but high up the tidal zone. Like an insignificant prey item released from the maw of a distracted predator, I clambered for the high ground of the dune. Coughing and sputtering, I looked back to the light post to see a series of waves dash over the very place I had been standing. I climbed all the way back up to the main street and staggered, cold, desperately tired, alive, back to the hotel.

'Hello, again,' I said to the desk clerk as I dripped salty water onto the marble floor.

'It's still raining, is it, sir?'

I woke up feeling like a survivor. Attitude was different. It felt like the rest of my life was a gift. At about ten o'clock, I went downstairs. I poked my head into the casino and was surprised to see it in full swing. I looked over to the craps table and there were Ron and Susan. No, it wasn't them. It was just a couple who resembled them. I looked at the waitresses. They appeared to be the same girls but actually they were a different shift. All the table operators looked the same but were different people. This interchangeability was surreal but it gave a sense of the true nature of the casino: it was a machine with interchangeable parts that serviced a necessarily interchangeable clientele. The only constant human element were owners bent on the incubation of their eggs with the money that should have been used to incubate those of the clientele. They did this with the promise of money for nothing — a promise they never considered keeping.

Then I saw Ron at the American Express money machine.

'Putting it in, or taking it out?' I asked. As if I didn't know!

Back in the Lincoln on our way back to New Paltz, Ron was fuming.

'Never, never tell me how to gamble again, Rudy. You fucked up my system. If you hadn't told me what to do, I would have gone ahead with my own plan and I would've won. If you ever do that again ...'

'Ron,' said Susan, 'Rudy was just trying to help. You were losing a ton at that point.'

'I know what I'm doing!' he screamed. 'Don't tell me what I know. I would have won. I win all the time, don't I. How did we come to be at Atlantic City in the first place!'

Rudy defended himself, 'You're always telling us, Ron, that the reason you win on games is because you're the bookie. At Atlantic City you're not the bookie. You *pay* the bookie there. That's why you lost. Not because you listened to me.'

'*Fuck you!* I would've won. I can't listen to this bullshit anymore. I know what I know. You two idiots know nothing. My problem is that I listen to fuckin' idiots. Shut the fuck up, both of you. Just shut the fuck up!'

And he hit the steering wheel with both hands. Nobody spoke for two uncomfortable hours. I was appalled at this public display of anger from a man who was so naturally an utter gentleman. I grieved at the gambling sickness of this otherwise gifted man. I cursed the gossamer web of false expectation that had held him at the table. And I looked forward to a new phase in my life, one that was closer, I believed, thanks to my experience of near-death at Atlantic City.

15

The End of the Road

In Atlantic City, Nature, tossing insignificant me here and there, amplified the reality of my life. For the last seven years it had been completely beyond my control. What could I do to take it back? However slowly, The Dingoes' machinery was still grinding away. Rudge was still planning our victory. Any day now we could get a call that might say, 'A&M wants to release the record by such-and-such a date. Get ready. You're going out on another tour. This time you'll be touring with the so-and-so band! Sex, fame, respect, money and happiness will be yours by X month! You can count on it.'

And so, like the casino players at Atlantic City, I waited. But the inertia of my counterfeit existence, kept on track by the forever just-out-of-reach massive pay-off, stymied other, more robust possibilities, more natural possibilities such as family life, home life — *a life*. In waiting on, counting on, sex, fame, respect, money and happiness, I had gambled with my youth. Even though that promise seemed tangible at times, pursuing it was a high-risk strategy. Just as the gamblers waited for their winning streak while their life savings were whittled away, I waited for sex, fame, respect, money and happiness while time inexorably eroded my youth. But at twenty-eight, these seductive goals not only seemed less likely to be achieved, they were also less desired. One day, back in New Paltz, I was walking alongside the rapids of the Wallkill River with Kerryn. I noticed a tiny crow's foot leading from the corner of his eye. *Jesus Christ,*

I thought. *We're getting old. It's really happening.* I was embarrassed to be approaching thirty. I was suddenly struck by the thought that I would rather be an old teacher, an old sailor, banker, architect, business executive — anything — than an old rock'n'roller gumming out the words, 'I wanna make love to you, babee.' As much as I still treasured my musicality, I came to think that the rock'n'roll stage should no longer be my forum. Perhaps I had always been an impostor.

Or was it rock'n'roll that was the impostor? An impostor of an art form.

'Kerryn, I think that's a crow's foot I see, extending from yon eyeball.'

'Yeah? And that's the beginning of a big bag hanging from *yon* eyeball,' he said, pointing to my eye.

'Christ. It's time for us to flame out of this rock'n'roll game, mate. We've got to go honorably, though. What d'ya say? Electrified by guitar? Choke on our own vomit? Cocaine OD?'

'My trouble is, I don't hope I die before I get old,' said Kerryn.

'Ah! You're not a true rock'n'roller then, are you, mate. You're a pretender, an impostor, just like me! It's not like that in country music, is it? You can be George Jones, Willy Nelson — he's just starting out at fifty! I reckon that's because rock'n'roll is so targeted, so specific to adolescence, that it sort of seems juvenile. It loses its charm because we grow out of its target audience.'

'But we shouldn't be knocking rock. Isn't it our fault that we become blind, deaf to its charm? I mean, when a person becomes so old he can't see, that doesn't mean the *Mona Lisa* becomes a lesser painting.'

'You've got me there, mate.' I thought about this for a minute. 'No. The best sorts of art forms should involve all generations and not die once you reach a certain age. Your old man's appreciation of the *Mona Lisa* may not have changed at all. Her smile still remains in his memory and is just as beautiful there as it was in real life. The trouble with rock'n'roll, both the new crop and the old crop remembered and reprised over and over again, is that it becomes less beautiful, less relevant and whatever else, the older you get. Let's blame it — and go easy on ourselves.'

'It's funny. We are a rock'n'roll band. But none of us would spend too much energy defending rock'n'roll. But we would go to war to protect the blues, and country music, the forms it came from.'

I nodded in agreement and we hopped off the bank and onto a rock two feet into the river. It had been worn smooth by thousands of years of rapid water. Yet small seashell fossils embedded in it told me the rock itself was formed from sediment at the bottom of a long-gone sea. We hunkered down on its slope about six inches above the gurgling eddies of the local water.

'Look at Muddy Waters, Ray Charles, Doc Watson, Duke Ellington.'

'Satchmo!' said Kerryn in a Satchmo voice.

'What is it about Muddy Waters that he can be singing I'm a M-A-N into his fuckin' seventies. But the same thing from a rock'n'roll man like Mick seems so bizarre. It's all fuckin' wrong. It's rock'n'roll that's the impostor, not us!'

I became enraptured by the dynamic of the current. We sat for about five minutes and then Kerryn got up to go.

'You go, Kerryn. I'm going to hang for a while.'

He jumped back onto the bank and headed for Ron's farmhouse. I stared at the water watching a crimson leaf as it rotated slowly in a near-the-bank backwater. Here, where the water was slow, a little shelf of ice had formed. The leaf, its upper surface dry except for a few beads of water, floated toward a fast-moving sluice between two rocks and immediately disappeared in the firmament of the rapids. I spat into the fast water. My foam blended instantly with the foam of the rapids. I fell into serial trances, states where only the rapid water existed — no interpretation, no sensation, no emotion; just the white noise, just the firmament — rushing to the great flux of the Hudson and onto the ocean.

A light snow-shower began to fall. I sat on the rock without knowing that meanwhile, back at the ranch, Stockley was answering a call from Peter Rudge.

When I returned, The Dingoes, Ron and Susie were sitting around discussing it.

'He said he wants to talk to us, didn't he. You can draw your own conclusions,' said Stockley. 'He wants us to all drive down to Sir tomorrow.'

Acting! In front of Brod's Land Rover. Cast: Brod, as an Aryan the cat dragged in; Stockley, as a refugee; me, as a French resistance fighter; J.L., maybe a gypsy. This is a publicity shot whose purpose has been long forgotten, circa 1974.
Photographer: Philip Morris

top:

Top row: Mal Logan (who contributed brilliantly to The Dingoes' first album); Broderick; Stockley, just out of hospital, showing his bandages after receiving a random bullet from an Allen crime-family crime spree. Bottom row: me, J.L., Kerryn.

Photographer: Philip Morris

bottom:

Publicity shot, USA, circa 1976. My muscles inflated by gentle pressure of underlying hands. Can't figure out who is tickling Broderick!

Photographer unknown

top:
We visited and jammed with Greg Quill's band, Hot Knives, at Morrissey Tavern in Davenport, Toronto, 1976. Left to right: Sam See, Dennis Pinhorn, Tony Bolton, Kerryn, Greg Quill.
Photographer Kevin MacLean

bottom:
Same Toronto session. Left to right: me, J.L., Brod, Kerryn, Chris.
Photographer: Kevin MacLean

top:
John Lee in Toronto, 1977.
Photographer: Kevin MacLean

bottom:
Broderick Smith in Toronto, 1977. David Stone on guitar.
Photographer: Kevin MacLean

opposite:
Me in Toronto, 1977. Note actual size of biceps.
Photographer: Kevin MacLean

top:
Kerryn Tolhurst in Toronto, 1977.
Photographer: Kevin MacLean

bottom:
Chris Stockley in Toronto, 1977.
Photographer: Kevin MacLean

top:
At the Station Hotel, Prahran, 1976. Brod parries with the mic stand; Stockley strums his Gibson SG.
Photographer: Andrew Chapman

bottom:
At the Station Hotel, Prahran, 1976. Ray Arnott rockin' on drums, me enjoying the ride. Biceps actual size.
Photographer: Andrew Chapman.

top:
At the Station Hotel, Prahran, 1976. Kerryn on lap steel. Note dinner menu ... wait, it's showing coming attractions: Wendy Saddington, Jeff St John and Ariel.
Photographer: Andrew Chapman

bottom:
Punters at the Station Hotel, 1976.
Photographer: Andrew Chapman

opposite top:
Times Square, New York, 1977. The whole message said: *New York City Welcomes ... The Dingoes.*
Photographer unknown

bottom:
Peter Rudge. True believer! Managed the Rolling Stones, The Who, Lynyrd Skynyrd and ... The Dingoes. His main source of revenue was Lynyrd, and when their plane went down he had to drop some of his acts. Still, he kept The Dingoes on. And even when A&M dropped us, he supported Kerryn and me for a time.
Photographer: Broderick Smith

The cover photo for our second album, *Five Times the Sun*. Mount Tamalpais, Marin County, California. I am almost invisible due to either punishment for out-of-control behaviour whenever idiotic A&M execs are present, or the recognition by savvy A&M execs of my total lack of charisma.

Cover of *Orphans of the Storm*, 1979, showing The Dingoes in 1903, New York, New York. Recorded at The Hit Factory ... wasn't a hit, however, despite John Anthony's best efforts.

Outside Elliot Mazer's His Master's Wheels studio, San Francisco, 1977. He gave us confidence because he loved our band and he had just recorded *The Band*.

Photograph courtesy of Janice Azrak

Latter-day Dingoes outside Kerryn's studio during *Tracks* recording, 2010, Tucson, Arizona.
Photographer: Perry Smith

top:
Kerryn caught in the act of producing *Tracks*, Tucson, Arizona, 2010.

bottom:
Rip Van Winkle, awakened to record *Tracks*. In the words of promoter Michael Chugg: 'What *happened* to you?'

top:
Folkways reissue of Broderick, during *Tracks* recording, 2010, Tucson, Arizona.

bottom:
Chris Stockley during *Tracks* recording, 2010, Tucson, Arizona. 'You're a barrel full of laughs, John ... pity the barrel's empty.'

top:
Me outside the Arts Centre Melbourne just before our induction into the ARIA Music Hall of Fame.

bottom:
Punters thirty years later. The author, dragged off stage by the adoring crowd at Northcote Social Club, 2011, for a group photo.
Photographer: Broderick Smith

I don't know what I was expecting for this final meeting. But there it was, more dooming than funereal cellos, more final than a football siren, Rudge's fey face. We sat in a semicircle around Rudge's desk as mercantile West 57th bustled below. It was cold and sunny outside. Rudge stood looking into the street, talking without expression, saying words, conveying that A&M were just not interested anymore. They wanted none of it.

Then he walked to his desk, took an antacid tablet, and said bluntly, 'There's nothing more I can do. I'm going to have to let you go, too. I'm still a big fan. It just didn't happen. I'm sorry.'

Rudge averted his eyes. We averted our eyes. After a long, barren pause, Stockley said, 'You win some. You lose some. Some as big as your fuckin' head.'

'You'll have your tickets home. I don't think we got you down on record properly. I'm sorry. I still like the first album — the Australian album — the best. Maybe we should have released that first. I don't know. My name's Peter Rudge, not fuckin' Jehovah. I don't know,' repeated Rudge looking at his appointment book and swivelling his chair back and forth as though he were ready to move on to the next thing in his life too. 'If Skynyrd ... If, if, if.'

That was it. Rudge could have wrung his hands more. But what for? We were all (except for Stockley) ready to move on to the next thing. Besides, The Dingoes had a good shot, but we had gone as far as we were going. I thought for an instant what it would take hours to tell: I was glad we were finished — I was ready for something new.

On the way out, Bill This-and-That, who must have been appalled at the amount of non-returnable money we were draining from their kitty, was emotional. 'Peter will never understand why you guys didn't make it. He loved you. You should hear him when you're not here. He talks about The Dingoes all the time.'

I said, 'You said we were going to make it — that's false how's-your-father. I'm suing you for every penny you've got (if we didn't get it already).'

He laughed. We slid out.

I wanted to avoid a long goodbye. I called the airline and booked a flight that day for a Midwestern town. Brod and J.L. shook my hand.

'Why don't you wait a couple of days and we can fly out together,' said Kerryn.

But I was firm. Kerryn and Stockley came to Kennedy Airport to see me off. They stood on the observation deck, under the clouds, now lowering and gloomy, heavy with suspended water. They waved as my jet pulled away from its berth. Even half a mile away, I could still see Kerryn's red bandana tied around his neck. But then the plane turned to take its position at the head of the runway. I was on the opposite side to Kerryn and Stockley. I hated myself for dwelling on why that was, instead of contemplating the separation from my friends. On a ship I simply could have walked to the rail on that side. On a smaller plane, I could have leaned over and still seen them. That demon, dehumanising technology, again. But, maybe on another day, when the wind came from the other direction, the plane would've taken off from the other end. This random weather event (or was it random, since weather is a concatenation of events that) ... Shut up, John!

I don't know if they were waving as the fuel started to burn and the big ship pulled at its brakes. I don't know if their eyes were moist as the mighty engines roared and shook. She built up to take-off thrust. The captain said he was willing and the tower said, 'Roger.' Slowly, then faster, the huge jet began her take-off roll. I thought of Kerryn's red bandana. Did he take it off to wave? Did Stockley rub his scars with one hand and wave with the other? I bet they popped in for a quick one at the airport lounge. I bet Stockley said, 'One for the *frog and toad*, mate?'

But a new set of thoughts would soon take the place of those of my friends. My chin twitched as I fought back tears. I grieved partly because I would miss them, and partly because I knew I would get over them quickly — they deserved better. But we would go crazy, I thought, if we were devastated by every separation. I cried tears of separation — and release.

The plane was still in a sharp climbing attitude when the captain turned off the *No Smoking* sign. I lit up a cigarette, and, with sweaty hands, looked at the destination on my ticket. We penetrated the clouds. Suddenly the sun appeared, flooding me with warmth and a feeling of bright potential. I looked down on the low clouds, then up into the deep-blue. The sky is always blue, I thought, it's just a matter of your point of view.

16

Way out West

That was in 1978. Then, in 1992 I received a letter from a friend back home. It contained this article written by David Dawson for the 'Weekend' section of the Saturday 30 May 1992 edition of the Melbourne *Herald Sun*.

> When a chartered plane fell from the sky into a swampy thicket at Gillsburg, Mississippi, on October 20, 1977, the career of revolutionary Australian band The Dingoes exploded. On board were hell-raising southern rock band Lynyrd Skynyrd with whom The Dingoes were scheduled to tour the US. Three Lynyrd Skynyrd members — singer Ronnie Van Zant and guitarist Steve and sister Cassie Gaines — perished in the blaze and other members were seriously injured. Although The Dingoes shared management with Lynyrd Skynyrd and the Rolling Stones they lost their bite and split. But now, after a James Blundell-James Reyne No. 1 hit of the 19-year-old Dingoes song Way Out West, band members are rising phoenix-like from the ashes.

Actually, I am staying troll-like, well-hidden under the ground.

> And, like the surviving Lynyrd Skynyrd members, they are doing it on their own on two different continents. Despite the ravages of

> time in the beer, whisky, and wine mines, none of the band is an alcoholic, junkie or desperado.

That is true.

> Guitarist Kerryn Tolhurst wrote Pat Benatar's hit 'All Fired Up', singer Broderick Smith will release a new single and album in July and guitarist Chris Stockley has recorded six new tunes with Melbourne's hottest cover band, Scarecrow. Drummer John Lee is in big demand on Melbourne's live circuit and ...

Last but not least:

> ... bassist John Bois is a teacher and musician in a black high school near Washington DC.

The school is a browny-red colour. I used to brag about my rock'n'roll past hoping it would endear me to the kids. But they don't believe me. The disconnect struck home at the Spring Concert this year. The musical director thanked me for playing. He said to the audience: 'Let's give him a big round of applause. On bass guitar ... *Mister* Bois!'

They let me teach biology because I spent five years from 1985 getting a Master's degree.

> The Dingoes' debut album has been released on CD and previously unreleased material, recorded 14 years ago in New York, is about to become available on a compilation CD featuring tunes from their three albums. This is not your average nostalgia-fueled soap-opera acted out on copycat commercial radio stations. The Dingoes' survival story is a real life drama where two members, Stockley and Tolhurst, fought death continents apart more than a decade ago. Pint-sized Stockley clung to life after being shot by complete strangers — a notorious underworld gang headed by the late Dennis Allen — as he carried a carton of beer into a Brighton party in 1973 ...

Just before the shooting Stockley was heard to say, 'You ratbags better not touch my beer!'

> The guitarist and latter day restaurateur still has fragments of the bullet, which entered his back, lungs and liver, floating around his body.

And big bloody scars to prove it.

> And Tolhurst, long-time resident of New York, fought a protracted battle with cancer of the spleen before Benatar had a No. 1 hit with a song he originally recorded with Melbourne band The Rattling Sabres.
>
> Early in the '80s a vast galaxy of Australia's best-known musicians staged a benefit in Sydney and Melbourne to raise funds for Tolhurst's cancer treatment in the US. Tolhurst, who has been given the all-clear, now performs and records in New York where he also produces other artists. Stockley and Smith are elated with the re-recording, production and success of the Blundell-Reyne hit 'Way Out West'.

I was elated, too, especially because, when it was first released, Kerryn, as a gesture of thanks to the band, split the songwriting royalties among us. Twenty years later, when it became a hit, we did nicely from it. But it should be said that Kerryn, alone, wrote it!

Epilogue

(2011)

'What a great story,' Joanna says.

She is the archivist of The Dingoes exhibition to commemorate our being inducted into ... wait for it ... the Australian Music Hall of Fame. And I am in the basement of the Arts Centre Melbourne. It is climate-controlled for temperature and humidity so that none of the artefacts age. Joanna is many years younger than I; she is intellectual, efficient, very professional and probably saucy. She reminds me of one of those young heroines of a British mystery series set in the 1930s, the kind that has a crush on her older superior. She is fizzy, but she is hip. I am flattered that she seems to think The Dingoes are also hip. I secretly lament the fact that I find her just as desirable as I would have if I were still her age.

'If only I could be in as pristine condition as these mementos.'

She smirks. 'I don't know. I think you've held up pretty well ... over here is your file.'

She glides through the file stacks.

I brought her a few things from the US to flesh out our exhibit: an album cover, a couple of pictures. They have aged terribly. She is giving me a courtesy tour of the archives. She pulls out The Dingoes' drawer. There I am. There we are. An Australian institution!

I suppose the others weren't as shocked as I was. After all, they have been here; even Kerryn has been back several times; they have witnessed the creation of the Dingoes legend. I have lived in the United States since we broke up. I became a teacher, a profession that is many things; but it is not great for financing trips to Australia. And so I am shocked to suddenly receive all this attention, to be archived at the Arts Centre Melbourne.

The *great story* to which Joanna is referring is not this book. She is talking about my Rip Van Winkle act.

'I know,' I say. 'Who gets to rock out after a hiatus of thirty years ... at fifty-nine.'

She pulls out an eight-by-ten photograph of Brod and me. He is in a Nazi uniform and I am a leather-jacketed French resistance fighter with my hands in the air. In the background is Brod's Land Rover. Joanna looks at me as if to say, *Why*?

'It was a photo shoot,' I explain. 'And ... I have no clue *why*.'

'But what is it with you lot and the Nazis?'

I give her a look.

'It's in *The Dingoes' Lament* ... The Afrika Corps ... Brod and the Rommel threat ... Jolly good, Corporal.'

'How do you know about that?'

'I read the first two chapters online. You don't know?'

'Of course I would know that.' I stand back to size her up. 'Wow, you're such a thorough researcher.'

'I bet you say that to all the archivists.'

Is she flirting with me? No, a woman her age can do that with a man my age because she is sure no assumptions are being made.

Joanna takes out another picture. It is me at twenty-four. She runs a finger around the line of my face. Her hands are delicate, fingernails deep-red and short.

'What do the others think of your *Dingoes' Lament*?'

'They say I always write to show myself in the best possible light.'

She holds my picture up.

'But you always were the best-looking Dingo.'

Now, I didn't make that up. She said that. It's a direct quote! Should I not report it exactly as it happened? Wouldn't it be dishonest to leave it out ... a sin of omission? Besides, there is so much in the book that is not quite true; it is about time to start facing facts.

I don't want to be coy about this. I wrote the story under the expectation that The Dingoes were never to be heard of again. How was I to know that so many musicians were inspired by our example, and that they would pay homage to us by getting us nominated to the Hall of Fame? This was not the plan. The plan was that my book would be so monumental that The Dingoes would be rediscovered and make us all millionaires. But now there is a problem: we have become minor celebrities; people are interested in knowing our story. And so I am afraid that my book will be bought under the false pretence that it is the true story of The Dingoes. Then, upon finding out that there are some slight exaggerations, some minor discrepancies with the historical record, the readers may want some redress — or, worse, a refund. But going back into the entire book and weeding these out would be tedious and pointless.

For example, in Juárez, the residents did throw fruit at us. But Mad Dog did not bring out a gun. This was because, not only did he not have a gun, but also because he did not exist! His real name was Eddy, who also did not have a gun. But he did, however, posses only one leg, and he liked to hammer the prosthetic just like I said he did. Do you see how confusing it can get if I have to iron everything out? Let's leave it at this: all the major plot points, every single one of them in *The Dingoes' Lament*, are absolutely, without question, upon my honour, guaranteed true — except for two.

Joanna pulls out another photograph. It shows The Dingoes just before we left for the States. On drums is not J.L. but Ray Arnott, another great drummer.

'How ... why did you make that change?'

'A too-long story. But briefly: J.L. had left us earlier to try his luck in London. When we got the call from the Rolling Stones office, we felt it would be better, more like the thing they had invested in, right, if J.L. met up with us in the States. Did you know that John had passed away?'

'Yes.'

'Personalities ought to change with age ... he couldn't deal with getting older.'

'Do not go gentle ... and all that?'

'Not really. He was Champagne Charlie:

Champagne Charlie is me name,
Drinking Champagne is me game,
I'm the idol of the barmaids,
Champagne Charlie is me name.'

She looks to see if anyone else is around to hear me sing.

'It's all good when it's champagne and good times with your mates ... then your mates are home with the wife and kids ... and all that's left for you is the champagne. And in the end his liver packed it in.'

A night with J.L., listening, perhaps stoned, to Joni Mitchell's *Hejira* and finding God in Jaco Pastorius's basslines put me in touch with a higher reality. The next day was a struggle to resume my own existence. J.L. was not prepared to do that quite as quickly.

'He was the most off-the-cuff player. You know, some drummers will map out the song and have it down beat by beat. John just played it every time, right off the top of his head ... wow!'

'That was exhilarating? Or anxiety making?'

'The former, usually. He took in song arrangements organically ... he wouldn't do it by rote. I think this made us sound natural ... spontaneous.'

'I suppose his champagne was a problem for you in the band?'

'No, never. He was always on top of things when we played ... professional, you know. I think I had more of an issue with that than he did. There were some issues off stage — wives of certain celebrities turning up to our US gigs and whisking him off (women couldn't get enough of him), exploits in the bathrooms of certain record company executives ... but he always came ready to play. He came alive on stage ... couldn't deal with life off stage. I wasn't around for the grand descent. I doubt he would have heeded anyone, anyway.'

I have not written that much about J.L. We may not have been friends if not for The Dingoes. Our only confluence of interest was music: R&B — Al Green especially —and reggae, any reggae. While playing we had great musical chemistry and communication. I remember I saw him in another band once, a great band, but like the time when I was fifteen — I saw The Easybeats and was fixated on George Young's rhythm guitar — I was fixated on J.L.'s performance to the exclusion of the other players. He was just such a natural. And he was very generous. We used to use his little Mini Minor for band transport ... always a death sentence for the car, if not the driver. He would share anything he had. Unfortunately, at the end — and even a considerable time before the end — he didn't have much and depended on the kindness of lovers. But my contact with him was musical. If anyone, even me, would bring a song, he would praise it, making it seem like it was going to be the next big thing. Then he would play a part with open delight. I loved that about him. But, like a couple that have an intense sexual relationship yet have nothing to say beyond the bed, we couldn't really hold up a conversation together. In truth, we were two very different spirits ... me the more prosaic, I fear.

'So who plays drums at the Hall of Fame Awards?'

'Ashley Davies.'

'God!' she laughs. 'It's like Spinal Tap for you guys.'

'You should be too young to know about that ...'

'My father—'

'Right.'

She pulls out another photo. More incriminating evidence.

'So who are these guys and where is Chris Stockley?'

'Err ... Chris was not with us by then ... that is Andy Hardin and Smiggy ... Robert Smith.'

The day before, after rehearsal for the Hall of Fame show, Stockley and I had gone to his favourite pub and shared several beers. I asked him what he thought of my manuscript. He said it threw him into a fit of depression ... about the way I described his playing. I didn't mention it before, but during our soul-destroying stay in New York, near the end but before *Orphans of the Storm*, we sent Chris Stockley off to Canada. It was one of those moves when a band is foundering and you have to do *something*. Depression probably made it seem like he wasn't into The Dingoes, and it may have — no, I am sure it did — affect his playing. In any case, it was a terrible mistake. The Dingoes were never The Dingoes without Stockley. In the book, and as I said to Stockley over the beers, I tried to capture him as a character for the ages. I enjoyed his idiosyncrasies so much I know I hammed them up. Cartoons are fun. Chris Stockley is and was fun but he is and was much more than a cartoon. But I had hoped my characterisation, the fact that I had featured him and that he was a big personality, would make him happy. Stupid me almost expected an embrace. But he didn't view this as much of a prize. He would rather hear good words for his guitar work. I argued that I had praised his guitar as embodying the essence of rock'n'roll, an essence that was at the heart of our character. He said he has been struggling with depression for many years, probably starting back then. After I sent him the original manuscript he went so low he went to see a shrink. He was told there are two kinds of depression. One is caused by a chemical imbalance, the other by some emotionally traumatic incident. 'Congratulations,' said the shrink, 'you've got both!'

Joanna brings out a photo of the band. As I'm looking at it I say in a distracted tone, 'Chris Stockley adores the *chemistry* of The Dingoes. We all brought flavors to the mix — Brod: the blues. Kerryn and me: country-rock, R&B and blues. J.L.: R&B and reggae. And Stockley: rockabilly, rock'n'roll and blues. But Stockley sees the value of the mix. He sees this more, I think, than anyone.'

She looks at me as if to say: *Did we just start an encounter session or something*?

'Excuse me, but the irony of us letting him go ... it still makes me wince.'

'Not to worry. You're all back together now ... except for J.L., of course.'

I make arrangements for Joanna to send me some photos after the awards exhibition closes. She walks me up the stairs and out into Melbourne winter.

'See you at the awards ... and thanks for the tour of Dingo nostalgia.'

'Yeah, come to my table and say hello.'

We shake hands. I measure the time of our hands clasping in milliseconds. Pathetic male brain.

Pathetic male brain, indeed, I think, as I release the contents of my stomach on the Westgate Bridge. The night before, after I said goodbye to Joanna, friends from the old days had feted me. And now, on my way to a weekend at Lorne, I just told my friend she had to pull over or suffer vomit in her car. She stopped where there is no breakdown lane. She is focused on the rear vision mirror. I think she is being discrete by not looking at the serial fountains of yellow chunder as they catch the early sun's rays. No, she is terrified of being rear-ended as cars swerve to avoid us. Australians beep at us. A couple of cars seeing my suffering call out, 'No worries, mate!'

Welcome home.

Six days later we play at the Hall of Fame Awards show. It is being televised live around Australia.

The Forum Theatre
Melbourne, August 2009

Well, here we are, each Dingo sitting at his own table with friends and relatives surrounded by music-industry folk. As Rip Van Winkle, no-one has seen me since 1976. Chuggi, former manager, says, 'What *happened* to you?' He is referring to my ageing physiognomy. Richard Clapton strides on to induct us. I haven't seen him since 1976. He's older, wiser and bigger. Richard tells anecdotes about how great The Dingoes were, especially our songs. He says he and J.L. walked into a club where INXS were playing and they all bowed to J.L., saying: '*We're* not worthy ... *we're* not worthy.' Richard says, 'The Dingoes were the real shit.' I'm beginning to feel a little less Rip Van Winkle–like.

To the sounds of Stockley's *Come On Down* we mount the stage. Kerryn gives a great speech. The speech is humble and devoid of industry talk. He makes a moving tribute to J.L., whose parents are in the audience. I stand there trying hard not to look like Rip Van Winkle. Kerryn says,

'It has only been thirty years since we played together. But if you stick around, we're going to make a bit of noise in a minute.'

We play. First is *Boy On The Run.* In Australia there is a conspiracy to not show me on TV ... a YouTube clip from 1974 has me obscured by a huge bubble around Broderick. To remedy this, I walk behind him so that I will be included in his bubble. People recognise this song as a classic now. They are staring at us as if we are celebrities, museum pieces, or accident victims.

Next is *Way Out West*. Jesus! This song is almost an anthem now. People are not just staring at us; they are smiling at us like beloved family members. And our rehearsal paid off — we sound polished. Even Van Winkle can still play. The applause swells into a standing ovation ... the first of the evening. Some are crying!

After we play, I go downstairs to the men's room. Several men are at the urinal. One says, 'Weren't The Dingoes *great*!'

'It's great to hear them after thirty years.'

I look at them and say, 'You can say that again.'

They recognise me and laugh. 'Good one, mate.' I go back upstairs to Joanna's table. She is there with others from the National Art Gallery.

'So how did we do?'

'Sounds like 1976 all over again.'

'Okay ... but *looks* like ...?'

'Looks aren't everything.'

'Say no more.'

'Oh, I'm teasing, you silly thing. What a great band. How was it up there?'

'It felt great. Wow. Don't know if we can just leave it there.'

Later that evening, at an after-show party, Kerryn is saying, 'Sounded fuckin' great, John. I'm talking to David Minear about doing another CD ... in Tucson.'

The fairy tale is over. Rip Van Winkle is back at his day gig: biology teacher at the eighteenth step, three years away from retirement. The kids ask me why I didn't stay in music.

Every Dingo but one has stuck with music.

J.L. was a drummer until he died.

Stockley has continued to play, write and help manage a catering business, serving the film industry, that he and Jenny own. He has formed several successful bands — Stockley, See and Mason was an all-original band that was highly regarded. Stockley is also in demand as a session player. When producers need the classic rock and roll sound that's who they call.

Brod has a solo career and a new CD called *Unknown Country*. After a rehearsal he invited me up to his house in Castlemaine, a Victorian country town where he is universally known and loved as both gifted eccentric and wit. He played his CD. It had not yet been released. I was taken by several tracks. In a song called *The Ring*, he sings in character as a boxer. There are great lines like, *I work the body, till the head dies.* It has the best rock'n'roll scream I have ever heard. I play it over and over, much to the surprise of concerned drivers stopped next to me at a red light. The title track is about moving into a post-relationship phase — there is poetry in the lines: *How did I fall into the shadows? Did the devil take it all? Except my simple wits ... enough to keep me ... breathing ... shallow.* There are songs about bushrangers and tow-truck drivers; it is Australian through and through, and I believe he is the best rock'n'roll/blues/ whatever singer Australia has produced.

Kerryn had been living mainly in New York but has moved to Tucson, Arizona. He travels to Australia often, to produce and play on an array of interesting projects. He produced a beautiful compilation of Australian surf music called *Delightful Rain*. He wrote international hits for Pat Benatar and Little River Band. He is greatly respected in the US and Australia. Indeed, as the composer of *Way Out West*, *Pay Day Again, Waitin' For The Tide* and *Singing Your Song,* he is increasingly being considered one of Australia's best and most underestimated songwriters. And I second that opinion!

In terms of Darwinian fitness, Brod and I are the winners — we both have three children. Kerryn and Stockley have one a piece, and J.L. did not pass on his genes, alas (I suppose this means there will be fewer drummers in the next generation). Stockley is the only grandfather as of this epilogue.

So, why didn't I stay in music? When we had kids, my first wife and I decided I needed to get a day gig. I had come close a couple of times with a recording deal; I had produced a stunningly unsuccessful CD for the stunningly gifted songwriter Cheryl Wheeler. But none of these activities promised to produce an income. So I went to college at the Harvard University Extension School and later graduated from the Harvard School of Education with a Master's degree. I started writing this book as an exercise in a writing class. At forty-one, I was teaching at Northwestern High School in Maryland. I have been there ever since. I kept my hand in by playing with the school's gospel chorus, jazz band,and various Latino bands.

'So can you come to Tucson at Christmas to record?'

This is Kerryn a couple of weeks after the Hall of Fame visit. I am back in Maryland trying to learn the names of 150 high school students. I love my job but this still sounds like a get-out-of-jail card!

'Fantastic!'

'We're picking songs, so send the ones you want and we'll take a vote.'

The CD has to be done on the cheap. This sad fact leads to a discussion between Kerryn and me.

I say, 'But one of the most important bits of this band is the rhythm feel between the bass player and drummer. And if I'm playing with a drum loop, it's just not going to be the same. I mean, I can do it ... but it's not going to be the same.'

'Yeah, I know ... but I have done this a lot. And put on drums later — it's a lot easier, quicker and, what's more important here for us, it's cheaper.'

Kerryn has become a record producer. He knows about these things. And he is much more assertive than the days of yore. I think this is a good thing for him and the latter-day Dingoes. But it is not good for my current argument.

'What would it cost to bring in a drummer ...?'

'It would take too much time. It's not just the money. You have about a week, right? I can send you the loops. You can have all your parts set before you get here.'

'But that's just it! Parts are better when you work it up with a whole rhythm section ... that was kind of our trademark.'

'I know, John. But I've budgeted it all out — money, time ... I wish we had that luxury but we don't. And it really works, you'll see. It's gonna be okay.'

'Well, whatever you think, but I don't know ...'

But I *do* know. As Science Department Chair, I spent years trying to work around fiscal realities. A mentor's advice: *Don't spin your wheels.* And I do know that Kerryn would make it happen with a real drummer if it were possible. I trust his wisdom in this decision.

And so here I am in Tucson, trying to get hip with a drum loop that doesn't see me, can't touch me, can't feel me, can't play softer or louder, doesn't bleed, can't talk, laugh, understand, smile, eat or argue about semantics. It seems to me that the dialogue about artificial intelligence — *Can humans be replaced by robots?* — has just started. Then how come one of the first human faculties to be outsourced to a machine is musical ability? Music: one of the very things that define us as human!

But, despite this rapprochement with the machine, I don't bring as much anxiety to the session as the days of yore. I think I don't care as much ... or, rather, I maybe cared too much before. What level of anxiety is it that switches from driving productivity to destroying the creative spirit? When I see photos of myself back then, it really looks as if I'm not having any fun at all. Seriously, someone should have counselled me out of this career!

Right now, as a teacher, it is good to return to music. What a great story. Why, after the Hall of Fame thing, a local Maryland reporter did a piece on me entitled 'The Science Teacher is a Rock Star'. But how is it for the other three? The Hall of Fame Award has revived our currency. It is a vindication of our songs, particularly Kerryn's. If not for the great success of *Way out West*, there would not have been a Hall of Fame recognition. Stockley is also fired up and sees the award as a just dessert. Brod is not yet invested. Sees The Dingoes as part of his life, not its frame. He had to be persuaded to do this CD. But there is still some sort of chemistry he responds to, even if it's only an amused audience of me. Between vocal takes, I am videotaping him.

I say: 'Za Führer vill be pleased mit your vocals.'

'Za Führer? I don't like za Führer anymore ... za Führer was a vegetarian.'

'You're kidding.'

'No ... strange but true. A vegan.'

Then, in his Hitler voice, 'Nothing with lips touches this stomach. Let's attack Japan ... they have tofu! Mung beans! *Free* for every German. Muesli for the troops! *But Herr Führer the men are fainting.* I don't care!'

He drops into these comic routines instantly. He has still got it. But in this time, since he has been operating beyond my orbit, he has become more Australian than the Australians. He has created his own archetypal Australian. It is in the tradition of the swagman, vagabond storyteller. And as a professional itinerant, I'm not sure how the Dingoes system will fit into his archetype.

Still, we are all much more relaxed with each other. We are old high schoolers revisiting the days of pranks and levity. Stockley, in his continuing battle with the electrical realm, has new challenges. Contacting Melbourne has to be done with a new temporary mobile phone. And, as if to facilitate the evil electrickery, I hide the phone. After the third time, I confess, 'It was me all along.'

He says in a Yorkshire accent, 'You're a barrel full o' laughs, John. Pity the barrel's empty.'

I finish my bass parts. They're okay (I practised like hell to get some of my chops back!). Now comes the guitar layering. They are both putting on some amazing stuff. Kerryn tells Stockley to try some Chuck Berry on *Damascus Road* ... and it fires the song up. And Stockley's accompanying parts are paragons of good taste. Kerryn rips a flawless lyrical solo in one of Brod's songs. It is effortless for him. Brod belts out some blues harp — what a knockout!

New Year's Eve, coming up to 2010. We are seated in a Greek

restaurant somewhere in Tucson. It has great food and wine. Stockley is a happy man. He starts off with a designer beer of some kind.

'Here, what's that you're drinking, mate?'

He studiously observes the label, adjusts his glasses: 'It's something called ... beer ... John.'

'Do you think it will catch on?'

'Well, this is why I'm trying it. It's market research, isn't it.'

'Foster's not good enough for you now?'

'A bloke's moved up in the world.'

'Too bloody right, mate.'

The soup is served.

Brod says, 'You remember what Richard Clapton said during his Hall of Fame speech, how we took all of their Sydney women? I was sittin' there thinking, *What's he* talking *about? I don't remember us being like that.* Do you, John?'

'No, mate. Not at all'

'No, me neither.'

'Hang on. Yes, there was that one ... and another after the whiskey ... that's two ... and does Balmain count?'

'Yeah, it's all Sydney.'

'So ... three, four ... now, how about Parramatta?'

'Of course.'

'... five, six, seven ... Wollongong?'

'Sure ...'

'... eight, nine, ten, eleven. Stockley, what's that you got there?'

Stockley is perched to dismember an octopus.

'It's octopus, mate. Or half an octopus, anyway.'

'A quatropus. That's phylum *Mollusca* ... twelve, thirteen ... very clever animals, octopus ... fourteen.'

'What about that netball team in Gosford?'

'That's right ... fifteen, sixteen, seventeen, eighteen, nineteen, twenty and twenty-one.'

Kerryn says, 'What's your secret, John?'

While nodding, I smugly point to my crotch.

Near the end of the main course, a belly dancer comes out, all razzle-dazzle and a beautiful physique.

But Stockley is intent on his mollusc.

I ask, 'Can I have a tentacle, mate?'

'Not here, John. Later, okay.'

He slices off a piece of tentacle and drops it onto my plate. Flavour. Lemon, tender, not chewy.

'It's really great, Chris ... twenty-two.'

The conversation turns to The Dingoes. Kerryn is saying how glad he is that we weren't together in the eighties. He says we are all better musicians now, and it would have been hard to do our thing in that decade, 'And there is that dreadful drum sound that locks all music in the eighties ... in the eighties.'

I say, 'Yeah, like, I love Prince, but the drums make him sound like a period piece. So much of this is accidental. My son just happened to grow up in the time of heavy metal. It's almost like he has no choice about the kind of music he likes. And that's twenty-three if we're still counting Newcastle ... right, Brod?'

'Right, John. How come they don't have steak and eggs here?'

Brod has ordered moussaka, the cheapest meal on the menu, not necessarily because it's cheap but because it is not too opulent. Brod is just a regular bloke.

Stockley is irritated. Something I said has reminded him of my book.

'You were wrong when you said we couldn't make it in New York because of the punk scene. It was all about marketing, John. You see—'

'I'm sorry, I don't agree—'

'I know you don't, but there is one point about this, in that, in the punk era, we've got Joe Jackson, Elvis Costello, The Police ... none of those bands were punk, but they used punk icons and punk colours and that made them part of the time. But they were never ever, you know, punk bands or punk artists. And there was a whole bunch of people like that ... and it was a matter of marketing in that regard.'

'You speak with such authority, it's hard to argue ... except to ask: which side of the Murray is Albury, and does it count as Sydney? And if so … twenty-four!'

Bouzouki music is becoming more frenetic. So is the dancer. She is accepting tips from diners.

Brod has his back toward the gyrating belly. He is oblivious. He generally shuns occasions such as this. Right now I think he is making a comment on the over-the-top opulence, or at least indulging in a satirical role-play of the privileged life. He pretends to be the suave actor Roger Moore and in a lethargic English accent says, 'I'm having a wonderful time here at the hotel in Singapore. I'm with the FO, the Foreign Office. I'm staying with a young friend of mine who's a writer by the name of … Graham Greene … and there's a weird gang of fellows that hang around with … W. Somerset Maughan … and they're giving me the shits. He's with a portly guy called P. G. Wodehouse. He keeps talking about pigs with wings or something. I'm not sure what's going on. They put something in my drink.'

With that he pretends to pass out with his head plummeting to the table.

Meanwhile, right behind him, the belly dancer is building to a climax. She is making a mental note not to accept any tips from Brod.

Here comes the bill; it's a big one. Even though a good part of it is being taken care of as a gift from Kerryn's brother, Peter, we still have to fork over our share. Calculating our respective portions is never an easy task. And all members have been known to underestimate.

I say, 'Brod, how much was yours?'

'Twenty-two seventy-five.'

'Ooh, that sounds a little light. There's something wrong with your math. Here, check it again.'

'I had a cappuccino …'

'There's two cups of chino …'

'But I only had one … and I'm only paying for one. Moussaka and no drinks … that's twenty-two seventy five and a fiver for a tip.'

'Stockley, what was the damage on yours?'

'Mine was fifty dollars and twenty-five cents.'

'What did you put in for the tip?'

'I put in a hundred and I need forty bucks back.'

'Why not just leave in the hundred.'

'Because I want change ... and I don't trust you.'

After about fifteen minutes of this dickering, we stand up and, with the sounds of bouzouki music and dinner plates smashing into the fireplace, we head into 2010. Except where is Stockley? I look into the restaurant window and there he is, talking to the entire wait staff. They are laughing with him. That's my friend, Chris Stockley.

The next day, my last day, and it's back to Maryland. Thanks to Kerryn, the recording has been a breeze. His skill in this has grown with his experience. Harry Vanda and George Young of the Easybeats had unlimited studio time to nurture their recording/producing expertise. The Dingoes had to beg for recording time. What would have happened if The Dingoes had this kind of recording-company support? For now, I am grateful that Kerryn has gained it, mainly through tenacity, holding on to his love of music and belief in himself as an artist.

I returned to my high school after the Christmas break — two days after students. They were already aware that I was a minor celebrity of some sort. They ask me what the name of my group was. With a straight face I tell them, 'The Beatles.'

'I've *heard* of them, Mr Bois. You *were* famous.'

'Yeah,' I say. 'AC/DC used to open for us.'

They are even more impressed by this, which is, in fact, true.

I get a copy of *Tracks*, The Dingoes' first CD in more than twenty years. Kerryn has done the impossible: on a bargain-basement budget (despite my whining about a real drummer), he has bridged the span of years and made this CD sound like a natural progression — it is how The Dingoes *should* have sounded if they had stayed together. The songs, mainly by Kerryn and Brod (but one each for Chris and me), sound contemporary yet in character for what one might expect from a sixty-year-old Dingo (that is supposed to be a compliment). I can't wait to get back to tour Australia to promote it.

We are driving along the east side of the Blue Mountains in an eight-seater Hyundai van. Last night we played in Katoomba. The overlook at Echo Point takes in a vista as ancient as any in the world. The ridges and crags are the remnants of once-grand mountains. As an accident of its position on the planet, Australia happens to be geologically pacific. Unlike the basin and range region of the US, a system that is constantly forming and reforming mountains, the geology of Katoomba (and most of Australia) is what it always was if it had not eroded.

So, showing off my knowledge gained from five years of study in natural science, I say, 'Brodles, do you notice these ancient formations? They're close to what they always were as Australia slides northward on its continental plate.'

'Ay, and you think you can cum 'ere with your college education ... you think your better 'n us. Let me tell you a thing or two lad ...'

'Ay ... and he still stands at the urinal like the rest of us.'

Stockley says, 'Glass the cunt!'

'I'm just sayin'.'

Kerryn says, 'He was always insufferable ... now it's only gotten worse.'

We stop for a pee at a country footy field. We take a football and start kicking it around.

Back in the Hyundai, Kerryn is driving. He has taken charge of almost all things now: the recording, getting money for the recording, renting the van, booking flights and hotels (with the help of agencies that are his contacts). And the tour is organised and SNAFU-less ... so much so that Rip Van Winkle is experiencing symptoms of disorientation. He was expecting fleabag motels and continental crossings by road. But Kerryn has arranged all travel by plane. Stockley is his right-hand man and has played an important role in helping out with the money (advancing money until gigs pay up) and setting up a legal arrangement (some kind of incorporation) with Kerryn and me. Together, they have made this tour a dream ride.

But Brod doesn't want to be a part of this. He sees himself as separate, as having moved on. I don't mean that he felt superior, aloof or arrogant; just that he likes to put the Dingoes project in its right place — that was then; what he is doing now is now. We worried that this attitude could threaten the tour. In Tasmania, Brod had laryngitis. His performance in Hobart was shocking. The crowd was there to observe the second coming. Brod sang every song an octave below where it should have been. They stared in disbelief and did not give us an encore like they had for the warm-up act. Brod could have said something. I asked him why he didn't. He said he was afraid they would ask for their money back. But we were scared this was the beginning of a disaster; that Brod was going to studiously avoid a strong performance. There was suspicion that Brod would have liked to see the tour cancelled. We needn't have worried. Two nights later, in Melbourne, he was in top form. But off stage, he continued to act like an employee who was contracted for a certain number of performances. I said before that Brod has a stage persona that more or less vanishes off stage. He doesn't like to shmooze at all. For example, after the ARIAs, he jumped in his car and was fast asleep up in Castlemaine by the time we had our third beer at the after-show party.

For this tour, Brod asked for and got a guaranteed fee, like The Dingoes' extra cast members. But then we got an offer to tack on one extra gig, at the Northcote Social Club, a gig that was sure to put the band in the black. Brod said no, he wasn't going to do it because he had contracted for a certain number of gigs and he had fulfilled his part of the bargain. We were exasperated. After all the success of the tour, it was looking like we would actually owe money. But again, the workings of Brod's exceptional mind switched gears: 'I was focusing on my own thing. I didn't realise that doing that one gig was going to put the band out of the red. I thought about it last night ... I'm going to do Northcote.'

We descend a steep incline down to the Hawkesbury River, drive onto the ferry and open the van's doors to take in the Hawkesbury's moist air. The river is bounded by rugged country. As if to emphasise the heroic content, Kerryn puts on a Wagner CD. It's *Flight of the Valkyries*. We are taking on the world all over again.

We play Newcastle. The band is really starting to sound tight. All the arrangements are solid. The song sequence is good and it builds to a great encore-getting crescendo. It is — dare I say it — triumphant. Brod does a great imitation of enjoying himself. He is full of one-liners. Our audience is about our age.

Brod doesn't dance around the issue: 'Ladies, if you knew the band back in the seventies and you want to say hello, please wear a name tag.'

'Ladies and gentlemen, hang on to your colostomy bags for this next tune.'

The crowd loves him. His patter puts them at ease.

'Wow, it's a shock to see you all singing along with the words. Feels like ABBA. I remember when we used to play at a pub in Dubbo to an old man and a three-legged Jack Russell terrier.'

We have a few days off in Melbourne and then fly to Adelaide. As if we had something to prove, every gig now is hot. After this one, a Rose Tattoo member runs up to the stage and shouts to me, 'That was miraculous!'

Then it's Perth. Back in the day, we were very big in Perth. I had a sweetheart there. She was delectable. But she doesn't show up. In fact, none of my former sweethearts show up for the entire tour. I'm not sure if I should take this personally.

Kerryn says, 'What are the odds of that, John?'

So here we are, back in Melbourne at the Northcote Social Club. Just before we go on, I walk out on stage with my camera and ask the crowd to smile. I give the camera to Brod and jump into the crowd. He takes the shot. It's our last gig — probably my last gig with the band. And it comes off almost without fault. Everyone is on. I find out later that it is being recorded. It is going to be made into a double CD called *Live at Last*.

I am back in the USA. The double live CD has been released. I remember a man with a miner's helmet threading microphone cables. This turned out to be Mick Wordley, an engineer who worked with Kerryn to record and mix the performance. It is amazing — as good as we have ever sounded live. Brod's vocals, and particularly his harp playing, are phenomenal and committed! The groove is great — thank you, Ashley Davies. Chris Copping's keyboards are worthy of Procol Harum. Our harmonies were never great but Kevin Bennett has created a sweet blend. The three guitars (including Kevin's in-the-pocket acoustic work) are rockin' — it's a guitar-player's album! Kerryn has loaded the CD with biting lap steel guitar, brilliant down-home riffs and last-chance guitar solos. Stockley excels, not only in blistering solos, but also in incredibly tasteful accompaniment. It is The Dingoes. It is what we were. It is what we could have been. It is what we are.

I sent a YouTube clip of my favourite song, *No Rain No River (*one of Kerryn's) played live at Northcote to the faculty of my school. Mrs Creese, a matronly Jamaican woman, is swept away, '*No Rain No River*, Mr Bois ... now that is a hit record. Do you hear me, Mr Bois? A *number-one hit record.*'

'Thank you, Mrs Creese.'

'We should make it required listening for the students, Mr Bois. There are valuable life lessons in that song: *Just because you stumble doesn't mean you have to fall.* Every line in that song is *quality*. *Top* quality. Make some worksheets for the students, Mr Bois.'

And from that point on, I am Mr *No Rain No River*.

So, thank you, Broderick Smith, for being the great Dingoes frontman in spite of yourself. Thank you, Chris Stockley, for not being in the least bit surprised that The Dingoes' reputation has continued to grow, and that there is/was something special about our chemistry. And for driving this through, for holding fast like a terrier, for belief in the concept and, of course, your songs and bitchin' guitar and slide work, thank you, Kerryn Tolhurst.

What a great story!

ROLLING STONE, SEPTEMBER 22, 1977

Five Times the Sun
The Dingoes
A&M SP-4636

By Ken Tucker

FOR ITS AMERICAN debut, this Australian quintet comes on like a cross between the Band and Steely Dan. *Five Times the Sun* is a provocative mixture of rural remembrance, burly rock and plaintive balladry. The result is a sort of populist rock & roll that very few since John Fogerty have done convincingly.

Above all else, the Dingoes convince.

The band tends to set up tidy melodies and terse narratives and then rip through them with a careful intensity. Most of this tension is provided by guitarists Chris Stockley and Kerryn Tolhurst, but lead singer Broderick Smith adds his own sort of ragged power, sounding on the slow songs like an adolescent Neil Young and on the fast ones like an apoplectic Roger Daltrey.

All this rawness gives the group an ironic edge. The lyrics of such tunes as "Smooth Sailing" and "Shine a Light" are just clever cruise-and-booze sagas, but the cracks in Smith's voice and Stockley's and Tolhurst's livid, now-or-never guitar playing lift these jaunts into harrowing journeys through their past. Songs like "Way Out West" and "Waiting for the Tide to Turn" present visions of white, working-class existence which, if they are meant to be representative of Australia, could just as easily be set in the American Midwest.

Valley News Sept. 2, 1977

The Dingoes, a pack of five Australian musicians who take their name from their homeland's wild, hinterland dogs, have delivered a curious blend of earthy rock and beautiful melody to American shores. Their debut A&M release, **"Five Times The Sun"** (SP-4636), exhibits many of the qualities American music lovers seek and receive from very few of their own bands—music uncluttered by gimmickery and possessed with spirit.

Eight original compositions based almost exclusively on guitar, bass and drums run the gamut of sounds from strong rock to country ballad. In between, the Dingoes' sound is occasionally augmented by keyboards of The Band's Garth Hudson and session pianist Nicky Hopkins. A trace of harmonica by vocalist Broderick Smith combines with Hudson's carnival organ to give "Waiting for the Tide to Turn" a prairie flavor along the lines of the Band's "Life is a Carnival."

But musical similarities begin and end with that song; the seven remaining tunes stand on their own as valid expressions of Australian country rock. Smith's vocals are tinged with a powerfully raw and expressive edge which match the work of the band's hard-driving guitars. Acoustic guitars and harmonica are featured on the smooth country ballads.

The Dingoes have given us an impressive debut. Their chunky rhythms and infectious melodies could signal the beginning of an effective merger of American and Australian rock styles.

—**Jeff Snyder**

OCTOBER 2, 1977 Los Angeles Times

Pop Music

International Disc Derby: Emphasis on Rock 'n' Roll

BY ROBERT HILBURN

The Dingoes' "Five Times the Sun" (A&M SP 4636)—Broderick Smith has a lot of the raspy, gripping vocal conviction of Frankie Miller in "Singing Your Song," "Come on Down" and "Way Out West," the three most appealing tracks on this Australian band's first U.S. album. When added to the semi-Creedence undercurrents of tunes like "Waiting for the Tide to Turn," the quintet shows more than enough vitality to make its debut noteworthy. As it shows in "Smooth Sailing," however, the Dingoes can be slick and passionless. Don't let that song, which has been getting some airplay, mislead you. This is a band with point of view and skill. Like Creedence, its approach is simple but highly engaging. YES.

PAIR MAGAZINE October 1977 Dallas, Texas

Broderick Smith

The Dingoes • *Five Times the Sun* • A&M Records

Australia contains some pretty strange animals and the Dingoes are no exception by any means. Although three of the five members are British, this band works mainly in the land of koala bears and eucalyptus trees but "Waltzing Matilda" is not in the Dingoes' repertoire.

Vocalist Broderick Smith sounds like an in-tune Neil Young at times yet possesses a unique style of gritty shouting and countryish harmonizing. Guitarists Chris Stockley and Kerryn Tolhurst write the material, which ranges from the hard-rocking "Come On Down" to a laid back "Shine A Light" to country influenced songs like "Way Out West." Nicky Hopkins, who's played with almost everyone in the business (including the Stones), lends his piano genius on a majority of the tunes.

Judging from their bio sheet, their record company considers the band to be a bunch of ruffians who only show up at the office when they need money; it's about time someone screwed a record company, though.

Regardless of their motives, the Dingoes play some really nice music, similar to The Band and some early Dillard and Clarke, yet comparisons do little justice. It's some of the best stuff to come up from down under in a long, long time.

—d.u.

The Dingoes' Music Mood Comes From Way Out West — Australia

By GARY PETERSON
Special to The Sentinel

"ALL RIGHT, MILWAUKEE, are you ready for some rock and roll? Put your hands together and welcome a beer drinking band to a beer drinking city," yells The Dingoes roadie just before the first of two past midnight concerts at The Electric Ballroom.

Nearing the conclusion of a four month blitzkreig tour of the east, south and midwest, The Dingoes are looking toward the return to their current home base — San Francisco.

"I'm gonna go home, see the wife and count the kids," quips guitarist Chris Stockley.

Broderick Smith, vocals and harmonicas, shows his inclination by opening with "Starting Today (I'm Making My Way Home To You)," one of The Dingoes' arsenal of 50 plus originals. Smith has a 15 month old son he hasn't seen for awhile.

"There's only one woman who's after me," Broderick reveals, "and that's my wife."

SMITH, STOCKLEY and guitarist / songwriter Kerryn Tolhurst have known each other for 10 years, beginning in Melbourne, Australia, where Smith arrived from England in 1967 at the age of 19.

John Lee, drums, is also an English-Australian as is Stockley, John du Bois, bassist, and Tolhurst are Down Under natives.

Four and a half years ago they joined forces when all were fresh out of work and leaving their respective bands. After one LP on the Festival label and a bout with unsatisfactory management, The Dingoes transplanted themselves to Toronto, Canada in 1975.

This is a working class band to the hilt. Their dress offers no glitter or frills. Their stage presence abandons pretense for hard edged self-assurance hiding a gentle core. Their sound is something like early Rod Stewart, the fragile side of Neil Young or Peter Townshend / Ronnie Lane's Rough Mix.

THE DINGOES WORKED Toronto and Montreal clubs until they met Elliot Mazer, Neil Young's longtime producer, and hooked up with Rolling Stones' manager Peter Rudge.

Signed 18 months ago to A & M, whose Jerry Moss had sought the group for his label while they were still in Australia, The Dingoes moved to San Francisco in December of 1976 and recorded their second LP, "Five Times The Sun," at Mazer's His Master's Wheels studio.

Since then they've been mostly on the road from Colorado to New England playing everywhere except, oddly enough, San Francisco, Los Angeles and the rest of the west coast where they'll tour next beginning Oct. 14 at L.A.'s Roxy.

The Electric Ballroom, which — strictly from the point of view of those of us who like to breathe — could be a great hall given a little ventilation, echoes with wild dog calls prior to Kerryn Tolhurst's unrecorded "Going Down Again."

Broderick Smith, who before the concert spent half an hour doing a Rocky, pulls one of several harmonicas from his utility belt and, waving his arms frantically at the crowd says, "Any place that makes beer is good for us."

SOMEHOW THE COMBINATION of Smith's harmonica and Tolhurst's pedal steel conjures up a keyboard sound replacing the absent Nicky Hopkins-Garth Hudson accompaniments of The Dingoes' recent recording.

Their plaintive Australia born western music equally mirrors The Band, source of Hudson, and the Hopkins backed Rolling Stones (i.e. "Wild Horses" or "Honky Tonk Woman").

There is a tradition for this type of band, one that includes the rough edges of Smith's Rod Stewart like delivery, more full voiced and cracking less frequently than its Scottish counterpart.

"I Don't Want to Face Another Day Alone," again an unrecorded original, continues the homesick, lonely on the road motif right into the second encore, a reprise of "Starting Today." This brings The Dingoes full circle, ever mindful of their approaching journey home.

"We intend to stay together for a long time," says Tolhurst. "We stay more together by living apart off the road. We all have influences and we don't try to hide them," he continues. "We're influenced by all the people we're compared to."

"Dingoes," Kerryn explains, "are wild dogs. In Australia they built a 6,000 mile cyclone fence — the longest in the world — just to contain them."

Fortunately, it didn't work.

Chris Stocky, the Dingoes' guitarist: with his drink and his Buddy.

A recent Zoo Free Sunday which hosted **The Dingoes** from Australia was moved from East Dallas to the west side of Fort Worth at the last minute! Hence, a lot of people missed out on the unique band's performance, which is Australia's biggest box-office draw. Their music incorporates a myriad of influences–so many that it's hard to pinpoint the five-piece band's major influence–or is that because The Dingoes are a strange breed indeed: totally original. If you missed them and their sometimes rockin', sometimes laid-back, sometimes countrified music from down under, you haven't blown it. The Dingoes will be back. We talked to them backstage, where we discovered how *nice* they are (even after our weak rugby and kangaroo jokes, which they must've heard a trillion times). The feeling is mutual: The Dingoes think Texas is nice, "especially Austin," guitarist **Chris Stockley** told us. The band got a few days off in Austin, much to its delight. Chris couldn't praise the city enough: "I'd *live* there–maybe I will someday. I love it! Austin's got everything." Hopefully, when The Dingoes make it back to the metroplex, the sports will take some time to "tie their kangaroos down" long enough to get to know Dallas and Fort Worth better. Until then, if you'd like to know more about this refreshing group, they've got one album out, *Five Times The Sun,* on A&M Records, and are working on their second, to be released in early '78. . .

CHICAGO DAILY NEWS
CHICAGO, ILL.

Down-under rock and roll

By John Milward

Broderick Smith, lead vocalist for a promising Australian rock band called the Dingoes, has given me the perfect analogy for why a band from "down under" must come to America to hit the big-time.

My question: Why does the tasty brand of Australian beer we're drinking come in absurdly large 25-ounce cans? His answer: Because we couldn't fit 32 ounces.

By definition, rock and roll success in Australia is a limited concept, and before long a band with stars in their eyes must cross the Pacific to strike it big. America is the media center of the world, and pop music is nothing if not an entertaining example of this country's pervasive cultural influence. Here, with the corporate support of a big-time record company (A&M in the case of the Dingoes), a young rocker just might come up with a bottomless beer can.

For the Dingoes, their entrance to the New World was initiated when rock heavy Peter Rudge (manager of Lynyrd Skynyrd, among others, and road manager for past tours by the Rolling Stones and The Who) came across a tape of their debut Australian album. He liked what he heard, sent for the band, and helped them settle in Canada for some intensive practice. Before long, they settled into Marin County and recorded their American debut.

Broderick Smith

Smith likens their transition from Australia to the U.S. to an accelerating car. The Dingoes limited success in their native country showed them the ropes, but only as they transferred their experience to the American market have they shifted to the high gears required for mass acceptance. The difference in America, Smith says, is the level of intensity.

The critical reaction to their album, "Five Times the Sun," has been positive, with comparisons often made to The Band and, in the case of Smith's attractively husky voice, to Rod Stewart. Initially, their U.S. reception mirrors their Australian experience—high critical praise and limited commercial success.

"Our Australian audience seemed largely composed of drunks and perverts," notes Smith in a tone of wry camaraderie. "Ironically, this seems to be the same in America."

But for the Dingoes, traveling the highways of America, with their instruments in tow, is a thrilling experience. Who cares if the meager crowd at B'Ginnings in Schaumburg Wednesday had no idea who these funky pastoral-sounding Aussies were? They finally were playing rock and roll central, and if ever their beer cans would run over, it would be here.

The Bugle **Sept. 23-Oct. 6, 1977**
Milwaukee

Five Times The Sun — The Dingoes (A&M)

by Barry Patton

The front and back cover pics and the sleeve pic seem like a hats-off salute to **Dr. Byrds And Mr. Hyde**, faces obscured by a backlit setting sun. The little black circle stuck on the cover reads: "Never Bark . . . Always Bite!" The back cover says that Eliot F. Mazer (Neil Young's steady producer over the years...well sometimes steady) produced it. You get to the inner sleeve and you find not only has His Master's Wheels been the recording facility but Nicky Hopkins and Garth Hudson (an odd combo that) hopped aboard for keyboard support. What we have here is the debut Lp from a bunch of Australian refugees ("...Five who did it alone, banded together, and chose to call themselves what 6,000 miles of fence could not contain.") who go by the trademarked name of The Dingoes.

The opening strains of "Smooth Sailing" are going to flash immediate comparisons to two of the finer English pubberowdy bands, Ronnie Lane's Slim Chance and early Humble Pie, but there's a lot more thrown in for a truely ecclectic blend; bits of early Byrds rhythm guitar, touches of a Rod Stewart/Steve Marriot blend in lead vocalist Broderick Smith's pipes, even a bit of the old Unicorn dedicated love of American country rock. But where Unicorn played a pretty straight version of late Byrds with George Harrison harmonies, The Dingoes kick a fine pubrock with roll that puts them in a league all their own right now. "Come On Down" and "Smooth Sailing" are gritty guitar numbers with appropriately bloozy back-up vocals (goddamn, maybe this **is** Ronnie Lane in disguise!). Kerryn Tolhurst takes quite a few liberties and makes the steel guitar sound like something it hasn't, much in the style of Steve Howe's "Going For The One" exercises.

Dingoes also play smooth, but there's that working class edge to everything that initially made Rod Stewart so appealing. "Way Out West" and "Singing Your Song" work this mode particularly well, with the former boosted by a nifty Hopkins piano fill and a classy accordian back-up from bassist John du Bois. Singer Smith plays an authentic cowboy harmonica on a number of cuts. His performance on "Boys On The Run" adds the western touch effectively (even if they are roping kangaroos). Stuff like this puts Stewart's "Mandolin Wind" to shame for imported cowhide authenticity. For you Band fans, Garth Hudson's performance shows up on the closing "Waiting For The Tide To Turn" utilizing his carnival organ sound to the proper advantage.

This is one Lp that can sit on my turntable for an infinite number of spins.

SHOW INFORMATION	TRAVEL
Stage Call: 10 AM Sound Check: ANYTIME Doors Open: ALL THE TIME Showtime: NOON Your On: NOON W/ 1-60 MINUTE SET CAP: 500 FREE SHOW	AFTER SHOW DRIVE TO SANTA MONICA... APPROXIMATELY 217 MILES
Stage Call: 9:00AM Sound Check: 9:30 OR 10 Doors Open: ALL THE TIME Showtime: 11AM Your On: 11AM W/ 1-60 MINUTE SET CAP: 2000 FREE SHOW	 NEVER BARK... ...ALWAYS BITE!
Stage Call: TBA Sound Check: TBA Doors Open: 8 PM Showtime: 9PM & 11:30PM Your On: 9:PM & 11:30PM W/ SOUTHSIDE JOHNNY	
Stage Call: SAME AS ABOVE Sound Check: Doors Open: Showtime: Your On: W/	
	DRIVE FROM LOS ANGELES TO SAN DIEGO...APPROXIMATELY 122 MILES
Stage Call: 3 PM Sound Check: 4:30 PM Doors Open: 7 Showtime: 8 & 10:30 Your On: 8 & 10:30 W/ THE PERSUASIONS CAP: 400 2-45 MINUTE SETS - AUDIENCE DOES CHANGE	
	DRIVE FROM SAN DIEGO TO TUCSON APPROXIMATELY 415 MILES
Stage Call: 11:00AM Sound Check: 5:30 PM Doors Open: 6:30 PM Showtime: 7:30 PM Your On: 7:30 PM W/ PABLO CURISE CAP: 2349 1-45 MIN. SET	
5	DRIVE FROM TUCSON TO AUSTIN.. APPROXIMATELY 900 MILES
Stage Call: TBA Sound Check: Doors Open: 8 Showtime: 9 Your On: 10:15 Pm	AFTER SHOW DRIVE TO TULSA... APPROXIMATELY 455 MILES

The Dingoes Pedigree

Adderley Smith Blues Band (1964-70)
Smith; Tolhurst; etc

The Roadrunners
Stockley; etc

Delta Set
Stockley; etc

Cam-Pact (1967-69)
Stockley; Keith Glass, etc

Sundown (1970-73)
Smith; Tolhurst; Glass etc

Carson (1971-73)
Smith; Mal Logan; etc

New Dream (1969-75)
Bois; etc

Country Radio (1970-73)
Greg Quill; Tolhurst; Bois; etc

Mississippi (1972)
Tolhurst; etc

Axiom (1969-71)
Stockley; etc

Blackfeather (1970-71)
Lee: etc

Dingoes 1 (Original Line-up 1973)
Smith; Tolhurst; Stockley; Lee; John Strangio

Dingoes 2 (*The Dingoes* LP, Stockley shot! 1974)
Smith; Tolhurst; Lee; Bois; Stockley/Logan

Dingoes 3 (Lee joins Ariel 1975)
Smith; Tolhurst; Stockley; Bois; Ray Arnott

Dingoes 4 (bound for USA, *Five Times the Sun* LP, 1976-78)
Smith; Tolhurst; Stockley; Bois; Lee

Dingoes 5 (*Orphans of the Storm* LP, 1979)
Smith; Tolhurst; Bois; Lee; Andrew Hardin;
Robert (Smiggy) Smith

Southern Cross (Canada, 1978)
Quill; Stockley; etc

Big Combo (1979-81)
Smith; etc

Richard Clapton Band (80-81)
Tolhurst; etc

Stockley See & Mason (1978-81)
Stockley; etc

Broderick Smith (1982-2011)
9 Solo albums

Rattling Sabres (1986)
Tolhurst; Lee; etc

Jimmy Barnes Band (1984)
Stockley: etc

Locomo (New York)
Tolhurst; etc

Scarecrow
Stockley; Gary Young; etc

Backsliders (2007 – 2011)
Hurst; Turner; Collard; Smith

So Rudely Interrupted
Quill; Tolhurst; etc.

Hard Road
Stockley; Gary Young; etc

Dingoes 6 (Hall of Fame, Tracks, Live at Last, 2009-2011)
Smith; Tolhurst; Stockley; Bois; Chris Copping; Ashley Davies

Discography

The Dingoes *Mushroom, 1974, Melbourne, Produced by the Dingoes & John French*

Come on Down *(Stockley)*
Boy on the Run *(Smith/Stockley)*
The Last Place *(Tolhurst)*
Way out West *(the Dingoes)*
Payday Again *(Tolhurst)*
Going' Down Again *(Tolhurst)*
Aaron *(Tolhurst)*
My Sunshine Lady *(Tolhurst)*
Sydney Ladies *(Smith/Tolhurst)*
Dingoes' Lament *(Bois)*

Sunbury Live *Mushroom, 1974, Melbourne*

I'm a Dingo *(Ross Wilson)*
Payday Again

Live at the Station Lamington, 1976, Melbourne, Produced by Keith Glass

Marijuana Hell *(Nagle/Blakeley)*
When a Man Loves a Woman *(Lewis/Wright)*

Five Times the Sun *A&M, 1977, LA, Produced by Elliot Mazer*

Smooth Sailing *(Tolhurst)*
Shine a Light *(Stockley)*
Singing Your Song *(Tolhurst)*
Starting Today *(Tolhurst)*
Come on Down
Way Out West
Boy on the Run
Waiting for the Tide to Turn *(Tolhurst)*

Orphans of the Storm *A&M, 1979, New York, Produced by John Anthony*

Outside Man *(Smith/Tolhurst)*
Since You've Been Gone *(Tolhurst/Bois)*
Into the Night *(Bois)*
The Stand Off Game *(Tolhurst)*
I Never Seem to Get Through (Tolhurst)
Child in the Middle *(Tolhurst)*
The Last Place
High Living *(Stockley)*
Going Down Again
Johnnie's the Last One (Bois)

Way Out west – Best of the Dingoes *Mushroom, 1992*

Way out West
Boy on the Run
Sydney Ladies
Going Down Again
Smooth Sailing
Shine a Light
Singing Your Song
Come on Down
Waiting for the Tide to Turn
Into the Night
Since You've Been Gone
Child in the Middle

Demo versions recorded in Atlantic Studios NY:

Don't Want to Face the Day Alone *(Tolhurst)*
High Living
So Little for So Little *(John Lee & the Dingoes)*

Tracks *2010, Tucson, Produced by Kerryn Tolhurst*

Right To Your Door *(Tolhurst)*
Not Worth Fighting For *(Tolhurst)*
Rolling Around The Sun *(Bois)*
Try Anyway *(Tolhurst)*
No Rain, No River *(Tolhurst)*
Ribs Of The Land *(Smith/Walker)*
Blue Sanctuary *(Stockley)*
Snow-blind Moon *(Smith/Hyde)*
Damascus Road *(Tolhurst)*
Driving Home *(Smith/Bennett)*

Live at Last *Liberation, 2011, Melbourne, Produced by Kerryn Tolhurst*

Not worth fighting For
Come on Down
The Last Place
Rolling Around the Sun
Child in the Middle
No Rain No River
Going Down Again
Snow-Blind Moon
Smooth Sailing
Waiting for the Tide to Turn
Singing your song
Blue Sanctuary
Shine a Light
Way Out West
Try Anyway
Damascus Road
Boy on the Run
Sydney Ladies